AMERICA'S
KNITTING
BOOK

AMERICA'S KNITTING BOOK

Gertrude Taylor

ILLUSTRATED BY
Marjorie Tweed, Alan Howe, and Lyle Braden

PHOTOGRAPHS BY Saul Pliuskonis

CHARLES SCRIBNER'S SONS · NEW YORK

TO ALL MY STUDENTS,
whose many problems prompted
and inspired this book.

ACKNOWLEDGMENTS

Among those who have helped me in various ways with the preparation of this book, my thanks are due particularly to the following:

Eva Berg, a fellow teacher, for her "No Stair-step Bind Off."

Raye Gailus, a student, for her pin method in reading patterns.

Julia Bowman, a meticulous knitter and ardent student, for her beautiful new buttonholes, which will surely please knitters everywhere.

Marjorie Tweed, a student, for her original art work.

Sue Sivers and Pat De Sisto, students, for endless hours of typewriter pounding.

and especially to

Jessie Garwood, a lifetime friend, who passed away this summer. She helped me in many ways to perfect the manuscript, organize and outline it.

WHAT MAKES SO MANY HAND KNITS LOOK HOME-MADE

1. Baggy bottom ribbing
2. Sweater too long or too short
3. Sweaters that hang longer in front than in back
4. Cuffs too big
5. Sleeves too tight, or too loose
6. Sleeves too long or too short
7. Necks stretched out
8. Shoulders that sag
9. Bound off stitches showing in the seams at the shoulder
10. Sleeves set into the armhole incorrectly
11. Seams with the unevenness of the edge stitches showing
12. Side seams that are too tight and draw up
13. Improperly matched ribbing on sleeves and at the bottom
14. Uneven hems
15. Hems that show through to the right side
16. Pig eye buttonholes
17. Collars put on askew
18. Collars put on with a thick seam
19. Crocheted edges that are uneven
20. "Picked up stitches" leaving big holes
21. "Picked up stitches" where the two sides are not even
22. Stitches picked up incorrectly, causing the front edges to buckle
23. Stitches picked up incorrectly, causing the front edges to sag
24. Knitting on the wrong size needles: Too small needles cause hard texture knits—too large needles give a sleazy-looking garment
25. Uneven pattern caused by doing yarn overs incorrectly
26. Inconsistency in knitting cable patterns
27. Skirts that cup in under the seat or tummy
28. Putting trim on unevenly
29. Ribbon facings that are too tight causing the sweater front to draw; loose ribbon facings that may cause the sweater front to sag

30. Ends that are not worked in properly may poke through and show on the right side
31. Zippers that are put in incorrectly will buckle
32. Seams made with long loose stitches will have gaps
33. Seams will look bulky if you use yarn that is too heavy
34. Stitches improperly woven together in the Kitchener stitch will leave holes
35. Sweaters in more than one color showing puckering where the yarn was pulled too tight when changing colors, or showing holes where the yarn was left too loose
36. *Last, but by no means least,* improper blocking or no blocking at all.

CONTENTS

AMERICA'S
KNITTING
BOOK

Introduction

This book is for you. If you are a beginner, you can teach yourself to knit by following the complete instructions in this book. If you have already done some knitting and are a more advanced "amateur," you will find many hints and new ideas here that will help you to knit better. You will discover some helps toward more consistently even stitches, toward better-fitting garments; simple instructions for assuring correct fit of your finished sweater or dress; simple and correct methods for blocking and shaping the completed pieces, and, finally, brand new ideas for assembling and finishing the parts into the completed garment. You, too, will benefit from the step-by-step instructions that this book affords, and will be astonished at the new and efficient methods suggested in these pages.

The beginner should practice with yarn of knitting worsted weight (4 ply) and a pair of number 8 or number 9 short (10 inch) straight knitting needles. A light or bright color should be used, so that you will see what you are doing at all times. You must watch the stitches form. You must see what you are doing and why you are doing it. You must check each step to make sure it is correct.

Do not do anything automatically. Make sure you are reading every step. Study the diagram. In reading complicated directions in knitting books, the best method is to read and do the work by many little steps. Read a few phrases, then stick a straight pin into the page to show you where your place is; then do that much work. Then read the next phrase, move the pin, etc. With this method, your hands are free to do the work and the pin holds your place in the book. Always use this method when teaching yourself to knit. Take a straight pin to hold your place, and then start in, step by step, to teach yourself.

HOLDING YOUR PLACE

You must watch your hands. Be sure you are using the left hand when the directions say "left hand" and your right hand when the directions say "right hand." This may sound too simple, but many beginners get into difficulties because they are careless about this one thing.

If you are left-handed and are just learning to knit, you will do much better if you learn to knit the "Continental" way. With this method, you are going in the same direction as right-handed knitters, and you are forming the stitches in the same way, except that you are holding your thread in your left hand and your left hand is doing most of the work. Your yarn is going around the needle in the same direction as it is in "American" knitting.

See picture given showing position of hands on needles, and how the stitches are formed.

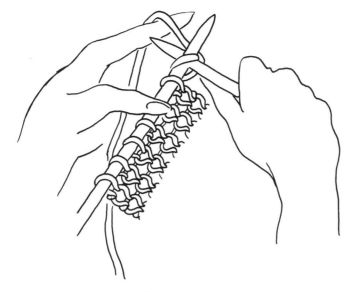

LEFT HANDED KNITTERS

If you are left-handed, you should *not* knit from left to right. Left-handed people write in the same direction as right-handed people do, so too, you should knit in the same direction as all knitters do, so that others will be able to help you.

CHAPTER I

Teaching Yourself
to Knit

INFORMATION ON YARNS AND NEEDLES

Materials

The beginner should have a slight knowledge of yarns. There are many kinds and brands on the market, and to familiarize yourself with yarns, spend some time in a yarn shop or department store browsing around. Much can be learned by simply reading the information on the labels. There are yarns of natural animal fibers and there are synthetic yarns, and combinations of both. Weights of yarn vary from very fine to bulky. The "ply" of yarn does not mean how heavy the yarn may be. It simply means how many strands are twined together to make the strand of yarn. There are heavyweight three-ply and four-ply yarns and lightweight three- and four-ply yarns.

4 PLY

HEAVY YARN

YARN PLY

Weights of Yarns from Very Fine to Bulky

Baby yarns	Very soft and fine
Dress yarns	Lightweight wool or synthetics
All wool fingering yarns Nylon and wool fingering yarns	For lightweight sweaters and socks
Sport yarn (3 or 4 ply), all wool	For socks, lightweight sweaters and children's sweaters
Nylane sport yarn (50% wool, 50% nylon)	Little heavier than all wool sport yarn, for sweaters, children's sweaters and socks
Knitting worsted or other yarns of knitting worsted weight (such as synthetics & machine washable wools & synthetics)	A medium-weight yarn for a great variety of sweaters, including ski sweaters
Bulky yarns	Any yarns heavier than knitting worsted, either wool or part wool and part synthetics.

The beginner should not be concerned with mohair yarns. See page 260 on mohair yarns.

NEEDLES

The beginner should use a pair of short (10″) needles for the swatch. But, purchase the 14 inch needles in most cases for other work so that the stitches may be stretched out across the needles and will not be pinched together. Single pointed needles may be purchased in either plastic or lightweight aluminum in a good brand. Your pattern will state the size and type of needles needed for your particular sweater.

Double-pointed needles (dp) come in sets of four. They are pointed at each end of the needle. They are used for making socks, mittens and neck ribbings. One uses double-pointed needles to knit tubular pieces, around in a circle with no seams. They come in a variety of sizes and lengths.

Circular needles are used for making tubular pieces, such as skirts without seams, or they can be used as straight needles; that is, to knit over and purl back, forming a flat piece of work. Raglan sweaters that start at the neck, or sweaters with circular yokes may also be knit on circular needles.

ROLLING THE YARN

Occasionally you may buy yarns in hanks. Before you start to use it, it must be rolled into a soft ball. Knitting worsted, for instance, may come in a hank which is really two hanks. Each half will make a ball.

Have someone hold the hank over her outstretched hands while you roll the yarn from the hank into a ball. Make sure you do not wrap the yarn too tightly. Yarn has a natural elasticity but if stretched too tightly it will lose its stretch and the garment made from it will not be soft and fluffy.

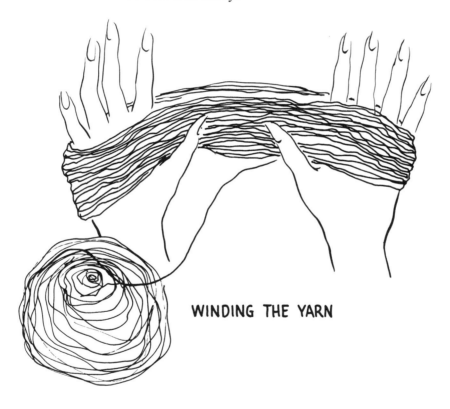

WINDING THE YARN

CASTING ON

Before you can learn to knit, you must put some stitches on the needle. This is called "casting on." These stitches are not

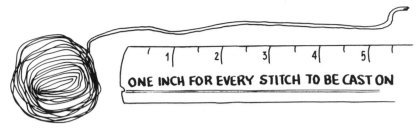

ONE INCH FOR EVERY STITCH TO BE CAST ON

CASTING ON

SLIP KNOT .....

simply looped over the needle. They must be cast on with two threads, so that the edge of a piece will be firm and straight with plenty of stretch. It takes practice to get these stitches onto the needle evenly.

To cast on use only one needle. On your yarn from the ball, measure off a length approximately one inch for each stitch to be cast on. For example, if you are going to cast on twenty stitches, measure to a point twenty inches from the end of the yarn. At this point on the yarn make a slip knot (by making a loop and pulling a second loop through the first loop). Place the loop of the knot on the one needle, having the short end of yarn coming from the Left Hand and the ball yarn coming from the Right Hand. Lay the short thread over the thumb and around the thumb of the Left Hand. With the needle in the Right Hand, slide the

(A)   MAKE A LOOP.....

(B)   PULL SECOND LOOP THRU....   (C)   PULL AND .....   (D)   TIGHTEN....

8

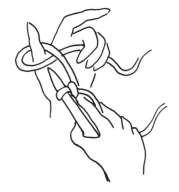
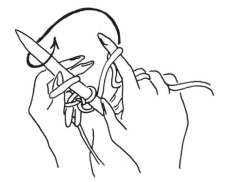
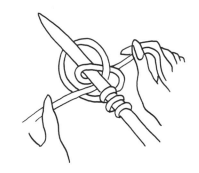

SLIDE THE NEEDLE IN ALONG SIDE OF THUMB

WRAP YARN AROUND NEEDLE FROM UNDERNEATH

WITH LEFT THUMB, FLIP LOOP OVER END OF NEEDLE AND TIGHTEN UP ON SHORT YARN

needle in alongside of the thumb, then with the ball yarn wrap the yarn around the needle from underneath to over the top. With the Left thumb, flip the loop over the end of the needle and tighten up on the short yarn. Continue for as many stitches as you wish to cast on.

Practice casting on until you are certain you are doing it correctly, working constantly to get the stitches even. The more you cast on the straighter and more even your stitches will become. Don't make the mistake of tightening the stitches too much, or it will be difficult for you to knit the first row. After you have cast on you do not use the short end of yarn again. If it is too long and is in your way, cut it off, leaving about a four-inch end.

Cast on twenty-four stitches for your practice piece or swatch.

LEARNING TO KNIT

Before you begin to knit, examine these stitches on the needle that you have just cast on. Take off one stitch and look at it. It is just a loop joined to the next stitch, which is another loop. In knitting you are going to take the loose yarn and pull another loop through the first loop of the cast-on stitches, then pull a loop through the second stitch, and so on to the end of the row. So you see, knitting is nothing more than loops pulled through the loops on the needle. We could do this by taking a crochet hook, pulling through a loop and putting it on a knitting needle. By knitting and using the needles to help you pull the loop through, you can do it faster and more evenly. The needles keep all the loops together and all the same size.

Directions for the Knit Stitch

Hold the needles so that the cast-on stitches are in the Left Hand and the empty needle is in the Right Hand. Insert the empty needle into the left side of the first stitch on the Left Hand needle on the side of the stitch facing you. Needles must be crossed and the empty needle lying under the full needle. Hold the ball yarn in your Right Hand, wrap it around the empty needle from behind,

EMPTY NEEDLE UNDER
FULL NEEDLE .....

WRAP YARN AROUND NEEDLE
FROM BEHIND.....

from underneath to over the top of the needle. Then draw the loop through the first stitch on the Left Hand needle; then drop the old stitch off of the Left Hand needle.

N O T E : In the knit stitch, the yarn must be on the *back* side of the work. A knit stitch is a smooth stitch.

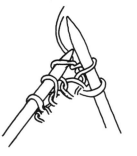

SLIDE UP ON TOP.....

SLIDE OFF ....

FOUR STEPS TO THE KNIT STITCH

1. Needle in
2. Yarn over
3. Slide up
4. Slide off

EXTRA TIPS ON KNITTING FOR THE BEGINNER

1. Always insert the empty needle from the left side of the stitch to be knit. *Never* do you knit in the back loop, always into the side of the stitch facing you.
2. Many self-taught knitters will wrap the yarn around the needle in the wrong direction. Make sure you are not doing this. The yarn is wrapped from underneath to over the top of the needle, that is—from right to left to right.
3. Hold your hands close to where you are working, not clear down near the knobs of the needles. Do not hold the needles like a pencil. Perch up on top of the needles.

DO NOT HOLD NEEDLES LIKE A PENCIL   "PERCH" ON TOP OF NEEDLES

4. Try to get a little tug against the yarn (tension); not too much, however, or it will be difficult to knit the next row.
5. Try to slide the needles as you knit. Your knitting will be smoother and you will knit faster. When doing step three (slide up), make a point of sliding clear up on top of the full needle and then do step four (slide off). This will make you knit up on the fat part of the needles. If you should be knitting on the very tips, the stitches would be too tight and then it would be difficult to knit the next row.
6. When drawing the loop through, be sure you are coming through the loop with just one thread and not pulling

through the back half of the same stitch along with the regular loop. This is one way you might get extra stitches and holes in your work.

7. Make sure the yarn is on the back side of work.

8. Turn work around to knit the second row. Your full needle in your Left Hand and empty needle in your Right Hand. Before beginning to knit the second row, examine the first stitch on the full needle. You will see that the first stitch has a big loop hanging right below the needle. Sometimes this big loop is larger than other times, but it is always there. Do *not* make the mistake of knitting in the big loop, thinking it is a dropped stitch. Knit only the stitches that are over the needle. Pull the big loop down and out of the way and start knitting the second row. If you should pull the loose yarn to the back side of work over the top of the needle, you would make the big loop into two stitches. Do not do this. So hold the big loop down then get yarn in back of work to knit the first stitch. The big loop has to be there because you must have stretch everywhere in knitting and so the big loop gives you the stretch you need on the edges.

9. Do not attempt to purl until you are knitting very well, or you may become confused. Learn one step thoroughly before you start to master the next step.

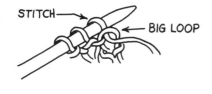

STITCH ⟶ BIG LOOP

LEARNING TO PURL

Everything about purling is the exact opposite from knitting. That is the reason why a beginner should have considerable practice at knitting before attempting to purl.

Directions for the Purl Stitch

Hold the needles in the same manner as for the knit stitch. Insert the empty needle in the first stitch, alongside of the stitches facing you, this time from the *right side* of the stitch. The needles must be crossed and the empty needle lying *on top* of the full needle. Bring yarn *forward* (toward you) *in front of the needles* and hold the yarn in your right hand. Wrap the yarn around the Right Hand needle going *over the top and down*. Then draw the loop through the first stitch, sliding it off, *through and out backwards*.

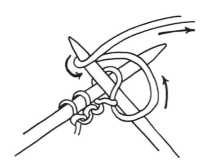

YARN IN FRONT OF NEEDLE,
NEEDLE IN FROM RIGHT SIDE .....

YARN GOING OVER
TOP AND DOWN .....

SLIDE THROUGH AND <u>OUT</u>
BACKWARDS .....

Then drop the old stitch off the Left Hand needle. NOTE: The yarn must be in front of the work when purling. A purl stitch is a "bump" stitch.

FOUR STEPS TO THE PURL STITCH

1. Needle in (from right side)
2. Yarn over (top to down)
3. Slide through backwards
4. Slide off

EXTRA TIPS ON PURLING FOR THE BEGINNER

1. Make sure you are taking the yarn over the needle in the right direction. It must go from over the top to down. You must always purl in the front half of the stitch, never in the back half. If you are wrapping the yarn in the same way you did for the knit stitch, your stitches will be lined up on the needle wrong for the next row, and you will get a row of twisted stitches. They will make an ugly flaw in your work.
2. When you are sliding through and out backwards, make sure you are coming through with only one thread. Peek over and watch the stitch coming through.
3. Look for the big loop on the first stitch of every row.
4. After you have purled one row, knit the next row. Look at the work. You will discover that your work begins to have a different look now. One side is smooth and the other side has all bumps. This is called Stockinette Stitch, and in order to do it, you knit one row, then purl one row.

13

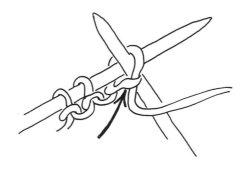

THE LITTLE "BUMP" IS JUST UNDER
THE NEEDLE

When you purl, you are making bumps, and when you knit, you are making smooth stitches. Recall, from the directions above that a purl stitch is a bump stitch, (the little bump is just under the needle), and a knit stitch is a smooth stitch.

5. As you practice purling, do so by knitting one row and purling one row (stockinette stitch). Do not have any bumps on the smooth side. In order to determine what is to be done on the next row, hold the work in your left hand ready to work the next row, then examine the work. If you see all bumps, make more bumps (purl), if you see smooth stitches, make more smooth stitches (knit). This is called "following your pattern." That is, you are doing what was done on the row below, bumps over bumps and smooth over smooth. Your work is "talking" to you, telling you what to do next. If you should rely on your memory to tell you that you have just done a knit row, and it is time to purl, you would make mistakes; because when you start and stop, unless you write yourself a note telling what you did last, you may purl (or knit) at the wrong time. If you can train yourself to watch your work carefully you will make fewer mistakes, and when you do, you will notice them immediately and can correct them. Get in the habit right now of watching everything you do and what it looks like in the row you are knitting and on the row below.

LOOK AT THE TWO KINDS OF STITCHES

There are basically only two stitches to learn in knitting. They are the knit stitch and the purl stitch. It is the variations of the knits and purls that make up most of the patterns used.

A knit stitch becomes a purl stitch on the opposite side, and a purl stitch becomes a knit stitch on the opposite side. (When you are knitting, you are making the stitch smooth on the side facing you and the bump is going on the back side. When you turn your work around, you see the bump.) Since the knits and purls look different on the other side, you must realize that when you are working the second row, you are coming back from the opposite direction and you see a bump that was a smooth stitch on the side you just finished. It is important that you consider how the stitch looks, *only as you are working these stitches,* and not how they look on the other side until you get to that side, then you will decide what you do with them at that time. Hold your work always with the full needle in your Left Hand and the empty needle in your Right Hand, *then* examine your work and if you are to "follow your pattern," you will do what the work tells you to do. If you see smooth stitches, make more smooth stitches, or if you see bumps, make more bumps on top of those bumps.

Twisted Stitches

It is most important that you do not have any twisted stitches in your work, as they will cause an ugly flaw in the completed fabric. If you are knitting correctly, your stitches will all be lined up on the needle properly, and you will not have any twisted stitches. However, if any stitches come off the needle, or if you have to rip back for any reason, you must make sure that you have not twisted any of the stitches as you put them on your needle. Learn to recognize twisted stitches. Actually a stitch is only

TWISTED STITCH

NOT TWISTED

one thread going from the front side to the back side of the needle. However, in order to explain this more clearly, assume that the stitch has two halves, the half closest to you and the half on the back side of the needle. Hold your work in the Left Hand and examine the stitches that you just put back on the needle. The half of the stitch facing you must always be closest to the point of the needle, whether it be a knit stitch or a purl stitch. If upon examining these stitches, you should find the back half of the stitch closest to the point, simply turn the stitch around on the needle and it will not be twisted.

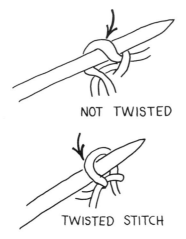

NOT TWISTED

TWISTED STITCH

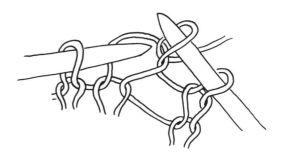

RIPPING BACK - STITCH-WISE

INSERT NEEDLE INTO HOLE WHERE YARN IS COMING OUT

Ripping Back Stitch-Wise

Don't be satisfied with any mistakes in your work. Your work should be examined closely so that errors may be detected and corrected. The sooner you notice mistakes, the less ripping you must do. Watch your work so that errors may be detected immediately. If an error is on the row you are working or on one row below, do not take the work off the needles. Instead, learn to rip back one stitch at a time. If you discover an error before you finish a row, do *not* turn work around. Instead, insert Left Hand needle into the hole where the yarn is coming out, with the needle going in the direction *away* from you, then pull out the old stitch. Slip off stitches thus until you have reached the point of error. After the correction is made, finish the row. No stitches will be twisted. Ripping is done in the same manner for either knit or purl stitches.

The only difference is that to rip out a knit stitch, the yarn is in back of the work; and to rip out a purl stitch, the yarn is in front of the work. If you have just finished a row, and turned your work around ready to work the next row, then discovered a mistake, *work must be turned back around,* then rip according to the directions above.

Attention!!!

All of these various topics and stitches just explained, and much more to come, must be tried out on your swatch. Rip back some stitches and do a little of each of the things explained here, so that when the time comes that you must do these things, you will have had some experience and can proceed.

LEARNING TO WORK RIBBING

Ribbing means you are making knit and purl stitches in the same row. Most sweaters have ribbing at the bottom, at the cuff, neck, etc. This combination of stitches makes deep grooves of smooth and bump stitches. It results in an elastic or stretchy texture. When you are working ribbing you must make sure the yarn is in the right position. That is, yarn is in back of work for knit stitches and in front of work for purl stitches.

EXAMPLE: Knit two, Purl two ribbing across row.

First, you must use a number of stitches divisible by four, or your work will not come out right on the next row. (That was why you started out with twenty-four stitches, which is divisible by four.) If you do not have a number divisible by four, take off some stitches until you do have the right number. (Simply pull them off and let them go.) To work ribbing, make sure the yarn is in back of your work, then Knit two stitches. Now change the yarn between the two needles (bring yarn forward between the two needles into purl position) and Purl two stitches. Change the yarn again between the two needles into Knit position and Knit two stitches. Continue in this manner across the row. It is wise to look at your work and make sure you are getting two smooth stitches and two bumps as you are going across the row. The little bumps are right under the needle. When starting the second row and all following rows, hold your work in your Left Hand and

Ribbing, K2, P2

Ribbing, K1, P1

examine it. If you see two bumps, make two bumps over those of the previous row, if you see two smooth stitches, make two smooth stitches on top of those smooth stitches. (Bumps over bumps and smooth over smooth.) This is called "following your pattern." That is, you are doing exactly what was done on the previous row. WATCH and THINK what you are doing. If you forget to change the yarn between the two needles, the yarn will drag up over the top of the needle and give you an extra stitch, and then your whole pattern of two's and two's will be thrown off. This cannot be, and must be ripped out stitch by stitch. There are many kinds of ribbing, but if you can do the simple "knit two, purl two" ribbing, you can do the "knit one, purl one" ribbing or any other combinations of ribbing.

OTHER STITCHES DESCRIBED

Garter Stitch

When you work row after row of knit stitches, you are making garter stitch. It looks alike on both sides. It consists of a ridge row (bumps) and a smooth row. This is a border stitch. That is, it can be used as an edge for the bottom of a sweater or the edge of a side front. It does not roll or curl.

Garter Stitch

Stockinette Stitch

Stockinette stitch is different on the two sides. One side is smooth and the other side has all the bumps. Usually the side that is smooth is used for the outside of garments, but occasionally the bumpy side is used. If so, it is called reverse stockinette stitch, and if your pattern calls for reverse stockinette, you must know that they mean the bumpy side out for the right side. To do stockinette stitch, you knit one row and purl one row. Stockinette stitch is not a border stitch. You will find that it curls and rolls on the edges and sides. Do not be alarmed, that is natural. That is why you must use a hem, border pattern, or facing with stockinette stitch to keep these edges from curling.

Border Patterns

Besides the garter stitch mentioned above, there are several other border patterns. They are Ribbing and Seed Stitch, and Double Seed Stitch. There are also some pattern stitches that are the same on both sides and are a combination of knits and purls that lend themselves nicely as border stitches.

Seed Stitch

Seed Stitch

Usually seed stitch is done in knit one, purl one across the first row. On the row following, instead of putting a smooth over a smooth and a bump over a bump (this would give you knit one, purl one ribbing) you would make a smooth over a bump and a bump over a smooth. Try a little seed stitch. It is easy and pretty, too.

INCREASES, DECREASES AND BINDING OFF

Shaping of Knitted Pieces

If you are going to make a sweater or *anything* that is not a straight piece, it will be necessary for you to knit the shaping as you go. Your pattern will ask that you "increase" or "decrease" or "bind off." You must understand that you are doing these things because you need to make your piece smaller or larger (lose or gain stitches). If you are told to bind off all stitches, that will finish off the piece.

Decrease

Decrease means getting rid of *one* stitch at a time. If more than one stitch is to be taken off, you must then bind off. To decrease, if you are on a knit row, knit two stitches together; if on a purl row, purl two stitches together.

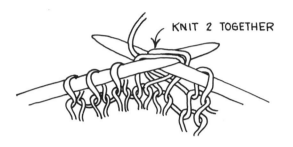

KNIT 2 TOGETHER

DECREASING

Increase (*Knitting*)

To increase knitting, knit in the front half of the stitch, then pull up, stretch out, but do not slide stitch off; then knit in the back half of the same stitch, then drop old stitch off. Two stitches have been made from one stitch.

NOTE: You may notice a little purl bump-type stitch below your new extra stitch. This is correct. Later on you will find directions given for increasing without leaving the little purl bump. However, when your pattern asks that you increase, use this method, unless pattern states otherwise.

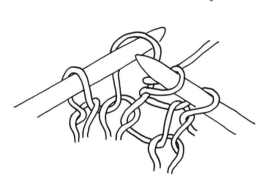

KNIT IN FRONT HALF OF STITCH

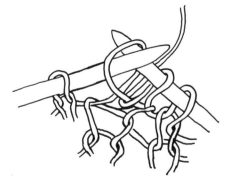

KNIT IN BACK HALF OF STITCH

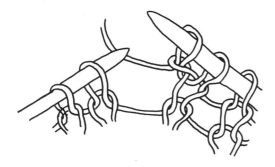

TWO STITCHES MADE FROM ONE

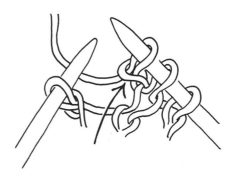

THE PURL"BUMP" STITCH IS UNDER NEW STITCH

Increase (*Purling*)

To increase purling, purl in the front half of the stitch, then change the yarn between the two needles, so that the yarn is in knit position, then knit in the back half of the same stitch. Then change the yarn back to purl position. Two stitches have been made from one stitch.

PURL IN FRONT HALF OF STITCH.....

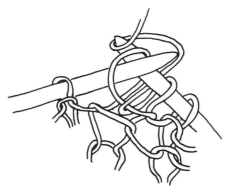

KNIT IN BACK-HALF OF STITCH

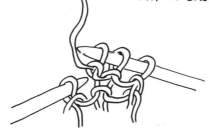

TWO STITCHES HAVE BEEN MADE FROM ONE STITCH

Binding Off

Binding off means getting rid of more than one stitch at a time. Binding off can be done only at the beginning of a row. To bind off, work two stitches onto the empty needle, now lift stitch number one up and over and past stitch number two and over the tip of the needle, dropping stitch number one completely off the needle. Knit (or purl) stitch number three onto the right-hand needle. Lift stitch number two over stitch number three in the same manner. Continue doing this for as many stitches as are to be bound off. Count as bound off only the stitch that goes over the point of the needle. Always bind off in pattern, if working in a pattern.

BINDING OFF
LEFT STITCH NO 1 -UP AND OVER
PAST STITCH NO 2

BOUND OFF STITCHES

N O T E : If you are working on a knit row, the two stitches will be worked over onto the right-hand needle *knitting,* and each time you work another stitch over onto the right-hand needle, it must be knit. If you are on a purl row, all stitches are worked *purling.* If you are doing ribbing and binding off in ribbing, it is most important that you work the stitches over onto the right-hand needle in the ribbing pattern. If you bind off in ribbing using all knit stitches, you will make an ugly ridge row at the end of your work, but if you work them in the ribbing pattern, the edge will ripple in and out in the ribbing pattern.

If you are to bind off all stitches, you will end up with one stitch on the right-hand needle. Then break the thread and pull the loose end through the last stitch on the needle, thus fastening off and locking the last stitch. You must be very careful that you do not bind off too tightly. Most new knitters tend to bind off tightly. After you have bound off a stitch, and you are left with one stitch on the right-hand needle, before you work another stitch over to the right-hand needle, pull up and loosen that one stitch, because it will be the stitch to be bound off next time. Practice binding off *loosely.* You must have stretch everywhere on your knitted pieces, and if you bind off tightly, the seams will draw and pull and you will not be able to get that professional look you must have.

CORRECTING ERRORS

Ripping Back Row-Wise

If it is necessary to rip back quite a bit of work, the only thing you can do is to take the work completely off the needles and rip it to one row past the mistake. You must be very careful that you get the stitches back on the needles correctly, or you will have a whole row of twisted stitches and they will make an ugly flaw in your work. Hold work in the left hand with the loose thread coming from the extreme *left* end of work. With a very fine needle (number 0 or number 1) and holding it in the right hand, insert the needle into each stitch from the *right* end of the work through the BACK of each stitch, with the point of the needle pointing toward yourself. When all the stitches are picked up, work the next row with the regular size needle. No stitches will be twisted.

NOTE: If you attempt to pick up the stitches with the regular size needle, you may pull out succeeding stitches.

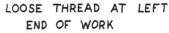

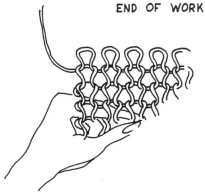

LOOSE THREAD AT LEFT END OF WORK

HOLD WORK IN LEFT HAND

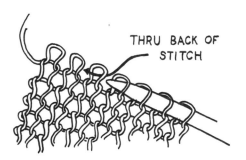

THRU BACK OF STITCH

INSERT NEEDLE INTO EACH STITCH FROM RIGHT END OF WORK *THRU* BACK OF STITCH POINT TOWARD YOU....

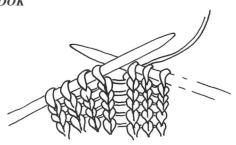

YARN IS FROM RIGHT HAND NEEDLE

Direction of Knitting

If it is necessary to stop in the middle of a row, make sure you start again in the right direction. Remember that the yarn is always hanging from the last stitch you worked and belongs in the right hand. When you start in again, make sure that the yarn is coming from the *right-hand* needle. If it is not, turn your work around.

Correcting Errors With a Crochet Hook

If you find that you have made a knit stitch where you should have made a purl stitch, you can correct it by letting down the stitch and picking it back up with a crochet hook. There are several other types of errors that can be corrected with this method. If you notice a thread behind a stitch, on the wrong side of your work and not going through the stitch, this can be corrected by the crochet hook method. If you have a split stitch and have left a fuzzy loop, this can also be corrected with the hook. Practice doing this on your swatch so that when it is necessary for you to do this in your work, you will be able to do so smoothly.

Let down the stitch that needs to be corrected and let it run, like a runner on a stocking, until it is one row past the mistake. Now hold your work so that the knit side is facing you and insert the crochet hook through the loop with the hook going in the direction away from you, then with the hook reach behind the loose thread and bring this thread through the loop already on the hook. Continue up the ladder of loose threads until you reach the top, then put loop back on the needle. Make sure that the stitch is not twisted when it goes back on the needle. If this row of hooked stitches looks smaller than the other stitches on either side of it, you were not pulling up enough before you went on to the next ladder. Practice again.

If you have gone part way across the row, have put your work down, then picked it up again and started in the wrong direction, you will have two more rows on one end of your work than on the other. This is an error that cannot be corrected except by ripping back row-wise. See "Direction Of Knitting" and this will not happen to you again. (Page 26.)

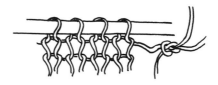

TIE A KNOT ... 3" ENDS...

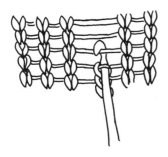

CORRECTING ERRORS....
REACH BEHIND <u>LOOSE</u> THREAD
WITH HOOK

NEW YARN COMING IN AT SIDES

OTHER PROCEDURES

Joining New Yarn

It is better to join new yarn at the side of a garment. If it is necessary to join in the center of the work, tie the new yarn to the old in a simple loose knot leaving about three-inch ends. Proceed to knit. If the knot comes through to the right side, let it remain there until the piece is finished. When the piece is finished, all knots are brought to the wrong side and untied and worked in. See page 61 (Working in Ends). If you join yarn on the edge of work, you may either tie a knot there or simply knit with the new yarn, leaving at least three-inch ends. See *picture* above. If you come upon a knot already tied in the yarn, this knot will probably be a hard knot with short ends. Untie this knot or cut it off, re-tying a simple loose knot, and proceed as above.

Knitting On

"Knitting on" is a term used in knitting. It is a form of casting on. If it is necessary to add on new stitches and you have only one thread, you knit on instead of casting on. Do not ever use this form of casting on in place of the regular casting on for the start of any piece—it gives an ugly, flimsy, loopy edge. Many patterns will ask that you cast on ten stitches (or any amount) at the end of the next row. To do this, you must knit on because you have only one thread available. Here you will be using this edge to form the inside of a seam and it will not matter if it is ugly and flimsy.

DIRECTIONS FOR KNITTING ON

Turn your work around; hold the empty needle in your right hand. Knit into the first stitch on the Left Hand needle, but do not take the old stitch off. Instead, pull up the new stitch, twist it, and put that new stitch on the Left Hand needle with the rest of the stitches. Now knit into that new stitch you have just added on, in the same manner, putting it on the Left Hand needle. Repeat for as many stitches as required. Then work across the row.

NOTE: If you are on a purl row, you may "purl on," or "knit on" as per directions above, then purl across the row.

KNITTING ON

PULL UP ON NEW STITCH .....

KNIT INTO FIRST STITCH ON
LEFT-HAND NEEDLE ....

PUT WITH REST OF STITCHES...

Buttonholes

HORIZONTAL BUTTONHOLES

Most pattern books ask that you do the regular horizontal buttonholes. To make a horizontal buttonhole, you usually start at the center front edge.

EXAMPLE: Work two stitches, bind off the next three stitches, work to the end of the row. In order to bind off these stitches you must actually work stitches #1, #2, #3, and #4. Then bind off stitch #3 over stitch #4, work stitch #5, bind off stitch #4 over stitch #5, work stitch #6, bind off stitch #5 over stitch #6 (three stitches bound off). Then finish the row. On the way back, work until you come to the hole where the stitches were bound off. Then *turn your work around,* get the yarn in back of your work, *knit on* three stitches (according to directions on page 28) over the three bound-off stitches in the previous row, *turn work around,* and finish row (last two stitches). See *picture.* This buttonhole must be hand finished when all work is complete and after blocking. See page 239.

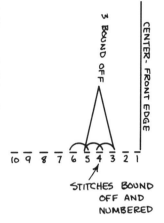

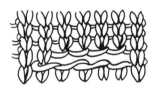

COMPLETED BUTTON HOLE

VERTICAL BUTTONHOLES

If you are working your border in ribbing stitch, your pattern will give you instructions for working the horizontal buttonhole explained above. But, you will have a much prettier buttonhole if you work a vertical buttonhole whenever you have ribbing or garter stitch on the border. The buttonhole will disappear in the ribs and will be very inconspicuous. If, on the other hand, you should work the horizontal buttonhole that your pattern asked you to, at every buttonhole the border would peak out, and then draw in between the buttonholes, giving the border of your sweater a very unattractive, uneven look. Always use a vertical buttonhole whenever you have ribbing or garter stitch on a border.

How to work vertical buttonholes

Divide the ribbing stitches in half and, starting at the center front edge, work the first half of ribbing stitches with the original ball of yarn, (ball #1). Lay in ball #2 and work the other half of the ribbing stitches and the remainder of the row. See *picture*. Jot down that you have done one separating row.

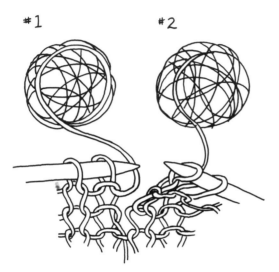

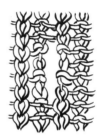

COMPLETE VERTICAL BUTTON HOLE

Next row: With ball #2, work across the stitches and half of the ribbing stitches, set aside ball #2, take up ball #1 and finish row, (last half of ribbing stitches). Jot down that you have done two separating rows.

Next row: With ball #1 work across first half of ribbing stitches, set aside ball #1, take up ball #2 and work last half of ribbing stitches and the remainder of the row. Jot down that you have done three separating rows.

Next row: With ball #2 work across all of the stitches on the needle, thus closing the vertical buttonhole. Cut off ball #1, leaving a four-inch end. This buttonhole will accommodate any button up to $\frac{3}{4}$ inch. If you are using a larger button make four separating rows before joining. This buttonhole does not need to be hand-finished, but all ends should be worked in at the same time that other ends are worked in before washing and blocking. See page 247.

CHAPTER II

Starting
a Project

INTRODUCTION

Why Sweaters Do Not Fit

If you have had the unfortunate experience of knitting a sweater, and, when it was finished, finding that it did not fit properly, the cause of this tragedy may be one of two things. Either you did not choose the correct size in the first place, or you did not knit an accurate stitch gauge. Far too many sweaters when finished do not fit. There is no excuse for this. You can know to the exact inch what size your sweater will be *if* you know how to choose the correct size and *if* you knit an accurate stitch gauge.

You may select the wrong size if you do not realize that sweater sizes are not standardized and most designers do not keep to the measurement charts given either in front or back of pattern books. Do not guess at sizes. Measure yourself and know your actual measurements, and from these you can find out what size is right for you in each different sweater pattern.

But even when you have selected the right size—you sometimes still end up with an Elephant Sweater.

Where do Elephant Sweaters come from?

Elephant Sweaters are those which are five to ten inches too large for the victim. They usually come when your stitch gauge is off by only one stitch per inch. Soon, those stitches add up into inches—far too many inches.

On the other hand, if your sweater turns out too small, much too small, in fact, a Midget Sweater (from five to ten inches too small), it too is the result of the stitch gauge being off one stitch per inch, this time in the other direction.

Learn how to knit an accurate stitch gauge, and knit one for *every* garment you make.

Choosing the Correct Size

Be sure to choose the right size. Sweater sizes are not standardized. If a size twelve fits you in one pattern, do not think that all size twelves will fit you. Each designer has her own idea of size and each one may vary. Take no chances and do not guess. Scrutinize the picture of the sweater and determine if it is tight in the picture, or loose and baggy. Be sure you are satisfied with the looks on the model. Usually, a sweater size twelve is quite small and would fit a person with about a thirty inch bust measurement. If you measure thirty-two inches at the bust, you probably will require the next size larger to give you about three inches more at the bustline.

Sweater pattern sizes vary and they are seldom the size of ready-made clothes. Because you wear a size twelve dress will *not* mean you should knit a size twelve sweater.

Choose the right size by measuring your bust line to get your actual measurement.

EXAMPLE: Actual bust measurement thirty-six inches.

For a cardigan add approximately three inches—(39″)
For a Chanel jacket use actual measurement—(36″)
For a pullover add approximately four inches—(40″)

NOTE: To get an idea of how your sweater should fit, hold the tape measure out to three inches more than your actual measurement, and by the time those three inches are distributed evenly around your bust line, you should have a perfect fit for a cardigan.

In order to choose the correct size, pick out the size you think will fit, then add up all the stitches given in the pattern for the fronts and the back just before the underarm shaping. (Glance through the pattern until you find the number of stitches they are using when you come to the underarm shaping for the back. Jot down that number. Then glance through the directions given for the front or fronts, and find out the number of stitches given. Add the two fronts to the back and you have the total number of stitches for the entire sweater at the bust line.) If you are figuring for a cardigan, deduct one overlap. (You can find out how many stitches the pattern uses for the front borders by looking through the directions for the front. Since one front laps over the other front at the border, you would only want to count the number of border stitches once, therefore, deduct one overlap.)

EXAMPLE:

92 stitches back
59 stitches front
59 stitches front
----
210 total stitches
−10 deduct one overlap
----
200 total stitches at bust line

Now, divide the complete number of stitches at the underarm (200) by the stitch gauge (given in your pattern) to get the finished measurement in inches. 200 stitches divided by 5 stitches per inch on the gauge equals *40 inches* (the size).

$$\left\{ \frac{200 \text{ stitches}}{5 \text{ stitches per inch}} \text{ equals 40 inches or size 40} \right\}$$

NOTE: In reading through the directions for the number of stitches required on the back and the fronts, remember that some patterns require increases up the sides before the underarm shaping, so make sure that you have the correct number of stitches *just before* the shaping for the underarm. If the first size you tried out was not correct, keep trying the various sizes until you come upon a size closest to the size you need.

When choosing the correct size for men use the same procedure—that is, take careful measurements at chest, length and sleeve length (measured approximately 2½ inches to 2¾ inches from armpit to wrist). Be sure to take the hip measurement where the bottom of the sweater will come. Many men's hand-made sweaters have a poor fit through the hips and most men want a tight fit there. See page 144 on how to adjust. Take his shoulder measurements from shoulder bone to shoulder bone. In deciding what size to work from, you will need to add the stitches given in the various pattern sizes as you did when figuring what size to work from for yourself. A good allowance to add for men is three inches more than the chest measurement for both cardigans and pullovers.

Choosing the correct size for children will be found in full detail in Chapter XI, KNITTING FOR INFANTS AND CHILDREN.

Stitch Gauge—Why and How

A stitch gauge is a sample of your knitting to see how many stitches per inch you are getting. Because all patterns in knitting are based on a given number of stitches per inch, it is most important to knit a sample gauge before starting *any* garment. If you, the knitter, do not knit a sample gauge, you will not know what size the garment will be until it is finished. The knitter *can* know exactly what size her finished sweater will be before she casts on the first stitch. It takes only a few minutes to knit a gauge, but it takes many hours to rip out and re-knit a garment that does not fit. If you meet the gauge on several sweaters, you must not think that you are an average knitter, and therefore do not have to knit the gauge thereafter. Some knitters knit with a different tension on different sized needles. For example, on fine needles, some knitters have a tendency to tighten up, and they may knit looser or tighter on circular needles than on straight needles. You must not assume that you do not need to knit the gauge. It is not worth the risk you run of ending up with a too large or too small garment.

A fact that few knitters know is that you are matching your knitting to the knitter who designed and made the sweater pattern. As all knitters vary, so do these pattern designers vary in their knitting. You must knit to the designer's gauge.

For your gauge, be sure to use the yarn you intend to use for your sweater. Sometimes yarns vary even in the same brand, as sometimes the dyeing process has made the yarn heavier or thinner. If you are knitting with two colors, and one color looks thinner than one of the other colors, be sure to knit your gauge in the color used most throughout the pattern. Or better still, knit the gauge with both colors and follow a small portion of your graph, enough for the amount of stitches required for your gauge.

DIRECTIONS FOR KNITTING AN ACCURATE GAUGE

A gauge must be knit for every garment. A four-inch gauge is the only accurate gauge. Take the size needles suggested in the pattern and cast on sufficient stitches for a four-inch piece.

EXAMPLE: Five stitches equal one inch; seven rows equal one inch. To make a four-inch piece, cast on five stitches times

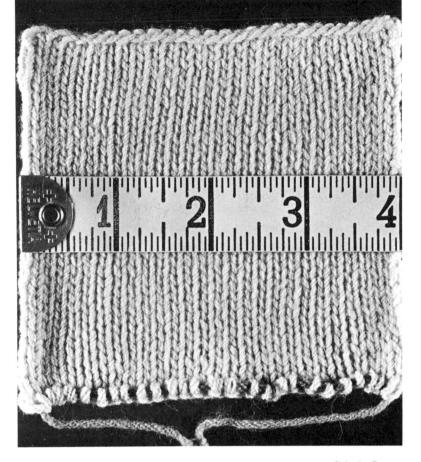

Stitch Gauge

four inches, or twenty stitches, and work for twenty-eight rows. Then the swatch is taken off of the needles and put on a yarn holder and measured. Do not bind off. See photo. If it does not measure exactly four inches by four inches, you are not on gauge and an adjustment must be made. If your piece measures three-and-three-fourths inches in width, knit another gauge with the next size larger needles. If your gauge measures four-and-one-fourth inches in width, knit another gauge with the next size smaller needles. NOTE: Gauge must be knit in pattern stitch if the sweater is in a pattern stitch. If two sizes of needles are given in pattern, use the size intended for the main body of the garment. Use the yarn you intend to use for the sweater. Do not ever attempt to adjust your knitting if you do not meet the gauge. Knit in your regular tension and adjust your needles if necessary. You are more concerned with how the gauge measures in *width*. Many of the patterns are knit inch-wise instead of row-wise. Usually, when you meet the gauge width-wise, you will also meet the gauge row-wise. If it is important that you be on gauge row-wise (such as for stripes or pattern graphs which require a given number of rows), you must obtain gauge row-wise or else an adjustment must be made to the pattern so that you will not knit the pieces too long or too short. It is important that you be on gauge row-wise if you are knitting a raglan with a given number of decrease rows. See page 146.

You are not going to send any of your hand knits to the cleaners. Solvents are not good for hand knitting yarns. Sweater soap and cold water is good for your yarns; therefore, since you are most concerned with how your knit will fit *after* the washing and blocking process, your stitch gauge should be wet and blocked out, then dried before you decide upon the gauge. Many yarns are synthetic or made of part synthetic yarns, which have a tendency to "grow" when wet and do not have as much elasticity as all-wool yarns. Many of the new yarns are of a *looser twist* which may "grow" when wet. Any pattern which draws up as you are knitting it (such as any of the rib patterns or fancy pattern stitches) must be blocked before deciding upon the gauge. Pattern stitches such as seed stitch or other patterns of knits over purls will "grow" when wet in many cases. Block your little gauge by getting it completely wet, drawing it out to what it must go to, then when the piece is dry, measure it. In many cases, a regular four-inch gauge before blocking will measure four-and-one-fourth inches when wet and then dried. You must know this, so that your needle size can be adjusted if necessary. It is most important that your gauge measure four inches *after* it has been wet and then dried. In the above-mentioned example, you would try another gauge with one size smaller needles. It is advisable to measure your gauge before and after blocking. Make a notation of the measurements before and after, and pin that information on your gauge. You will find it useful to use as a comparison as you proceed on your knitting.

WHAT WILL HAPPEN IF YOU ARE OFF GAUGE

The reason why a four-inch gauge is the only accurate one is because it gives you a large enough sample of your work so that you will not deceive yourself into thinking you are on gauge. If you knit a one- or two-inch gauge, you could push the stitches together or spread them out and make it come out to the one- or two-inch piece. But with the four-inch piece, if you are off one-fourth inch in four inches, that would only be a fraction of a stitch per inch. These fractions of stitches add up to stitches and stitches add up into inches. Therefore, if you were off one-fourth inch in a four-inch piece and proceed to knit the sweater anyway, you would find that in eight inches you would gain one-half inch, in sixteen inches you would gain one inch. If you were striving for a size 40 sweater, for instance, your sweater would turn out to be a size $42\frac{1}{2}$ inch.

The same holds true if your gauge should be off in the other direction. Instead of gaining one-fourth inch in every four inches, you would be losing one-fourth inch in every four inches. Now your sweater would turn out to be two-and-one-half inches smaller than you intended. Your size 40 would measure $37\frac{1}{2}$ inches which would be a bit tight for you.

Now, if you should be off one stitch per inch, you would soon be face to face with an Elephant Sweater. For example, let us assume that the total number of stitches required for a man's size 40 sweater at five stitches per inch is 200 stitches. If the knitter did not knit a sample gauge, but was knitting four stitches per inch instead of five, the sweater would measure 50 inches at the chest line, instead of 40 inches. The total number of stitches at the chest line including the stitches from the back and fronts was 200. Divide that number by the stitch gauge of five stitches per inch and you get a size 40 sweater. But, if you are getting only four stitches per inch instead of five, divide 200 by four and you get a size 50 sweater. Learn how to knit an accurate stitch gauge. Remember, it is the fraction of a stitch that makes the difference. Get as near to the gauge as it is possible to get, and a small difference can be blocked out.

Supply Kit

The following items should be in your knit bag with your

knitting at all times, then when you need one of these items, it will be available and ready to use.

Tape measure
Box of ring markers
Crochet hooks, sizes 0 and 00 (steel)
Package of little gold safety pins
Straight pins
Pair of size 0 knitting needles (for repair work)
Scraps of different colored yarn (for yarn holders and markers)
Pair of scissors
Tapestry needles
Scratch pad and pencil

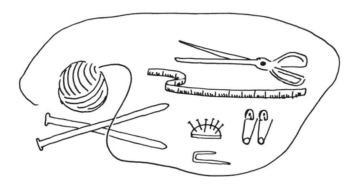

NOTE: Make sure that the yarn you intend to use as yarn holders and yarn markers is of good quality. These markers remain in the garment during the washing and blocking process and should they be of poor quality, they may run and fade on your garment.

Standard Abbreviations

The following is a list of the standard abbreviations used in most books:

Beg	Beginning
St	Stitch
K	Knit
P	Purl
Inc	Increase
Dec	Decrease

MC	Main Color
CC	Contrasting Color
Incl	Inclusive
Sl St	Slip Stitch
Tog	Together
YO	Yarn Over
*	Asterisk—means to repeat instructions following the asterisk as many times as specified
PSSO	Pass Slip Stitch Over
RH	Right Hand
LH	Left Hand

For Crochet

Ch	Chain
Sc	Single crochet
Dc	Double crochet
Hdc	Half double crochet
Trc	Treble crochet
Rnd	Round

Interpretation of Directions

You must learn to read every comma, period, semicolon, etc., when reading knit directions. Many people have difficulty reading through the directions and do not understand what the writer means for them to do.

EXAMPLE: "Work until piece measures 10″." The writer means that you are to work until the *entire* piece, including hem or ribbing measures ten inches. If the writer means to measure from above the hem or ribbing, the writer will state, for example, "Work until piece measures 10″ above hem."

If the writer states "Work in pattern for 4″, ending on a knit row," she means that you are to *end on a knit row, knit across that row and end on it.*

If the writer states "Work even for 6″," she means to follow your pattern as established, *without any shaping* for six inches.

If the writer directs: "K1, with yarn in front, sl 1 as if to purl." Many people cannot figure out how you would knit one with the yarn in front of work. If you notice where the comma is placed, it is right *after* the knit one. So you would knit one first, then notice the comma; that means you will start the next step which is to place your yarn in front of your work, then another comma, then slip one as if to purl. The commas set off each little step you are to do. Read from comma to comma, and the directions will make sense.

If the directions state: "Purl the next row, inc at even intervals to 176 sts." The writer means that you are to increase across that purl row, spacing evenly, all of the stitches needed to make 176 stitches. The writer does not mean that you are to start increasing up the sides, one stitch each side, at even intervals, as many readers interpret.

STARTING YOUR FIRST PROJECT

Now you have learned to knit, purl and rib, to decrease, increase and bind off, and you have learned to correct your mistakes. If your knitting looks quite even, you are ready to start your first project. Practice on yourself first. Select a pattern for yourself of a simple pullover or cardigan in a wool of knitting worsted weight. Choose a light or bright color for the first project. Use the yarn the pattern calls for; do not substitute. Select 100% wool worsted, as it is easier to control in the blocking process. Buy a pattern from a reliable pattern company; use A-One quality yarn, and needles from a good needle company. There is no substitute for quality. Yarns of poor quality may streak and run, or fade, or shrink, or stretch, and may not hold up through many washings. Poor yarn does not deserve your time and work. The same is true with patterns. Pattern books and yarns put out by good yarn companies are reliable, and show the latest fashions.

Choosing the Correct Size

Read through the directions for choosing the correct size and for knitting an accurate stitch gauge. Make sure you understand why you must do both of these for *every* garment you knit. You must understand that when you are knitting, you are making your own material. But, you have no paper pattern to lay on your material and you cannot cut your material if you have made it too large.

You must knit each piece properly and to your own measurements. Do not guess at sweater lengths or sleeve lengths. Use your own lengths. See Page 47 on "Measuring Sleeve and Sweater Lengths."

Take out your pattern book and in the upper left-hand corner of the book on the page where your directions are found, put down your *actual size* (your actual bust measurement). Then on the right-hand corner of the same page, put down your knit measurements.

Actual size 36	Knit size—39
	Length—14
	Sleeve length—15
	Overall—
	Overall sleeve—

Of course, you will be putting your own measurements into this chart. These measurements will be in front of you while you are knitting your sweater and you may desire to check measurements from time to time as you are progressing. When the time comes to match sweater pieces and block your sweater pieces, your planned measurements are there, and there is no last minute measuring. At that time you will insert the overall measurement (from neck to hem) and overall sleeve measurement (from top of cap to end of sleeve) of your finished pieces. It is most important that you get these measurements correctly. When it is time to block your pieces the overall measurements will help you to block the armholes to the correct length.

Abbreviations and Directions

Before you start your project, learn the abbreviations used in pattern books. See Page 39. Do exactly what is said, and do not read very far ahead or anticipate what you are to do until you get to that point. Remember, you are shaping sweater pieces, and when the pattern asks that you bind off, or decrease, this means that you are shaping for armholes, shoulders, neck, etc. You will start to *see* pieces being formed. Most pattern books give fairly complete knitting directions, and a key to reading the directions will be given at the start of the pattern. If the pattern calls for several different weights of yarns, determine what group your yarn comes in. Make sure you are reading in the right column. Make sure you are picking up the numbers for *your* size. An excellent method to use is to circle your size throughout the pattern. Be alert. If you do not understand the directions, read them over and over again until you do understand. Learn to think things out for yourself.

Diagram

The best way to knit accurately is to draw up a diagram of your sweater pieces. Draw them as you need them. Use all the little crutches mentioned in this book. They will help you to knit accurately.

Learn to use a simple diagram for everything you knit. A diagram is a picture of your piece and it tells you where to shape and when. Use of a diagram will improve your knitting 100% and you will make fewer mistakes and knit and measure more accurately. You will be able to know where you are at all times. If you should put your knitting away for several weeks, you can pick it up and go right on because you can tell by the diagram just where you left off. If you learn from the very beginning to draw up a simple diagram, and learn to use one, then when you become more skilled and are making some intricate project, where a diagram is absolutely necessary, you will be in the habit of using one and it will be easy for you to follow a difficult pattern. Get in the habit of drawing up a very large diagram. Use a full-sized piece of paper and start at the bottom. Your markings must not be crowded. If you are to be helped by this diagram, you must be able to read it easily. Leave plenty of room to show decreases and "stair step" bindings.

KEY TO DIAGRAMS

D = DECREASE

I = INCREASE

ER = EVERY ROW

EOR = EVERY OTHER ROW

工 = BIND OFF

⟨10⟩ = PLACE ON YARN HOLDER

Ϙ = YARN MARKER

To read this diagram: Cast on 87 stitches and rib for 1½ inches. Change to large needles and work until the piece measures thirteen inches. Shape the armhole at the beginning of the next two rows by binding off eight stitches. Tie in a colored scrap of yarn on the row of the first bind off. Then decrease one stitch at each end of the needle every other row, five times. Work even on 61 stitches until the armhole measures 7¾ inches. Then shape the shoulders: At the beginning of the next four rows, bind off six stitches, then at the beginning of the next two rows bind off seven stitches. Put the remaining 23 stitches on a yarn holder. See picture.

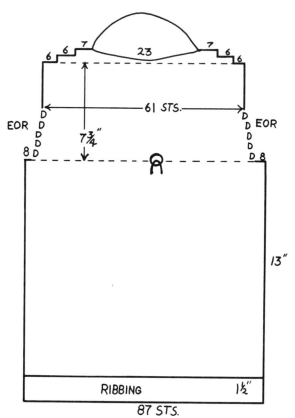

EXAMPLE OF DIAGRAM
BACK OF SWEATER

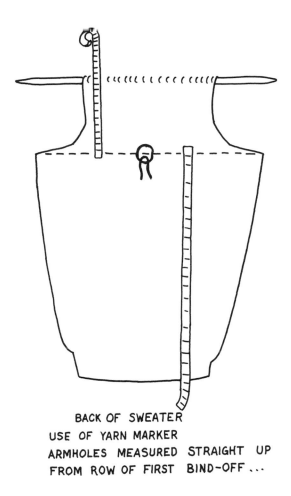

BACK OF SWEATER
USE OF YARN MARKER
ARMHOLES MEASURED STRAIGHT UP
FROM ROW OF FIRST BIND-OFF ...

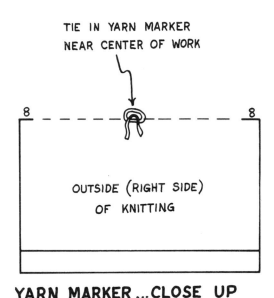

TIE IN YARN MARKER
NEAR CENTER OF WORK

8   8

OUTSIDE (RIGHT SIDE)
OF KNITTING

YARN MARKER...CLOSE UP

USE OF YARN MARKER

It is most important to measure the armhole accurately. Armholes are never measured around the curve of the armhole, but are measured straight up from the row of the first bind-off. That is why the yarn marker is used. You use it to measure from the first bind-off to the point of decrease for the shoulder. If you tie in the marker near the center of your work, your measurement will be more accurate than if you were to measure near the edge where there is stretch and sag.

The colored yarn marker is always placed on the outside of your knitting. In all patterns you start any new shaping or change of pattern on the right side of your work (outside).

Another use of the marker is to tell you when to decrease. If you are to decrease every other row, then when the yarn marker is facing you, you decrease, and when it is not facing you, you do not decrease. The importance of correct measurements cannot be stressed strongly enough. Since you do not have a paper pattern on which to lay your work, and have only the tape measure to rely upon, you must measure accurately, or the sleeve will not fit into the armhole properly. The sleeve is planned to fit the armhole, *if* measured exactly as the pattern states.

HOW TO KEEP YOUR PLACE ON THE DIAGRAM

You will know where you are at all times if you get into the habit of circling each part of the diagram as you do it.

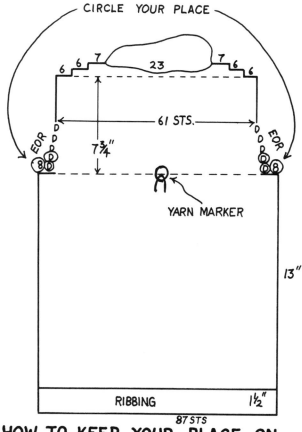

HOW TO KEEP YOUR PLACE ON THE DIAGRAM

EXAMPLE: As you bind off eight stitches at the beginning of the next two rows for the armholes, circle the eights. Then, when you decrease one stitch at each end of the needle every other row five times, circle the D's as you do them.

If you should have to lay your work aside after any of these decreases, you could quickly tell where to start in again.

MEASURING SLEEVE AND SWEATER LENGTHS

Although pattern books will give you the number of inches you are to work before shaping armholes or the number of inches for the sleeve length, you must consider that these dimensions are for the average person. If you want your sweater to fit you correctly, you must figure the lengths to fit your dimensions. If you are short, your sweater must naturally be a shorter length than the pattern asks for. If you are tall, you must make your sweater longer. Take careful measurements and make a note of them and insert YOUR measurements into the pattern. Stand in front of a full-length mirror and hold a tape measure to where you think

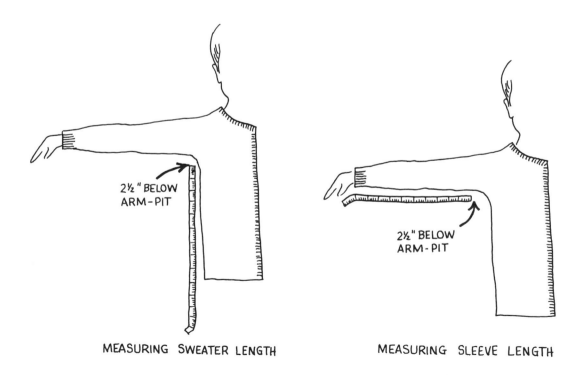

MEASURING SWEATER LENGTH   MEASURING SLEEVE LENGTH

the bottom of your sweater should come. Then measure the distance from your underarm to that exact length. When measuring from under the arm, do not hold the tape measure clear into the armpit. No sleeve ever fits clear into the armpit. Hold the tape approximately two-and-one-half inches below the armpit to the exact length you want your sweater to be. Most armholes start at a point two-and-one-half inches below the armpit. Occasionally some raglan sweaters will have a little longer armhole. When you measure your sleeve length, measure that, too, from approximately two-and-one-half inches below your armpit to the point on your arm which you want the sleeve to reach. If you are planning a full length sleeve, take into consideration that the sleeve will block down a little, and therefore, measure only to the wrist bone. A sleeve that is too long can be very uncomfortable. There is a way to cut off sleeves and reknit a new cuff if necessary, but careful measurement before starting your project will insure against having to take these drastic measures.

Needles and Needle Sizes

Most patterns require two different sizes of needles. The ribbing at the bottom (or hem) is usually worked on needles several sizes smaller. Then the main body is knit on a larger needle. The smaller needles are used again for cuffs, neck ribbing, etc. The reason for this is that ribbing is used to pull the edges in. This is what you want at the bottom of a sweater or on cuffs or neck ribbing. Follow directions in your pattern book and be prepared to change needles when the pattern asks that you do so. When changing from small to large needles, do not transfer the stitches to the large needle, simply knit off onto the larger size needle. You will be using one small and one large needle for the one row. From then on you will be using both large needles.

Using Yarn Holders

It is not good to use a metal holder in your work. If you are putting stitches off onto a holder for the neck, for example, the holder will remain in the piece through the washing and blocking process. If it is a metal holder, it may bother you during washing or it may catch and pull some stitches. A metal holder will pinch all of the stitches together, and you cannot stretch your work out again in the blocking. Always use a yarn stitch holder. Thread a tapestry needle with yarn of a different color and run the needle and yarn through the stitches (as if to purl). Then, bring the ends together and tie. Make sure your holders are making a loose loop that will allow you to stretch the stitches out so that they will lie flat.

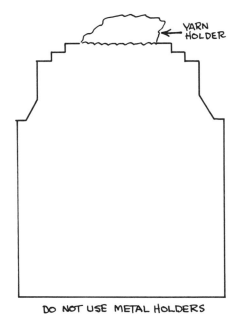

DO NOT USE METAL HOLDERS

AT LAST! READY TO KNIT!

After choosing your correct size, knitting your accurate stitch gauge and drawing your diagram, you should cast on and knit the back of the sweater, following all instructions.

Matching Edges

After the back is finished and before you start the front or fronts, examine the beginning edge where the stitches were first cast on. One side of the edge looks different from the other side. It is correct to use either of these edges for the outside, but it is very amateurish to use different edges for different pieces of the same sweater. Whichever edge was used for the outside on the first piece should be used throughout the sweater. Cast on for the

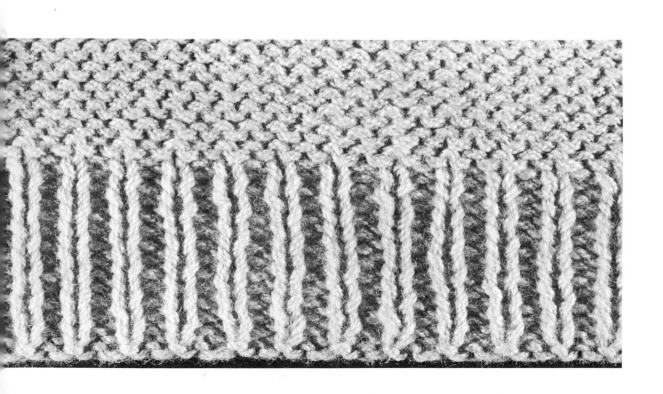

front (or one front, if a cardigan) and work a few rows. Then you will be able to see the difference between the two sides of the edge. Match the outside edge of the front to the outside edge of the back and mark the outside with a scrap of colored yarn.

Count Rows or Patterns

After the back is finished and as you are working the front or fronts, be sure to knit the fronts the same length as the back. Count the rows on the ribbing and knit as many rows on the front as you worked on the back. It is easy to count rows in stockinette stitch from the wrong side. See picture. Count the "bump" rows. If you have as many rows on the front as there are on the back (or within a few rows of the same number) when the time comes to assemble, you can use the "pick-up eye" method. If you do not have equal rows, you will have to use the back stitch. Remember that when you are binding off, you can bind off only at the beginning of a row. Therefore, you will be binding off one row higher on one piece than on the other piece. This cannot be helped and will not matter.

Knitting Two Fronts for a Cardigan

If you are ever in doubt about where the front edge is to be on a cardigan, or which side should have the underarm shaping, simply hold the piece up to your body with the outside colored yarn marker out, and if you are knitting the left side first, hold it to your left side. Then you can see which end of the needle

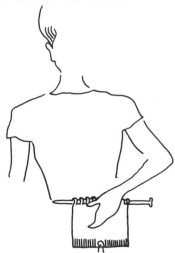

COUNT THE BUMP-ROWS

HOLD PIECE UP TO
LEFT SIDE

will have the front border and which end of the needle will be for the underarm shaping. When you are ready to work the other front piece, work a few rows, then mark the outside of the work so that the starting edge matches the other edges. If you will continually hold the piece up to your side, there will be no danger of your making two pieces for the same side. On your second front, the pattern will not give you complete directions, but will ask that you reverse all shaping. This, you can easily do, by holding the piece to your body on the side intended and shaping accordingly. Use the diagram you used for the first front you made. *See example diagram.* If you have circled all the shapings, then put an "X" over the circles as you do each step to keep track of your place on the diagram.

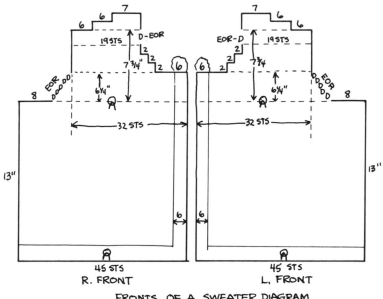

FRONTS OF A SWEATER DIAGRAM
EXAMPLE – NECK SHAPING

NECK SHAPING FOR THE FRONTS

When it is time to shape the front neck for the left front, the distance from the yarn marker should measure $6\frac{1}{4}$ inches. You have 32 stitches on your needle. Work across the row until you come to the six border stitches. Do not work them, slip them onto a yarn holder for later use when you are finishing the neck. On the next row, bind off two stitches at the neck edge, and finish the row. Circle the first two stitches bound off on your diagram. On the next row, you do not shape the neck. You will shape at the neck every *wrong* side row until you have bound off all of the twos and have circled them. Then, on the next right side row, decrease one stitch at the neck edge. Circle the one stitch decrease. Now all of the neck shaping has been worked and according to the diagram, you have nineteen stitches left on the needle. Count to see if you do have nineteen stitches. You will work on the nineteen stitches now until your armhole measures 7 ¾ inches from the yarn marker. Then, you will take your shoulder shaping starting all of your bind-offs from the *armhole* side. Your left front is finished.

Work the right front to correspond to the finished left front, and if you would be helped by drawing up another diagram showing the shaping for the right front, do so. See diagram, page 52.

NOTE: Since you can bind off only at the beginning of a row, your bind-offs will all start from the opposite side from where they started on your left front.

MARKING POSITION OF BUTTONHOLES

Patterns will ask that you first knit the front piece that does not have the buttonholes (left front for women, and right front for men). After the piece is finished, you will mark the position of the buttons with safety pins or colored yarn. The pattern will give you the position of the first and last buttons, and ask that you evenly distribute the others.

EXAMPLE: Mark the position for seven buttons, the first button one inch above the starting edge and the last button one-half inch from the start of the neck shaping. Now if you have the first and last buttons marked, measure the distance with a tape measure from the first to the last and if you have seven buttons, you will need six spaces. (You will always need one less space than the number of buttons.) That will give you the distance between buttons. If the distance between the first and last button marking is eighteen inches, your buttons should be marked three inches apart (eighteen inches divided by six spaces), and you would fasten in the little gold safety pins on the border three inches apart.

As you knit the side with the buttonholes, you should keep

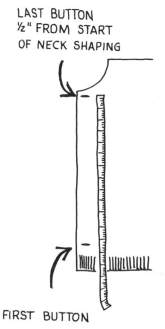

LAST BUTTON ½" FROM START OF NECK SHAPING

FIRST BUTTON

comparing it to the first piece, and when you come to the marked button position, you will make a buttonhole. If you are using the vertical buttonhole, you must start the buttonhole one-fourth inch below the marker; but if you are using the horizontal buttonhole, start at the marker. When comparing the second piece to see if it is time to work the buttonhole, lay the second piece over the first piece, as shown. Do not try to compare exactly on the edge because there is stretch and sag. If you are making a vertical buttonhole, start it when the top of the needle touches the pin, (that will be about one-fourth inch below the marker). Do not count rows between the buttonholes. It is best to use the comparison method given above.

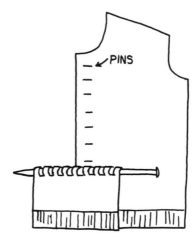

LAY SECOND PIECE OVER
FIRST ONE ... DO <u>NOT</u>
COMPARE ON EDGES ...

KNITTING THE FRONT FOR A PULLOVER

You may want to use the same diagram for the front that you used for the back of your sweater until you come to the front neck shaping. Most patterns ask that you knit the front the same as the back until you reach the point where the neck is to be shaped. The instructions which were used as an example for the back diagram continue on for the front:

"Front—Work same as back until armholes measure 6″. There are 61 sts on needle. *Next row:* Work across 38 sts, slip the last

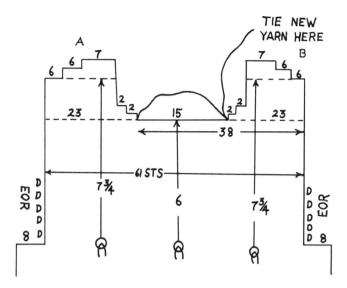

PLACE NEW YARN MARKER IN CENTER OF
SIDE AS STATED

15 sts on a holder for neck stitches, work to end of row. Continue working on each side with a separate ball of yarn binding off 2 sts at each neck edge every other row twice, shaping shoulder the same as the back when armholes are the same length."

Draw up your diagram for the front as shown in the *picture*.

Take your underarm shaping as you did on the back of your sweater, circling all of your markings as you did before. Now, when your armhole measures six inches from the yarn marker, it is time to shape the front neck. Work across 38 stitches from the right side of work, then thread the last fifteen of those 38 stitches onto a yarn holder (that will leave you with 23 stitches remaining on the right-hand needle). Then you will finish the row, across the 23 stitches on the left-hand needle, working them over to the right-hand needle. Since there is a large space between the two pieces, and you will have to work these two pieces separately until you come to the end of the shoulder shaping, you will need to tie in another ball of yarn at the side of the fifteen center stitches so that you will have yarn on that part of your front to continue on up to the top. (NOTE: You will have had to move the position of the yarn marker, because it was in the center of your work and you took off the stitches at the center of your work. Place new yarn markers in the center of each side as they are placed in the diagram so that you can measure from the markers on the separate pieces.)

Now you will be knitting two separate pieces with two separate balls of yarn. To simplify this procedure, label the left section of the front "B" and the right section of the front "A". Hold them to your body with the right side out to make sure that you have labeled them correctly. Use little scraps of paper and pin these papers right onto your knitting, tagging the sides "A" and "B". (After you have done this once or twice, you will not need to label the separate sides.) Your yarn is now at the arm edge of section "A". Work across section "A". Now tie in the new ball of yarn on section "B" at the neck edge. Just after you tie in the new ball of yarn, bind off two stitches at the neck edge, circling the two on your chart as you bind them off, then finish the row. On the next row work across section "B" with no shaping, then take up the other yarn and work across section "A" binding off two stitches on the neck edge and circle those two on your diagram. Finish the row. On the next row, work across section "A" with no shaping, take up the other ball of yarn for section "B" and bind off two stitches at the neck edge for the last of the neck shaping for that section, and finish the row. On the next row, work across the section "B" without any shaping, take up the other yarn, for section "A", and bind off two stitches at the neck edge for the last of the shaping for section "A" and finish the row. Now all of your neck shaping has been done and you will continue working on each piece with its separate ball of yarn until your work measures $7\frac{3}{4}$ inches from the yarn marker. It is now time to bind off for the shoulders. Do so and your piece is finished.

Sometimes your pattern will have you finish one half of the front with the original ball of yarn, then tie in a yarn at the neck edge on the other piece and work it separately until it is finished.

Knitting the Sleeves

If the sleeve has ribbing on the cuff, make sure that the starting edge is the same as the starting edge on the back and the fronts. When measuring the sleeve to determine when to put in increases, always measure near the middle of the work, away from the edges where there is stretch and sag. Plan on increasing on the right side (or "outside") rows, always measuring from the bottom to just under the needle. Do not measure the distance between the increases or count rows. If the work does not quite measure what it should and yet another row would make it more than needed, put the increases in as near to the measurement as possible on an outside row, and as you are always measuring from the bottom of the work the spaces will average out. The important thing to remember is that your increases must all be made by the time you reach the last two inches before you are ready to bind off for the armholes.

If increases are to be put in every inch twelve times and the ribbing is two inches, the first increase would come when the piece measures three inches; the second increase would come at four inches, and so on. Mark the increases each time with a small gold safety pin in the center of your work, or circle the increases on your diagram. By using one of these methods, it will be easy for you to count your increases and know how many you have made and how many more are needed. When all of the increases are in, work even until you reach the number of inches you decided upon for your sleeve length. Then, you are ready to shape the cap.

Draw up a diagram of the cap of the sleeve. Be sure to tie in your colored yarn marker at the point of the first bind off. See diagram. The second sleeve is to be made exactly the same as the first sleeve.

NOTE: If your pattern asks that you put increases in every three-fourths of an inch twelve times, you may want to change it to read every one-half inch six times, then every inch six times.

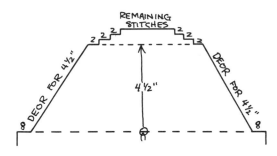

EXAMPLE OF DIAGRAM FOR CAP OF SLEEVE

It is much easier to measure in the halves and wholes than in other fractions of inches.

If the pattern asks that you increase every twelfth row, for example, find out by checking your stitch gauge how far that is in inches, and then substitute inch measurements.

EXAMPLE: Six rows equals one inch—the increases would come every two inches.

Most sleeve directions in pattern books are for sleeves too long for the average arm. Make sure to knit your sleeve to the correct length for you. You may find it necessary to plot your sleeve on scratch paper to make sure that you will get in all of the necessary increases before it is time to shape the cap. *See plot of sleeve length.* You must not still be increasing just as you are ready to bind off to shape the cap.

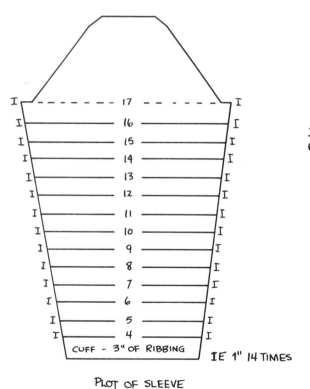

PLOT OF SLEEVE

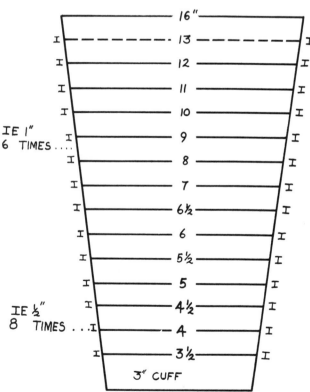

ADJUSTED SLEEVE LENGTH AND ADJUSTED INCREASES

This sleeve will need to be adjusted to have all of the increases in by the time the sleeve measures fourteen inches, and still allow for working even at least two inches before binding off to shape the cap.

ASSEMBLING

Preparation Before Assembling

MATCHING SWEATER PIECES

After all pieces have been knit and before you block the sweater pieces, make sure that each piece is knit properly. Lay like pieces (two sleeves, two fronts) together and make sure that they are exactly alike. Make sure that the side edges of the back are the same as the side edges of the fronts. Make sure that

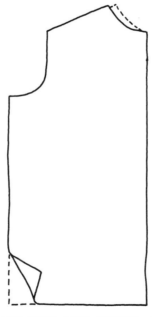

MAKE SURE LIKE PIECES ARE
EXACTLY ALIKE

MATCHING SWEATER PIECES

bound-off shoulders, necks, etc., have plenty of stretch. If not, rebind. Then, when you are sure that all pieces match and are knit correctly, work in all of the ends. Then the sweater pieces are ready to wash, block and assemble.

All trim, collars, neck ribbing, pockets, etc., are done after blocking.

After matching the pieces, be sure to make a note of the over-all back measurement, and the over-all sleeve measurement. Put these measurements with the other knit measurements that you have, so they can be used when the pieces are being blocked out to the correct size and length.

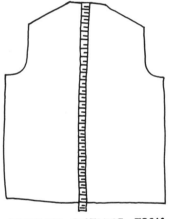

MEASURE DISTANCE FROM
VERY TOP TO VERY BOTTOM

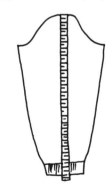

MEASURING OVER-ALL SLEEVE
AND BACK

Do *NOT* take out the yarn markers you used to measure your armhole lengths and your outside markings. They are intended to be left in through the blocking and assembling. However, you must remove any safety pins which have been used for marking.

WORKING IN ENDS

All ends should be worked in before the pieces are blocked. The only ends not worked in are those that are coming from the yarn holders.

If you have a knot in the middle of your work, make sure that it is on the wrong side. Untie it and work in as follows: End No. 1 must go through hole No. 2, and end No. 2 must go through hole No. 1. Then, each end should be worked through several back

WRONG SIDE

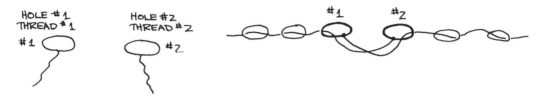

KNOT UNTIED

loops and clipped off. Ends that were tied in at the edge of work should also be crossed and worked in as above, then worked up and down several edge loops in the opposite direction. Ends that are on an outside edge should be crossed, then brought to the

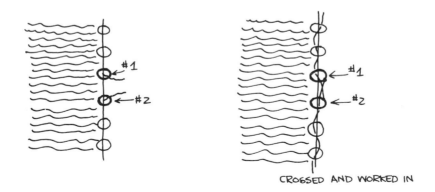

CROSSED AND WORKED IN

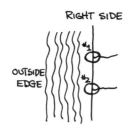

WORKING IN ENDS
RIBBING BORDER

RIGHT SIDE

OUTSIDE
EDGE

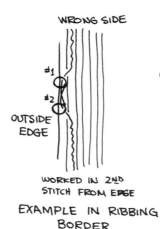

WRONG SIDE

#1

#2

OUTSIDE
EDGE

WORKED IN 2ND
STITCH FROM EDGE

EXAMPLE IN RIBBING
BORDER

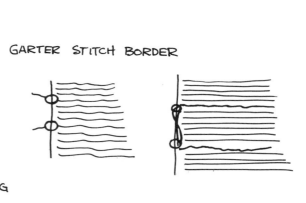

GARTER STITCH BORDER

wrong side and worked into the second row or the second stitch in from the edge. This will conceal the thread better than if it had been worked in on an outside edge.

WASHING

All sweater pieces get soiled while they are being knit; therefore, they should be washed before blocking and assembling. Then when the sweater is finished, it will look brand new and clean. Do not be afraid to wash and block knit pieces. Water and sweater soap are good for your wool. Solvents and cleaning fluids are not gentle to wool yarns. Solvents tend to make knits hard and sometimes colors become grey after many cleanings. Water, on the other hand, will not harm yarn. If you have hard water, use a *good* water softener. (If the water is hard, it will be difficult for you to rinse out all of the soap. This causes matting.)

Do not attempt to assemble sweater pieces that have not been washed and blocked. You cannot possibly sew a straight seam in your sweater if the edges are rolling and curling. It is easy to block to the exact measurements while your sweater is in pieces, and it is very difficult to block to these measurements if the sweater is already assembled. To get a professional look to your sweater, you should always first block the sweater pieces, then all the trim should be added after blocking and during assembling.

Washing Do's and Don'ts

Do's	Don'ts
Use cold water	Never use warm water
Use a good sweater soap	Never use excessive amounts of soap
Use the amount the package recommends	Never over-soak
Allow sweater pieces to soak three minutes	Never rub pieces together
Handle pieces very gently	Do not hold wet sweater pieces up and let them sag
Swish the sweater pieces around in the suds	Never leave pieces rolled up in a towel
Press out the soapy water (bring pieces to edge of bowl and push out the soapy water)	Never dry in the sun or near direct heat
Rinse at least four times in cold water	
Press out excess moisture	
Lay pieces out on a turkish towel	
Block immediately	
To hasten drying in a cold room, change towels under pieces twice a day	

BLOCKING

Pieces will block nicely if you leave lots of moisture in them. Do not roll the pieces in a towel until you are ready to block each piece. Roll them very quickly so as to leave the pieces quite wet. In trying to block pieces which have been rolled in a towel so that most of the moisture is taken out, you will find it difficult to remove wrinkles and that the pieces will be stubborn and refuse to conform to your measurements. Re-wet the pieces so that you can control them.

Block the pieces in a place where they will not have to be moved during the drying process. Use clean padding under sweater pieces to absorb moisture; towels or pieces of quilted bed pads will do nicely. Lay out your knit measurements (those you jotted down at the top of the pattern page). Start with the back piece, and lay it out with the right side up. Smooth it from the center out, until it meets the measurements you have jotted down. The back should measure half of the knit measurement at the bust. (Knit size 40—block back out to twenty inches plus seam allowance of approximately one fourth inch on each side.) Next, make sure that the length is correct. Always measure from the yarn marker to the exact length you have jotted down. If the piece appears to be too long, you must push it up with the palms of your hands. If the piece is too short—working from the center, push both up and down. Make sure that the edges are even and straight. Work with them, pinching them to a straight line. The ribbing at the bottom should be blocked completely out. Next measure the "over-all." If the "over-all" is not the exact measurement you jotted down the adjustment must be made in the upper part (opposite the armhole), measuring up from the yarn marker. When you are satisfied that the piece fits the measurements and is straight on all of the edges, rub out any unevenness with your fingers, then "press" the piece all over with the palms of your hands to make it flat. This will remove most wrinkles.

If your sweater is a cardigan, the next step is to block the fronts. Lay out one front, pressing it out or pushing it in to the

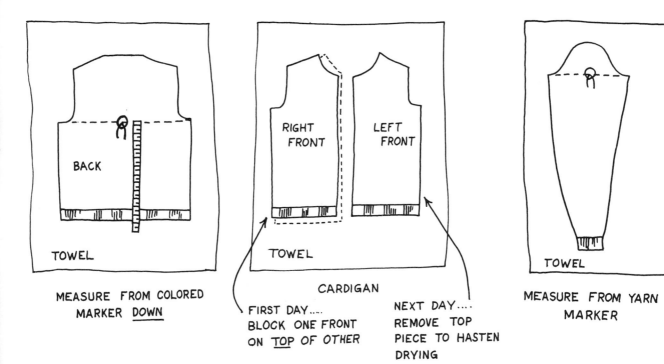

BACK

TOWEL

MEASURE FROM COLORED
MARKER <u>DOWN</u>

RIGHT
FRONT

LEFT
FRONT

TOWEL

CARDIGAN

FIRST DAY....
BLOCK ONE FRONT
ON <u>TOP</u> OF OTHER

NEXT DAY....
REMOVE TOP
PIECE TO HASTEN
DRYING

TOWEL

MEASURE FROM YARN
MARKER

measurements, as you did on the back. For the bust measurement, use one-fourth of the knit size (size 40—one front is ten inches). Be sure to measure from the *center* of the front band and allowing one-fourth inch for one side seam. When you are satisfied that the piece fits the size and lies straight, lay the other front on top of it, right sides together. You do not need to measure this second piece, because you have carefully measured the first front. Like pieces are blocked together so that they will be exactly alike. However, on the second day, the top piece should be removed in order to hasten the drying process. Lay it beside the other piece with the right side up. Move the piece carefully.

Now block the sleeves. First, do one sleeve laying it out as above to the measurements you have jotted down. The width of ladies' sleeves before the start of the cap shaping should be at least fourteen inches (or divide the number of stitches on the piece at that point by your stitch gauge to get the exact measurement). Measure lengths accurately from the yarn markers. Make sure that the over-all measurement is correct. Then, lay the other sleeve out on top of the first sleeve right sides together just as you did for the fronts. Move the top sleeve off on the second day.

If your sweater is a pullover, the front should be blocked on top of the back to make sure that they are exactly alike, then moved on the second day.

Extra tips to the new blocker

If sweater pieces seem to grow and you have trouble pushing them back to the desired length and width, re-wet the pieces in cold water and do not press out all the water. The wetter the pieces are, the easier they are to push back in. If you are having trouble making the sweater wide enough (i.e., as soon as you lift your hands off of the pieces, they begin to creep back in again), weight down the edges with something heavy (such as fruit jars or drinking glasses). Do not pin the pieces down. It is too hard to remove the little peak marks left from the pins after the pieces are dry.

Assembling

THE OLD VERSUS THE NEW IN ASSEMBLING KNIT GARMENTS

The lovely coats, suits and dress patterns now available deserve that "tailored" look. You can get that look with practice and correct methods.

Knitted garments may be put together in many ways. The old method was to finish the garment flat so that there were no seams showing on the wrong side. This flatness seemed to be an obsession with knitters, but in pursuing it they turned out garments with a home-made look. Now the new concept is for elegance on the outside, with the inside looking neat and perfect but with seams, either back-stitched on uneven edges, or with "picked-up eye" stitches on straight edges. These seams do away with the uneven look produced when seams were butted together to achieve the "flat" look, and all of the unevenness of the edge stitch showed. Never should you sacrifice the outside in order to have the inside flat; better to have the outside perfect and the inside neat, with seams if necessary. The hand knit can and does have an elegant "tailored" look, if pieces are first washed and blocked properly and the new, modern seam methods are used.

The hand knit deserves hand finishing. It is a shame to spoil lovely hand work by making seams by machine, or working button-holes by machine.

SEWING UP A SEAM (OLD WAY) WEAVING BACK AND FORTH

PROPER SEQUENCE

If the sweater has set in sleeves, sew the shoulder seams first using the *back stitch*. Then, set in the sleeve using the back stitch. Sew from the sweater side rather than from the sleeve side. Then, sew the sleeve seam and the body seam all in one. Split yarn should be used in most cases. If yarn is four-ply use two of the plies; if yarn is three-ply take one ply away. In doing the back stitch, anchor the thread without knots. Pull up the stitch and stretch out the seam after each stitch, continually looking back to see if the work is satisfactory. Stay in far enough so that the decrease and increase marks will not show from the right side. Do not let any of the ugly bound-off stairstep edge show in the seams. Each seam should be steamed out before any cross seams are made. If the seams have increases or decreases a back stitch must be used. If the seams are straight use the method of "picking up the eye." This is done from the right side. Do not attempt to use "pick-up eye" if the work is in a pattern stitch as it is too difficult to do this. Use the back stitch.

To give an extra professional look, all back-stitched seams should be carefully tacked back with sewing thread of a matching color.

If the sweater has raglan sleeves, all of the raglans should be seamed first. If the raglan is full-fashioned use the "pick-up eye" method. If the raglan is not full-fashioned (if the decreases are right on the edge), use the back stitch method. Then the sleeve seam and the body seam should be seamed all in one.

FINE POINTS OF ASSEMBLING

Assembling sweaters correctly is tedious monotonous work. If the work is done in a hurry you can easily ruin an otherwise beautiful sweater. If you find that you are getting careless, and that your stitches are not as small as they should be, put the work aside and go back to it later when you are not bored. Do not do a careless job. It takes a special knack to assemble a sweater nicely. If you do not have this knack, develop it by using the best methods and do not be satisfied unless it is perfect.

Be sure to examine the work at frequent intervals, then corrections can be made with a minimum of ripping. Do not ever attempt to assemble a sweater that has not first been washed and blocked. The edges roll and curl and it is most difficult to sew a straight seam. In order for your sweater to look hand made instead of home made, it must be blocked before being assembled.

Split yarn should be used whenever possible because you will have a much prettier sweater if the seams are dainty and flat. If the yarn is too weak after splitting; then, of course you must use full strength yarn. Do not use long strands of yarn in seaming as the yarn will become weak before you have used it up. Use a piece not longer than eighteen inches. Always anchor the thread near the seam you intend to sew. Go over the edge twice. See picture, page 68. Use fine tapestry needles, No. 18 or No. 20 for seaming.

Using the back stitch

This seam is always done from the wrong side. If you are sewing a stair-step shoulder seam, pin the two pieces together wrong sides out. Start at the armhole edge and anchor the thread (without a knot) near to the edge of one of the pieces, then weave

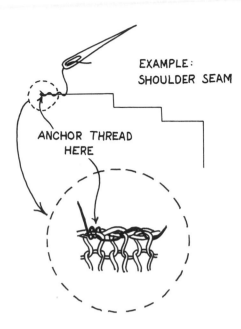

EXAMPLE:
SHOULDER SEAM

ANCHOR THREAD
HERE

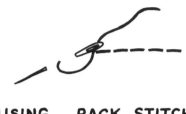

USING BACK STITCH

the needle through threads to get to the edge. In order to do this stitch, you must go back about one thread, then forward one thread, pull up on thread, stretch out on seam after each stitch in order to assure plenty of stretch on the seam. Stay in far enough from the edge so that the bound-off edge does not show. Taper up the stair-steps, do not jog. End the seam by going over the edge twice at the neck edge. If the neck stitches are on a yarn holder, fasten off your thread at the base of the first stitch on the yarn holder so that no stitches on the holder will be sewed into the seam and so that there will not be a gap between the seam and the stitches on the yarn holder.

Steam out all seams before any cross seams are made.

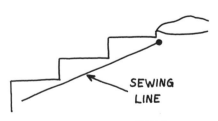

SEWING
LINE

TAPER UP STAIR STEPS
DO NOT JOG

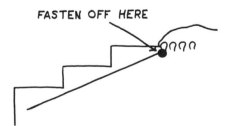

FASTEN OFF HERE

FASTEN OFF TO BASE OF
FIRST STITCH ON YARN HOLDER

Method of steaming seams

Knit pieces are *never* ironed. The weight of the iron *never* rests on the knit pieces. The ironing table should be heavily padded with Turkish towels. A steam or a dry iron may be used. You will be making your own steam with a wet Turkish wash-cloth. *Make sure the setting of the iron is no hotter than "wool".* An iron that is too hot may cause a color change on that part of the garment that is steamed. Lay the seam out on the padded surface with the wrong side of the garment facing you and the right side down on the ironing table. Now lay a wet wash-cloth (the cloth must be nearly dripping wet in order to make enough steam) over the seam to be steamed. Do not try to open out the seam at this time. Now touch the wash-cloth with the hot iron and you will hear a sizzling sound. Do not let any weight of the iron rest on the wash-cloth. You will be holding back the weight and just touching the iron to the wash-cloth.

After you have held the iron in position for a few seconds, remove the wash-cloth and test the seam to see if it is damp enough. If it is, then with your fingers, carefully open out the seam. This will give you a finish you cannot get in any other way. Your seam will look pressed open, but your knitting will not look ironed or matted. It will still retain that third dimensional look. *Never* iron directly on any part of the knit pieces, but always make steam with the wet wash-cloth method. If you are steaming out a sleeve seam, for instance, (or any other curved seam) you must do the work in many little steps in order to get around the curve and not stretch out the piece in any other place. Keep the seam close to the edge and point of the ironing table and proceed as before.

NOTE: It is most important that the wash-cloth be wet at all times. You will find that you will be continually wetting it in order to make the steam you need. Use a small square of Turkish toweling (a wash-cloth) instead of a large piece. The small piece will enable you to wet only that part of the sweater you intend to steam and will not drip all over other parts of your sweater. Make sure that you carefully open out all seams with your fingers. Do not rub the seam, press open with the fingers.

Setting in sleeves

After the shoulder seam has been seamed and steamed open

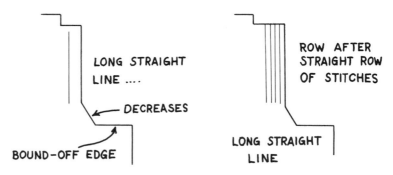

LONG STRAIGHT
LINE ....

ROW AFTER
STRAIGHT ROW
OF STITCHES

DECREASES

BOUND-OFF EDGE

LONG STRAIGHT
LINE

TO SET IN SLEEVES

you are ready to set in the sleeves. Notice that on the fronts and back at the armhole, you have a bound-off edge, then a curve, then a long line straight up to the shoulder. Examine that long straight line. You will notice that you have row after straight row of stitches there.

Plan on sewing in the sleeve in such a way that the seam will be straight and will not wiggle in and out of the rows. In other words, you must get in a groove and stay in it all the way up the long straight line. That is the reason why you must sew from the sweater side instead of the sleeve side. The sleeve side does not have a long straight line, it is curved all the way around. Many people are most careless and just pin the sleeve in place and sew it in with no thought about that straight edge groove. These people will have a poor amateurish job. It takes a great deal of practice in sewing to be able to stay in the groove because you are sewing from the wrong side of the work and cannot easily see the groove. Therefore, it is best that the beginner put in a guide line with split yarn or sewing thread of a different color. In order to do this, set in the guide line from the right side and have the guide line follow a groove about one-and-one-half stitches in from the edge. (This will be like a basting thread which will be pulled out after you have finished the seam, or pulled out as you are sewing the seam.) Make guide lines on all pieces and make sure that the groove follows through the shoulder seam and onto the other side of the armhole without a jog.

Now you are ready to pin in your sleeve. Find the middle of the cap of the sleeve and pin it to the shoulder seam. Place

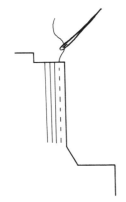

SET IN GUIDE LINE FROM
RIGHT SIDE OF WORK

in pins all around the armhole easing in any fullness. Start at one bound-off edge with the sweater side facing you, and sew using the back stitch near the bound-off edge and up through the curve where the decreases are, staying in far enough so that the unevenness does not show (approximately one-fourth inch), then when you come to the long straight line, get in the groove and stay in it.

Be continually looking back to see if your work is satisfactory. If there is a stitch that does not please you, rip it right out before you proceed. When you have finished the seam, steam out the seam, taking many little steps so as not to stretch out the piece in any other place. Open the seam with your fingers as you proceed. You should have a very professional looking job of setting in the sleeve by using this method.

If you should try to set in the sleeve after the side and sleeve seams have been sewed, you would find that you would have trouble crowding the sleeve into a little round armhole. But, if you use the method explained above, setting in the sleeve as a flat piece, you will find that you can get at the curves and can steam out your seams and do a first class job.

Now you are ready to sew the sleeve and body seam all in one.

Sewing the sleeve seam

If your sweater has ribbing at the cuff, start in above the cuff and anchor your thread without a knot. Since your sleeve has increases, you will have to use a back stitch. Pin the sleeve together so that the edges will come out right when you reach the point where the sleeve and the sweater meet. You should sew the cuff according to directions for cuff, given later.

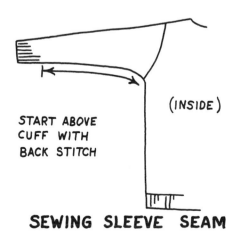

(INSIDE)

START ABOVE
CUFF WITH
BACK STITCH

SEWING SLEEVE SEAM

Sewing side seams

If your sweater does not have any increases on the side seams and you are in stockinette stitch (not in a pattern stitch), you can use the method of "picking up the eye." This is an unusually fine way of sewing a seam that is straight with no increases or decreases. From the right side of the work your sweater will look as though there is no seam there, but on the wrong side a small seam will show. It takes some practice to do a good job and still have a little stretch on the seam. If you are not pleased with the work take it out immediately.

Do not fasten off the thread you had left from the sleeve seam but when you come to the seam at the underarm, bring the needle and thread through to the right side because the "pick-up eye" is done from the right side of your work.

Picking up the eye

In order to "pick up the eye," you must have within three rows of the same number of rows on each piece. It is a good idea to count rows if you intend to "pick up the eye." "Picking up the eye" is done from the right side of the work with split yarn. (Do not attempt to "pick up the eye" in a pattern stitch. Use back stitch on patterns.) Work from the top to the bottom rather than from the bottom to the top.

Learning to recognize the eye

The eye is the little thread between two stitches. In order to find the eye, first find the "up" stitch, and the eye is just to the side of the "up" stitch. Examine the stitches near the edge of your

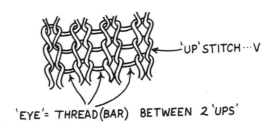

'UP' STITCH···V

'EYE'= THREAD (BAR) BETWEEN 2 'UPS'

SEAMS
PICKING UP THE EYE

work. A stitch starts in a hole, the thread goes up and under another stitch, then back into the same hole again. A down stitch is a stitch hanging down, but in reality it is not a stitch—it is half of two stitches. If you can see the stitch pointing up, you can find the eye, which is the little bar between two stitches. The stitches look like little "V's".

Do not try to "pick up the eye" on the very edge of your work. Your stitches are uneven right on the edge and so you will want to come in one stitch and "pick up the eye" between the first and second stitches.

If you have just seamed the sleeve and are ready to sew the body seam, bring your yarn and needle through to the right side of your work. Now "pick up the eye" between the first and second stitches in from the edge on one of the pieces to be joined, then go the eye (between the first and second stitches) and pick it up on the opposite piece. Working from side to side, pick up one eye on one piece, then one eye on the opposite piece. Do not pull the thread too tight. Stretch out the seam after every third set of eyes.

PICKING UP 'EYE'

WORKING FROM SIDE TO SIDE
PICK UP ONE EYE ON ONE
PIECE AND ONE EYE ON THE
OTHER PIECE.

STRETCH AFTER EVERY
THIRD SET OF EYES

NOTE: You cannot pick up the eye if there are any increases or decreases on the side seams.

Examine your work carefully as you are proceeding downward, make sure you do not get out of your groove. The eyes are lined up one on top of another and if you should come in too far, you will have a flaw in your seam which must be corrected. Keep comparing the sides to be joined at the bottom to make sure you will come out with both sides matching. If you have the same number of rows on each piece, you will come out exactly right at the bottom. If, however, you have several rows more on one piece than on the other piece, you must know this in advance so that you can distribute these extra rows so that they will not be noticeable.

EXAMPLE: Three rows more on one side than on the other. Place three pins in the side with the extra rows, one near the top, one near the middle and one near the bottom of the piece. As you are working the seam and picking up the eye, when you come to the pin mark, pick up two eyes instead of one. You should come out even at the bottom and your extra rows are distributed evenly and will not show.

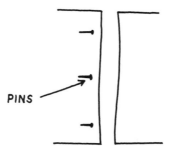

PINS

PLACE 3 PINS AT SIDE WITH
EXTRA ROWS

Steaming out a "pick up eye" seam

When you have finished "picking up the eye" seam, you may steam it very lightly on your padded ironing table with the right side down. Use a wet wash cloth as before but do not attempt to open out this seam. The seam is too small and therefore you must not try to open it out as you did for the back stitch seam. It will remain very flat.

Blending the ribbing

After you have seamed your sleeve and body seams the ribbing on the cuffs and at the bottom of the sweater is done.

Fasten split yarn where the ribbing begins and work down to the cast-on edge. If you blend the cuff correctly the ribbing will match exactly and you will not see any seam from the right side of the garment.

If your seam above the cuff has set your ribbing up so that two purl stitches are coming together, you can pick up the stitch in the middle of the purl stitch on each side to be joined and work from side to side the way you did for "picking up the eye," (you can be picking up the stitch instead of the eye). Now if two knits come together, pick up in the middle of each knit stitch and that will blend the ribbing completely. If one knit and one purl come together, "pick up the eye" at the side of the knit and the eye at the side of the purl to blend the ribbing. When you reach the cast on edge, go over the edges twice, then weave the needle through the edge stitches on the wrong side for about one inch, then cut off yarn.

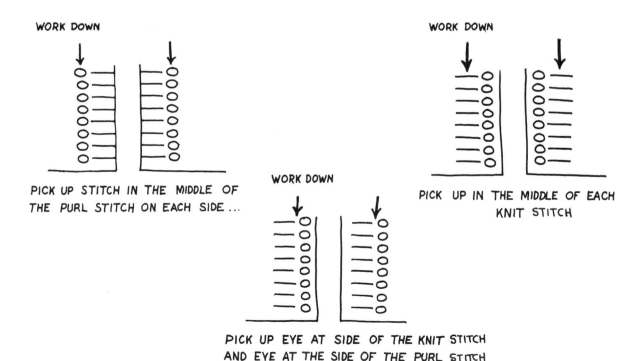

WORK DOWN

PICK UP STITCH IN THE MIDDLE OF THE PURL STITCH ON EACH SIDE ...

WORK DOWN

PICK UP EYE AT SIDE OF THE KNIT STITCH AND EYE AT THE SIDE OF THE PURL STITCH

WORK DOWN

PICK UP IN THE MIDDLE OF EACH KNIT STITCH

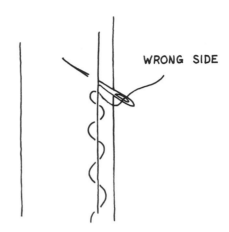

ALL BACK-STITCHED SEAMS SHOULD
BE TACKED DOWN WITH SEWING
THREAD OF MATCHING COLOR WITH
'SIDE TO SIDE' STITCH

Tacking back the seams with sewing thread

After your garment has been completely put together, all back-stitched seams should be carefully tacked down. Thread a sewing needle with the matching sewing thread, and anchor the thread near to the starting place without a knot. Use a little "side to side" stitch. First take a little stitch along the very edge of the seam, then take a little stitch in the sweater itself where the seam edge just touches the sweater. When sewing on the sweater side take up just a few threads of the yarn so that no stitches will show through on the right side. Do not pull up your stitches tightly or you will show an impression of the seam on the right side. You must leave some stretch in the seams. Stretch the seam out after every third or fourth stitch. Your stitches should not show on the wrong side nor on the right side. The next time you wash and block your garment your seams will stay nice and flat and will never need to be opened out again.

Adding neck trim, pockets, etc.

Any neck trim, pockets or collar, knitted or crocheted, are added after assembling. For details and instructions see pages 119, 129, 220, 223, 224, 236.

CHAPTER III

Improvement over the First Project

CHECKING ON THE FIT; A BASIC MEASUREMENT CHART

After you have knit a sweater for yourself, you should be able to tell a lot more about what you want in the fit of a sweater and what changes you will make on your second project. If your armholes seem too tight, make a notation of that fact, and decide what depth armhole would be better for you. If you have knit a raglan sweater, make sure that you are satisfied with the depth of the raglan. If you are not, decide upon what depth you want to use for your second sweater. If your sleeves seem too tight or too large, make a notation concerning the width of the sleeves. On your second sweater you can custom knit better and make all of these various corrections for a better fit. If your sleeves were too long or too short, make a notation to that effect and what sleeve length *you* need. If the length of your sweater is not correct, lengthen or shorten on the second sweater. If your bust is quite large, you may need to knit the fronts about an inch longer than the back to get a better fit over the bust. If you have made the fronts longer than the back, when you are sewing the fronts to the back, you will not be able to use the pickup eye method; you will need to use the back stitch, easing in the extra length of the fronts to fit the length of the back. Show all of the dimensions you need for yourself on a sketch, (see below), then adjust future patterns to your needs.

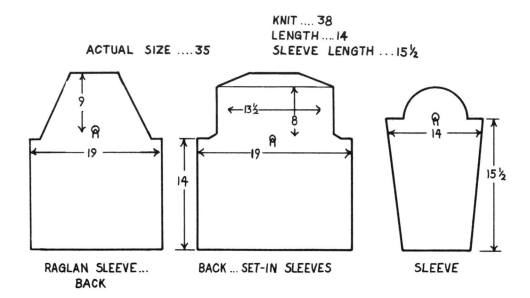

KNIT 38
LENGTH 14
SLEEVE LENGTH ... 15½

ACTUAL SIZE 35

RAGLAN SLEEVE...
BACK

BACK ... SET-IN SLEEVES

SLEEVE

Be sure to take into consideration what type of yarn you are using. If the yarn is quite bulky, or heavy mohair, you will need a larger sweater than you would need if you were using finer yarns. Certain sweaters do not look attractive if they are too short, others if they are too long. Make sure you are choosing the right length for you.

Did you cast on too tight? If you did, you probably had a hard time bringing your sweater pieces out to the desired width at the cast-on edge during blocking and perhaps they will draw the sweater toward the back as you wear it. DO NOT cast on too tightly on the next sweater. Remember that ribbing is meant to be blocked clear out. Look at pictures of ribbing in your pattern books. The ribbing is stretched out to its full capacity. The only exception to this rule is in the case of double neck ribbing where the ribbing is permitted to draw in to give the neck a tapered look.

Checking on your Stitch Gauge

To be on the safe side, even though you knit an accurate stitch gauge, you should check on your stitch gauge periodically to be sure you are still maintaining the same gauge. Sometimes, a knitter will loosen up when going faster, or knit too tightly when going slower. (Do not envy the fast knitter. Many times her knitting is not as even as that of the slower knitter. Your first concern is to obtain evenness, not speed.) A thorough check on the gauge should be made as you proceed on a skirt, for instance, because of the large number of stitches involved. If you are off stitch gauge by one-fourth inch in a four-inch piece, you will be considerably off in the finished garment. (If you are off only one-eighth inch in the four-inch piece, this small difference can be corrected in blocking. However, YOU MUST MAINTAIN YOUR STITCH

Measuring Stitch Gauge As You Are Working

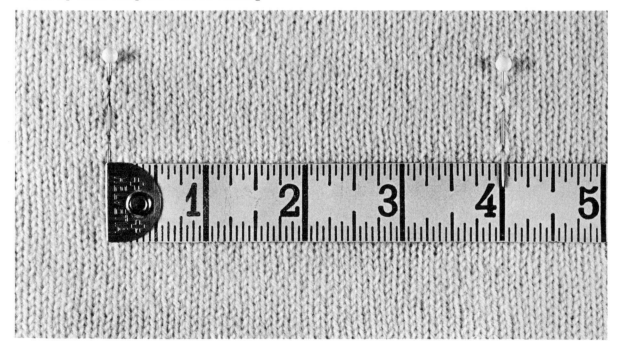

GAUGE, because your pattern was figured from that stitch gauge. If you are knitting more loosely as you go along, you must discipline yourself, and slow down to keep to the original gauge. *If it has been a long time since you have knit, do not knit your stitch gauge immediately.* You should practice knitting for a while to get your "pace" so to speak; then knit your stitch gauge.

To check your gauge along the way, insert a straight pin into your work then count out what would be equal to a four-inch piece (for five stitches per inch, count twenty stitches; for six stitches per inch count twenty-four stitches, etc.) then insert another pin. Measure between the pins with your tape measure to see if you are still on gauge. (See Photo, page 79.) Keep in mind how your work was affected by wetting the gauge, and take that fact into consideration when measuring your work as you proceed.

If you are off gauge, and have knit more loosely on the second piece of your project, and you are to count rows to match the first piece, not only will your piece be wider than it should be, but you will find that your second piece is a great deal longer than the first piece. Be on the alert to maintain gauge; slow down if necessary, to hold your gauge. Do not wait until a whole piece is knit to measure it. Measure as you go along.

CHAPTER IV

Crocheting for Finishing and Trimming

CROCHET

The finishing and trimming on many knit garments requires crochet. Learn to crochet with knitting yarns. It is much easier to see the stitches and to learn how to make the various stitches, than when learning on fine crochet thread. If you have never done any crocheting, purchase a #00 steel crochet hook and use knitting worsted yarn in a light color.

THE BASIC STITCHES

Chain Stitch (CH)

First, make a slip knot and attach the slip knot to the crochet hook. In crocheting, you must hold both your work and the loose thread in the left hand. The right hand holds the hook only. To work a long chain, hold the tag end of yarn left over from making your slip knot in your left hand between the thumb and *third* finger. Hold the yarn coming from the ball of yarn over your *index* finger. With the hook in your right hand, lay the crochet hook in front of the new yarn, wrap the yarn over the hook, then with the hook pointing *down,* take the new yarn through the loop already on your hook. One chain stitch has been worked. Continue working chain through chain for a nice length of chain so that you will get the feel of doing the chain stitch (about 30 chain stitches).

N O T E : You must keep moving your thumb and third finger up to hold the chain close to where you are working.

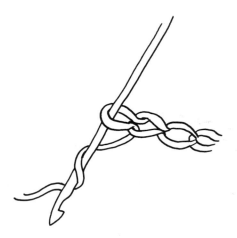

CHAIN STITCH

INSERT HOOK IN TOP TWO THREADS

SINGLE CROCHET

Single Crochet (SC)

If you care to use the chain you have just formed for the foundation of your work, you may do so. When working through a chain stitch, you should always insert the hook through two threads. See picture. Insert the hook in the top two threads of the second chain from the hook, put the yarn over the hook and draw a loop through (so that you have two loops on the hook), then put the yarn over the hook and draw the hook through the two loops on the hook (so that you have one loop left on the hook). One single crochet stitch has been worked. Work into each chain stitch, making a single crochet stitch in each chain stitch across your work. Chain one stitch (to count as one single crochet), then turn your work around. Now, put a single crochet in each single crochet of the previous row. Strive to make the stitches even.

NOTE: You must hold your thumb and third finger near to where you are working, and you must point your crochet hook down in order to pull another loop through. Do not have the loops on the hook too tight or it will be hard to pull new loops through. Work back and forth over these stitches working through both top loops until you are working evenly and easily.

If you would rather work some single crochet stitches directly on the edge of a knit piece, you may do so using the same directions, except that you will insert your hook into a hole near the edge of your knitting, yarn over and pull through, yarn over and pull through both loops on the hook. After you have learned to crochet, you will be given explicit directions on where to place your first row of stitches, through what holes, etc., on page 224, on Working Crocheted Edges.

Half Double Crochet (HDC)

To make a row of half double crochet stitches across the row, work as follows: Chain two to count as the first half double crochet stitch (one loop is already on the hook). Wrap the yarn around the hook, insert hook into the stitch, pull up a loop, yarn over and pull the yarn through all three loops on the hook. One half double crochet stitch completed. Work into each stitch across the row.

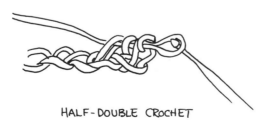

HALF-DOUBLE CROCHET

Double Crochet (DC)

To make a row of double crochet stitches across the row, work as follows: Chain three to count as the first double crochet stitch, turn work around, (one loop already on the hook). Wrap the yarn around the hook, insert the hook into the stitch, pull up a loop, yarn over, pull through two loops, yarn over and pull through two loops. One double crochet stitch completed. Work into each stitch across the row.

DOUBLE CROCHET

TREBLE CROCHET

Treble Crochet (TR C)

To make a row of treble crochet stitches across the row, work as follows: Chain four to count as one treble crochet stitch, turn work around, (one loop already on hook). Wrap yarn around the hook two times, insert the hook into the stitch, pull up a loop, yarn over, pull through two loops, yarn over, pull through two loops, yarn over and pull through two loops. One treble crochet stitch completed. Work into each stitch across the row.

Slip Stitch (SL ST)

To work a row of slip stitch across the row, work as follows: Turn the work around (one loop already on the hook). Insert the hook into the stitch, yarn over and pull through loop on the hook. One slip stitch completed. Work a slip stitch into each stitch across the row.

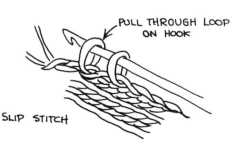

PULL THROUGH LOOP ON HOOK

SLIP STITCH

CHAPTER V

Variations on Stitches and Color to Create Designs

READING THE PATTERN

Marker on the Needle

The reason for putting a ring marker (a little metal or plastic ring) on the needle is to set off a given number of stitches, either for a border or for working a pattern stitch on a given number of stitches between the markers. If the pattern asks that you put a marker on the needle, slip the marker onto the needle so that it will show you where the pattern or border starts (or ends). When you are working across the rows, simply move the marker from one needle to the other. The marker will carry up, row after row, always on the needle.

RING MARKERS ON THE NEEDLE

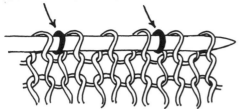

MARKER CARRIES UP ROW AFTER ROW

MARKING A STITCH

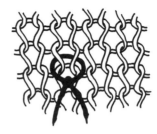

TIE IN COLORED YARN MARKER

(CAUTION) Many times a marker on the needle will cause a separation line which will not come out during the blocking process. If you see that you are leaving a separation line, do not use a regular commercial marker. Make one out of sewing thread and move it from needle to needle as you would a regular marker.

Marking a Stitch

If the pattern asks that you mark a stitch, you will simply tie in a colored yarn marker *through* that stitch. Such a marker will remain at that spot, and will not carry up through the rows.

Learning How to Read Pattern Stitches

Most pattern books will give you the directions for the pattern stitch before they go into detail on directions for the back, etc. And then, when you come to the part in the pattern book where they say, for instance, to change to larger needles and work the pattern stitch, you will look to the first part of the instructions to find row after row of the pattern stitch. Occasionally, your instructions will have you work some stitches in stockinette stitch, then put a marker on your needle and work the pattern across a given number of stitches, put another marker on your needle, and end with stockinette stitch. In that case, you will always work the extra stitches at the beginning and end of the rows in stockinette stitch, and all the stitches between the markers in the pattern stitch. Reading some of these pattern stitches is not always easy. Remember, pattern makers are very precise in their directions, and very *concise* also. In most instances they will not tell you any more than they have to. Do not assume that they mean something else. Do exactly what is said to do. Remember that you must change the yarn to the position for knits and purls, as you work some of these intricate stitches. Use the "straight pin" method in reading pattern stitches. See page 2. That is, read and do the work in many little steps. Read a few phrases, then stick a straight pin into the page to show you where your place is; then do that much work. Then read the next phrase, move the pin, and so on. With this method, your hands are free to do the work while the pin holds your place in the book. You will be able to use the pattern over and over again, because you will not be marking your book with little pencil marks. Make sure you know how to do all the stitches. Study the paragraphs on "yarn-overs", "slip stitches", etc. on pages 93, 94. Try out your pattern stitch on a few stitches of an experimental swatch. Be sure you have the right multiple of the number of stitches in the pattern. See page 88.

Learn to read the directions step by step. The asterisk (*) means that you must repeat instructions following the asterisk (*) as many times as specified. A dagger (†) is used in the same way. Whenever an asterisk is used in a pattern, you will find an ending asterisk also, and the sequence of the pattern is repeated between the asterisks.

EXAMPLE: K3, *P12, K5; repeat from *, end K3. Across the row you will work as follows: K3, P12, K5, P12, K5 (always repeating the P12, K5, until there are just three stitches left), then you will end K3. Now that means that you will end P12, K5, K3. You would have eight *knit* stitches at the end of the row. Now, if the pattern had read K3, *P12, K5; repeat from * ending K3 instead of K5; you will end with P12, K3 (leaving only three knit stitches at the end of the row).

If your pattern should read, as another example: K1, P2 * K12, P2, K1, P2, repeat from * three times—you will work as follows: K1, P2, do the work between the asterisks once, then repeat the work between the asterisks three times more (doing that work between the asterisks four times altogether).

Oftentimes daggers (†) and asterisks (*) will both be used in the same pattern. Sometimes, you may even be given double daggers (††). Sometimes, you may be given instructions referring you to some other row. For example: P2, K1, repeat between ††'s of row 3 twice, P1, K1, etc. Now to do this: P2, K1, then when you are told to repeat between ††'s of row 3 twice, you would look back on your pattern to row 3 and repeat what was given there between the ††'s *two times*. Oftentimes, a student will make an error at this point. Since she was told when doing row 3 to do the stitches between the ††'s once, then repeat twice, on row 3 she did the work altogether three times. Now later, on another row, if the directions refer you back to do the work between the ††'s twice, you should do that work only *twice*. In other words, they are not giving you the work first then telling you to repeat it twice. They are just asking that you do the work twice.

Sometimes a pattern book will use parentheses ( ), as well as asterisks and daggers. You should know how parentheses are used. For example: *K4 (K2 tog, YO) twice K7 (YO, sl 1, K1, psso) twice, K4, repeat from * twice. To do this, you start out K4, then take the work between the ( ) and do it *twice,* then K7, take the next work between the ( ) and do it *twice,* K4, then repeat from the * two times *more.*

Many times, patterns will refer you to twists, or popcorns, etc. They will go into *great* detail on how to do this work, then in parentheses they will state, as an example, "right twist made" or "left twist made". The next time they want you to do that they will refer to it as a right twist stitch. Make sure you know how to do all of these stitches correctly. See the paragraphs on "Working Difficult Pattern Stitches", page 90.

NOTE: All changes from one pattern to another will start when the right side of the work is facing you.

EXAMPLE: If you have been doing ribbing for the bottom of your piece, then are to start on a pattern stitch, the pattern stitch will always start on the right side. If this is not so, the pattern will tell you immediately, because the rule is always to start any changes on the right side. Such pattern will then read: Row 1: (wrong side), then proceed to give directions for this row, alerting you to the fact that you are to start the pattern on the *wrong side.*

Multiple

Whenever you work a garment with a pattern stitch, the directions will give you row after row of the pattern until one pattern sequence is completed. Then the directions will state, for example, repeat the six rows for pattern. Now you can see that it is going to take six rows to complete one pattern, but how many stitches is it going to take to complete one pattern going across? That is where multiple comes in, and you must understand what "multiple" means. Suppose you are working the simple checkerboard pattern of K3, P3 for three rows, then alternate and work P3, K3 for three more rows. You can see that your pattern takes six rows to be complete. And you can see that your pattern takes six stitches to be complete. But, you are going to want to end your row with the same square as you started, so your pattern is a multiple of 6, plus 3 extra stitches, so that it will end the same way it starts. Most pattern books will tell you what the multiple is for each pattern. In this case the *multiple* is *6, plus 3*. Now if you want to try this pattern out on a small number of stitches, you will need any number you can divide by 6, plus 3 extra stitches. Therefore, the pattern will come out "even" on 15 stitches (12 + 3), 21 stitches (18 + 3), 27 stitches (24 + 3), and so on. Suppose, for another example, your pattern was a multiple of 8, plus 5. Now you must find a number divisible by 8, plus 5 extra stitches: 21 stitches (16 + 5), 29 stitches (24 + 5), 37 stitches (32 + 5), etc.

It is a good idea to knit your stitch gauge and try out a new pattern at the same time. If on your gauge 5 stitches equal one inch, and you want to make a four-inch gauge, you will cast on 20 stitches. But, if your pattern will not work out on 20 stitches, you must select a number *more* than 20 stitches that is the multiple of your pattern. The nearest number might be 21 stitches. When you measure your gauge, measure 20 of the 21 stitches. The reason this pattern will not come out on 20 stitches is, that when you work this pattern, you first work across from one end; then on row two, you are coming back over these same stitches starting from the *opposite* end of your work. The stitches in the second row will not line up on top of the stitches in the first row as they must do to form the pattern. Thus, you would throw off the whole pattern on the second row, and of course, if the second row of the pattern is not correct, all other even rows will also be incorrect. *You must be on the right multiple.*

WORKING DIFFICULT PATTERN STITCHES

Do not attempt to work any pattern stitch until you understand what "multiple" means. If you are going to knit a garment that is done in a pattern stitch, you will be wise to learn to do that pattern on a small number of stitches. Then you will be completely familiar with the pattern stitch before you must do it on a great number of stitches. It is always a good idea to mark the right side of the pattern work with a colored yarn marker. It is also good to know if the right side rows are all odd rows or all even rows. You must be completely familiar with your pattern in any place on any row, because a certain amount of shaping must be done, and you must be able to keep to your pattern even while you are adding more stitches or taking some away. Try to learn your pattern so that you do not have to refer to the pattern book for each stitch. Do not rely on the pattern book or on row counters to help you to work this pattern except for the first times you are going over it. (If your pattern is a repeat of many rows, such as any number over 20, you may have to use a row counter. See article on row counter on page 92.) If you can train your eyes to watch every single thing you are doing, and to see what part of that pattern you are forming, and what these different stitches look like on the row you are working, and also on the row below, you can find some kind of a key to any pattern. Whenever you make a yarn over (YO), it will look like a slant stitch on the needle, and then on the next row, when you come back to it and it is

"YARN OVER" IS A SLANT STITCH ON THE NEEDLE

IT WILL LOOK LIKE A BIG LOOSE THREAD

YARN OVER

LEFT HAND NEEDLE

YARN OVER

Yarn Overs As on Lace Patterns

on the Left Hand needle, it will look like a big loose thread, and as you work it, it will leave a hole. This is correct. This is used on lace patterns. Try to line up the holes and see how many stitches come between holes; try to find good "landmarks" as you are "trying out" on your sample. You must learn what all these different kinds of stitches look like. Know what knit two together (K2 tog) looks like. You can see that you have made one stitch from

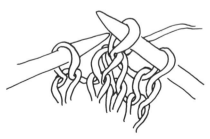

KNIT TWO TOGETHER
YOU HAVE MADE ONE STITCH FROM
TWO STITCHES

two stitches. You can see the two stitches below the needle after you have knit the two together. Train your eyes to see *everything,* then knitting these difficult pattern stitches will become easy.

In any pattern there is usually one plain row. If it is necessary to rip out your work, rip past the mistake to the nearest plain row, or nearly plain row, then count the number of stitches you have left on your needle to make sure you will be starting out again on the correct number of stitches.

Using a Row Counter

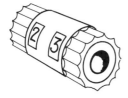

ROW COUNTER

Most row counters are made so that they fit on the end of your needle, but it is best to fasten this row counter to your work by running a little strand of yarn through the hole and tying it right onto the work. The weight of the row counter on one of your needles may bother you, or it may disturb the evenness of your knitting, because it makes that needle heavier than the needle without the counter. A counter should be used only if you have a great number of rows and it is not possible to use the trained eye method entirely. Because there is always a danger of forgetting to turn the counter, you must decide before you start to use the counter, that you do not turn the counter until you have *finished* the row. Then if you should stop in the middle of your work, and your counter reads 18, for example, you know that you have finished row 18 and are working on row 19. Even when you are using the counter, you must try to find some good "landmarks" to go by so that you are not doing any of the work automatically. Careful watching should assist the row counter. Know from the beginning if the odd or the even numbered rows are the right side rows. Make a little note to that effect on your pattern. If you find some good "landmarks" along the way, you may soon give up the

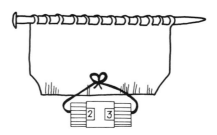

ROW COUNTER ON WORK

row counter and work the pattern without using the counter. After you have gone completely through all the rows of the pattern, and when you start to work these rows over again, keep comparing your work with the work you did previously on the same numbered row. Learn to detect errors immediately, then you will reduce ripping to a minimum.

Various Types of Stitches

SLIP STITCH

If you should be directed by your pattern to slip a stitch, it simply means that you move a stitch from the Left Hand needle to the Right Hand needle without working it. Unless the pattern states otherwise, you should slip the stitch as if to purl, that is,

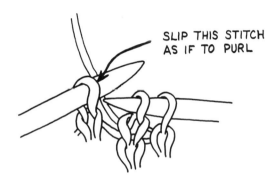

SLIP THIS STITCH
AS IF TO PURL

you will insert the Right Hand needle into the stitch on the Left Hand needle from the *right-hand* side of the stitch and move the stitch to the Right-Hand needle without knitting it. The yarn that would have gone through that stitch, (if you had worked it), will carry across that stitch to the following stitch. Usually your pattern will state, "with yarn at back of work, slip one stitch as if to purl", or, "with yarn in front of work, slip next stitch as if to purl". Usually, the yarn will carry across on the WRONG side of your work, where it will not show. This stitch is used to make the stitch look much larger than a stitch which was worked. You see, you are stretching a stitch to make it more than one row high, because you do not work another loop through that stitch. The effect is very good. Sometimes it is used to give a ribbed effect.

Knit and Slip Pattern

YARN OVERS

How to do a "yarn over" (YO) depends on what comes before and after the "yarn over". If you do not make the "yarn overs" correctly, and you are using several of the different kinds of "yarn overs" in your pattern, you will see that some holes left from the "yarn overs" are larger than others; some appear smaller than others. In order to make all the holes the same size, you must make the "yarn overs" correctly. There are four basic kinds of "yarn overs" as follows:

1. "K1, YO, K1"—To do this, you knit one stitch, bring the yarn forward, between the two needles, into purl position, and as you are knitting the next stitch, the yarn automatically goes over the top of the needle and gives you a "yarn over".

2. "K1, YO, P1"—You knit the first stitch, bring the yarn forward between the two needles, take the yarn up over

the top of the right-hand needle, around to the back side, then forward again between the two needles (back into purl position), and purl the next stitch.

3. "P1, YO, P1"—Purl the first stitch, take the yarn up over the top of the right-hand needle, around to the back side, forward again between the two needles, (back into purl position), and purl the next stitch.

4. "P1, YO, K1"—Purl the first stitch, do not change the yarn, then go ahead and knit the next stitch with yarn in purl position. The yarn will automatically go up over the top of the right-hand needle to give you your "yarn over".

If something comes in before the "yarn over" such as a slip stitch, you must consider that your yarn will be carrying across that stitch over the the next stitch. Make sure that your yarn is carrying across on the back side of your work. If your yarn is carrying across on the front side of your work, you will see a little thread before the "yarn over". You would not want this to show on the right side, so before you slip the stitch and before you do the "yarn over", make sure that the yarn is in back of your work, then follow directions for the "yarn over" when the yarn is on the back side of your work.

SLIP ONE, KNIT ONE, "PASS SLIP STITCH OVER" (SL 1, K1, PSSO)

Whenever your pattern asks you to slip one stitch, K1, and PSSO, this will indicate to you that you are going to make a

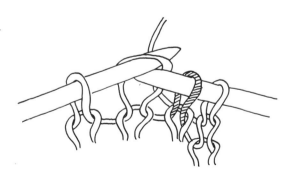
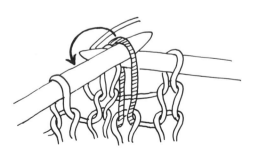

PASS SLIP STITCH OVER

decrease, PSSO means to pass the slipped stitch over the stitch you have just knit. PSSO in effect binds off the slipped stitch. The reason why you do not simply knit two together is that it would pull the stitch in the wrong direction. The general rule in most pattern books is to always slip as if to *purl* unless otherwise stated. (The exception to this general rule is when shaping for a raglan, where, in the case of Slip 1, K1, and PSSO, most times the pattern will ask that you slip *this* stitch as if to *knit.*) Be on the alert, however, and watch to see if the stitch is being twisted. The stitch that you bound over the knit stitch was the slipped stitch. If it was slipped as if to purl, then the bound-over stitch would be a twisted stitch.

TWIST STITCHES

There are many kinds of twist stitches. Your pattern book will go into great detail telling you how to do each twist stitch. Sometimes in the same sweater pattern you will have a right twist stitch and a left twist stitch. If you follow their directions step by step you will see how to do these stitches. Remember, if the book asks that you skip a stitch, simply pass by this stitch as if it were not on the needle and do to the next stitch exactly what they say to do. Then the directions will probably have you come back to the skipped stitch and work it either through the front or back of the stitch. *Do what the book tells you to do.*

EXAMPLE: "*K1, P1, Skip 1 st, insert needle from left to right in front loop of next st, K this st, leave on left-hand needle, K the skipped st, drop both sts from left hand needle, P1; repeat from *."

To do this, K1, P1, ignore the next stitch as if it were not on the needle and then K the next stitch in the front loop as you would regularly do. (When you insert the needle into the front loop, you must cross over past the skipped stitch so that your right-hand needle is crossed and lying underneath the left-hand needle.) See Photo. Wrap the yarn around the needle and pull the loop through, but do not drop the old stitch off. Then knit the skipped stitch in the regular manner, and *then* drop both stitches off. This will give you a right twist.

To do a left twist similar to the right twist, the pattern may read "*K1, P1, skip 1 st, insert needle in *back* loop of next st,

First Step of Right Twist

Second Step of Right Twist

Swatch of Twist Stitches

K this st, K the skipped stitch as usual, then drop both sts from needle". (There are many other kinds of twist stitches, and most directions will state exactly how to do them.)

Try these two stitches out. After you have done them, look at them carefully and you can see that they are turning to the right and to the left. Notice that if you skip a stitch, and then knit the next stitch, the second stitch (the one you have just knit) will pull to the right. Now watch the stitches form for the left twist. Notice that as you knit the second stitch through the back loop, then knit the skipped stitch, the stitch will pull to the left.

If your pattern requires that you knit in the back loop of a stitch or purl in the back loop of a stitch, it will probably say for you to do so. However, in some pattern books, they use simply a little letter "b" after the stitch to indicate that you should use the back loop.

EXAMPLE: "K3b or P3b" means to K3 stitches through the back loops or P3 stitches through the back loops. If they want you to K3 together through the back loop, they will say "K3 tog b".

PURLING IN BACK OF STITCH

Make sure you know how to purl a stitch through the back loop. This seems to puzzle most knitters, and they cannot see how to purl through the back loop. It is easy to do this after you see the drawing above.

Sometimes if you are working a difficult pattern stitch, you will not always have the same number of stitches on the needle for each and every row of the pattern. Sometimes the number of stitches will be decreased and then increased again on another row. But when the pattern ends, you will back to the original number of stitches before starting your second sequence. Or sometimes, you will increase to a greater number of stitches on one or more rows of your pattern, then on another row, you will reduce the number down to the original number of stitches you started with.

POPCORN STITCH

There are many kinds of popcorn stitches. Some are better than others. Some always hold the popcorn to the front side, and some methods will let the popcorn flip from the front side to the back side.

Here is a good popcorn stitch that will always stay on the right side. It takes two rows to work this popcorn; the wrong side row to form the popcorn and the right side row to close the popcorn.

ROW 1: P3 sts; form popcorn in the next st as follows: K in the front, K in the back, K in the front, K in the back, K in the front of next st (5 sts in 1), *P3, popcorn in next st, repeat from * across row, ending P3. (Note: when knitting 5 sts in one, YOU MUST STRETCH OUT BOTH

First Step of Popcorn

Second Step of Popcorn

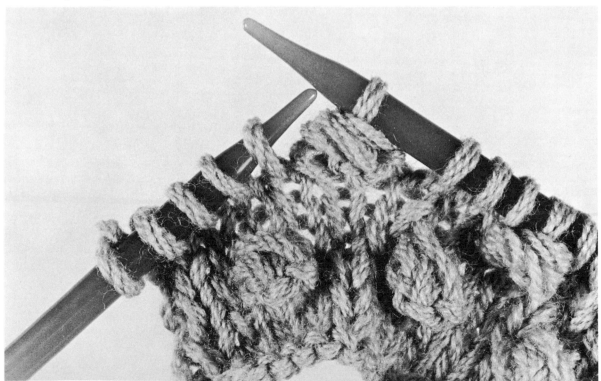

STITCHES WHEN CHANGING FROM BACK TO FRONT.)

ROW 2: K3, close popcorn as follows: Slip the next 5 sts as if to purl onto the right-hand needle. One at a time, bind off each stitch over the first stitch on the right-hand needle (4 sts bound off). Now knit in the *back* loop of the next st, *K2, close the next popcorn, K in the back loop of the next stitch, repeat from * ending K2. See Photo.

KNIT ONE, KNIT ONE IN THE ROW BELOW

If a pattern calls for you to K1, K1 in the row below, you will be doing a kind of ribbing, similar to machine knitting. It means that you can create a ribbing effect without purling any stitches. Actually, when you are knitting in the row below, you are dropping the stitch down to the row below, and instead of your stitch making a bump of one loop on the wrong side, the stitch will make a bump of two loops. When working the next row, never "knit in the row below" into the same stitch that you "knit in the

Swatch of Popcorn

STITCHES WHEN CHANGING FROM BACK TO FRONT.)

ROW 2: K3, close popcorn as follows: Slip the next 5 sts as if to purl onto the right-hand needle. One at a time, bind off each stitch over the first stitch on the right-hand needle (4 sts bound off). Now knit in the *back* loop of the next st, *K2, close the next popcorn, K in the back loop of the next stitch, repeat from * ending K2. See Photo.

KNIT ONE, KNIT ONE IN THE ROW BELOW

If a pattern calls for you to K1, K1 in the row below, you will be doing a kind of ribbing, similar to machine knitting. It means that you can create a ribbing effect without purling any stitches. Actually, when you are knitting in the row below, you are dropping the stitch down to the row below, and instead of your stitch making a bump of one loop on the wrong side, the stitch will make a bump of two loops. When working the next row, never "knit in the row below" into the same stitch that you "knit in the

Swatch of Popcorn

First Step of Popcorn

Second Step of Popcorn

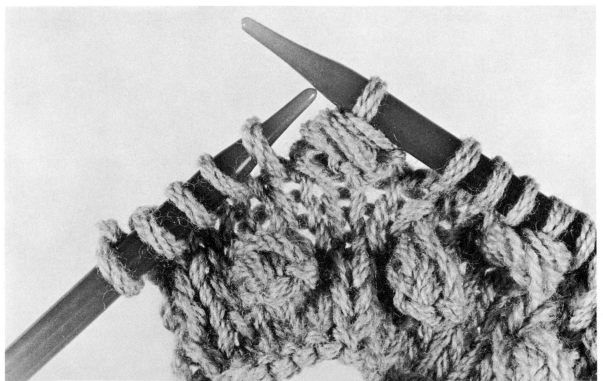

Knit In Row Below

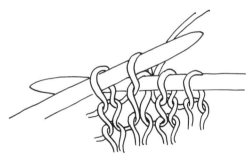

KNIT IN ROW BELOW

row below" in the previous row. In order to determine where to "knit in the row below", look for two loops right under the needle (that was the "row below" of the previous row) so simply knit that stitch, then "knit in the row below" on the next stitch. Never "knit in the row below" on the first or last stitch. You may have to knit two stitches at the beginning of the row or end with knit two.

If it is necessary to rip back this work one stitch at a time, do this according to the regular method given on page 25, and when you come to the stitch that was "knit in the row below" you will find that you have two threads over the needle. This is correct. Pick them up that way, then when all of the stitches are picked up, simply knit across the row, knitting these two stitches together, then knit one. If you must rip back by taking your work off of the needles, rip one row past the mistake, then pick up the stitches with a very fine needle as usual. You will find that you must pick up two stitches together, then one stitch. When you have picked up all of the stitches, work across the row, knitting with regular size needles, knitting one stitch, then knit two together (the two that fall together).

CABLE STITCH

Working cables

Cables are rope-like patterns knit into the garment. There are many kinds of cables; single, double, plait, and many more. If you can work the basic cable stitch, any of the other cables will be easy for you, even the complicated ones. Cables are worked by crossing one group of stitches either in front of or behind a second group of stitches. Cables are usually set off by purl stitches. The stitches which will become the cable are in stockinette stitch. Learn to use a cable hook, although one could use a double-pointed (dp) needle. If you are using a cable hook, there will be less chance of the stitches held in back or in front of your work becoming twisted. (A cable hook looks similar to a hairpin with one end longer than the other. Cable hooks may be purchased at any knitting department, ⊂▬▬▬ .) Cables are always turned on *right side* rows. There are always the same number of rows between cables. It is most important that all cables be even. If you do not count the rows properly, you may get more rows between some cables than others, and the consistent, twisted, rope-like effect is lost.

Usually the directions will have you work the pattern for about one-half the number of rows between cables, then turn the cable for the first time. From then on the cables are always turned on the same numbered row. The way most pattern books read is most confusing. It would be easier for the knitter to do this work if the pattern did not read row for row, but instead would set your work up for you in the knits and purls, and then tell you how to turn the cables and on what row. When working the rows between the turning rows, you simply keep in your pattern of knits and purls. An excellent way for you to work this out is to find out from your pattern how many rows the entire cable pattern requires. Jot down the rows.

> EXAMPLE: Row 1: *P5, K6, repeat from * ending P5
> Row 2: Follow your pattern in knits and purls
> Row 3: Follow pattern
> Row 4: Follow pattern
> Row 5: Turning row
> Row 6: Follow pattern in knits and purls
> Row 7: Follow pattern
> Row 8: Follow pattern

Now you can see that there are eight rows between each cable and you are turning your cable for the first time on Row 5, then after the first turning you will always turn on the eighth row. If you should be relying on your pattern book to guide you, you would have to work Rows 1, 2, 3, and 4, and then turn on Row 5, then work Rows 6, 7, 8, 1, 2, 3, and 4, and turn again on Row 5. The reason you turned for the first time on Row 5, an odd numbered row, and then all cables after that first one are turned on the eighth row after the first turning, is that you started to form your knits and purls on the *right side of your work,* and this was called Row 1. Now, if you turn on Row 5, this is also on the *right side* of your work, but when you start to count all over again from one to eight, you start to count your first row *on the wrong side,* so Row 8 will be on the *right side* of your work again after 7 rows of following your pattern between cable turns. It is easy to count the rows right on your work, and this will be explained in detail right after the explanation of how to *turn* the cables.

How to turn cables

Using the example for the cable given above, on the fifth row you are told to turn the cable as follows: "*P5, slip next 3 sts onto a double-pointed needle and hold in back of work, K next 3 sts, K3 sts from double-pointed needle, repeat from * end P5." To follow these directions, P the 5 sts, now use the cable hook instead of the double-pointed needle, and slip the next 3 sts onto the *short*

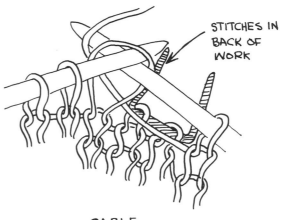

STITCHES IN BACK OF WORK

CABLE

point of the cable hook, letting the hook drop down on the back side of your work, then knit the next 3 sts. Now K3 sts off the cable hook, (bring the hook back to the front side of your work between the needles making sure that these stitches are not twisted, and that you are knitting from the *long end* of the cable hook), repeat from * ending P5.

NOTE: When you slip the stitches onto the short end of the cable hook, make sure you are going into the stitches as if to purl, otherwise the stitches will be twisted on the hook.

Swatch of Cables

Counting rows between cables

Do not rely on row counters or jotting down numbers of rows to tell you when to turn the cables. You *should* count the rows between each cable. Then you will never make the mistake of having different numbers of rows between cables. Note that whenever you turn a cable you have a hole where the stitches cross and turn. Put your finger in the hole where the cable was turned. Then skip the first row above the hole, because that was the row the cable was turned on. Then count up, starting with one, until you reach the number of rows, minus one, that you need, then turn the cable on the next row. In the example you have been using, you would insert your finger in the hole, do not count the row above the hole, then count up, starting with "one" until you reach "seven", then you will turn again on Row 8.

Rules to follow for cabling

When you are shaping your pieces, do not turn any cables as you are binding off or decreasing. At least three rows beyond a cable *turn* should be worked before binding off. Or do not turn that last cable at all, just keep your stitches in the knits and purls without turning cables. The reason it would be wrong to turn a cable as you are binding off or decreasing is that it would be most difficult to sew a seam where a cable had been turned right on the edge. The seam would be too bulky, and the stitches would be drawn together. The knit garment breaking this rule looks very amateurish. If you are working a sleeve, for example, and are doing an all-over cable pattern, and you are increasing up the sides, you should keep the new stitches in pattern (of knits and purls), but do not turn any cables until you have enough stitches for a full cable plus one extra stitch. Do not ever turn a half-cable.

BLOCKING GARMENTS WITH RAISED PATTERNS

In blocking raised patterns do not press the pieces with the palms of your hands to flatten them. For example, if you are blocking an Aran Isle sweater, where the design consists of raised lines, popcorns and cables, take the pieces out to the right size, then work with the pattern so that you will not spoil the three-dimensional look by flattening the pattern. If reverse stockinette stitch was used as a background for the raised line patterns, press down the background work with your fingers so that the raised lines will stand forward. Pinch and work with popcorns and bobbles to make them round and symmetrical. Make your cables stand out by pressing down on the background purl stitches. Press your finger into the hole of each wishbone cable to help form it. In other words, mold and work with your sweater pieces. This will pay big dividends in the looks of the dried pieces. Careless work here can spoil the best knit pieces. Remember that all ribbed patterns must be blocked clear out.

COLORED DESIGNS

There are many ways one can work colored designs. The designs can be knit in by using two or more balls of yarn, or the designs could be put in later in "duplicating stitch" (a type of embroidery stitch worked over the top of stitches), or the designs could be knit with one color at a time using the knit and slip method. If the designs are to be knit in and the colors are used throughout the rows, no bobbins will be necessary. You will simply knit with the colors called for and follow a graph. Read the color key to the pattern and jot down the colors *you* have chosen for the various colors—A, B, C, etc. In most patterns, the graphs will use X's, dots (·), slant lines (/), triangles (△), etc., to represent the colors A, B, C, etc. To read this graph, read from BOTTOM TO TOP. If you are on a knit row, read from RIGHT TO LEFT. If you are on a purl row, read from LEFT TO RIGHT. Each square

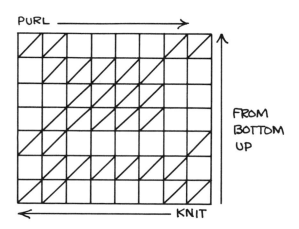

108

means one stitch, and each square high means one row. Colors may be either carried loosely in back of your work, or laced in every third stitch. If colors are laced in, there is no long thread on the back side of the work, but, in most cases, the lacing disturbs the evenness of your work, and the colors will show through from the wrong side to the right side.

Directions for Carrying Colors Across the Back of Work

In working a colored design with the colors carried across the back, the following method should be used when it is time to change from one color to the next: Get into position for the next stitch (insert needle into stitch to be worked), then take the old color to the left position, stretch out the stitches on the right-hand needle which you intend to carry across, and bring the new color up from underneath. Change in this manner on both the knit and purl rows. If you find that the work has a puckered look, you are

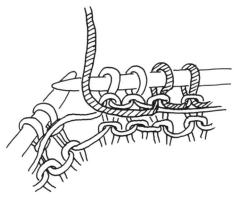

TAKE OLD COLOR TO
THE LEFT

BRING NEW COLOR UP

COLORS – CARRIED LOOSELY IN
BACK OF WORK

not carrying the thread loosely enough on the wrong side. When it is time to change colors, you *must* stretch out the stitches *more* on the needle that you intend to carry across so that the work will lie flat with the color that was not in use stretching across the back of your work. CAUTION! Be sure to practice this work carefully before attempting to work with colors on your garment. This will enable you to get the feel of how to change your colors and how to lock in your colors before you start your project. If you are not careful when changing colors, and do not use the method explained above, you will have a separation where the colors are changed. You must lock in the stitches when you change colors by taking the old color to the left, then bring the new color up from underneath. It is safe to carry across ten stitches. If your pattern wants you to carry across more than twelve stitches, it would be better to lace in, once or twice, the color you have been carrying across the back of your work.

You must keep your stitches even. Many people trying to do this work will be very conscious of carrying the thread loosely across the back of their work, and while keeping that thread loose, they may be *knitting* loosely, too. You must *not* do this. You must knit in your regular style with your regular tension. You cannot have some stitches much larger than other stitches. If you knit too loosely, you will not maintain your stitch gauge. If you do not maintain your stitch gauge your finished piece will not be the correct size. *Knit with your regular tension.* Practice!

NOTE: If you are knitting an all-over colored design, you must knit your stitch gauge with the two or more colors called for in the pattern. Follow part of your graph for this gauge.

Directions for Lacing in Colors

You must practice this well before trying to do it on your project. Work several stitches with Color A, then lay in Color B and knit two stitches. Carry the color not in use over the finger of your left hand; now lay the yarn from left-hand finger over the needle (wrapping the yarn in the opposite direction); now knit with Color B, using your right hand, and as you are pulling the loop through the stitch already on the needle, do not pull the loop also through the loop from the left-hand needle; then knit two more stitches with Color B and right hand, then lace in color again in the same manner. See picture.

Colors are changed and laced in the same way when you are working a purl row, although the color in the left hand that you will lace does not lie over the needle in the wrong direction, it lies over the needle in the same direction that a regular purl stitch would lie, then purl in the regular manner with the yarn in your

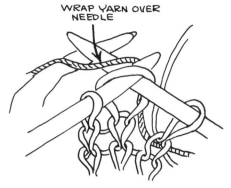

THREAD BEING LACED IN
IS ALWAYS HELD ON LEFT
FINGER

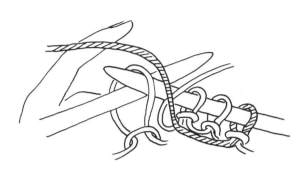

LACING IN COLORS ON PURL ROW

right hand, not pulling through the loop you laid over from the left hand. This takes considerable practice. Colors are very apt to show through from the right side and stitches may be more uneven.

Of the two methods given, carrying colors loosely across the back and lacing in colors, carrying colors across the back is considered the best method. If you have the necessary practice before the start of your project, your work will look very neat and the stitches will be even. (Photos of both sides, page 112.) The threads across the back of your work will block beautifully if they are carried without any puckering. If you are lacing in the colors, the back side will look very neat, but on the right side you may have uneven stitches and you may see colors showing through from the wrong side. You may be sacrificing the outside for the inside.

When and How to Use Bobbins

If your design to be knit is in "globs" of color with wide spaces between designs, you should use bobbins for each color, and a bobbin for each section of the main color between the designs. If your design is in blocks of different colors, you should use a bobbin for each color. There are little plastic bobbins on the market that are most satisfactory for this work. Wind as much yarn on the bobbin as the bobbin will hold. There is a slit at the top of the bobbin which lets you unwind one wind at a time, therefore

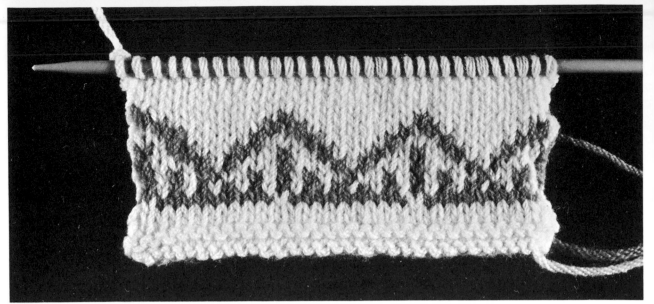

Two Color Knitting—Right Side

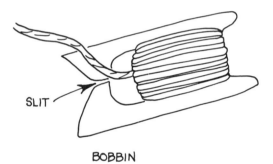

SLIT

BOBBIN

Two Color Knitting—Wrong Side

the bobbin can unwind only as far as you want it to. When it is time to change colors, you will change in the same manner as for the method of carrying colors across the back of work; that is, take the old color to the left and bring the new color up from underneath. This will prevent any separation between colors.

If your pattern uses very small areas of a color, or if lines are to be made with a color and these lines go up several rows, and over several stitches on each row, you may want to use just a strand of yarn for this work instead of a bobbin. In order to find out how long to cut the strand, count the number of stitches to be worked, then allow one inch for each stitch, plus a four-inch piece for each end. (The ends will be worked in later.)

Working Duplicating Stitch

In some patterns it will be to your advantage to use duplicating stitch instead of knitting in the design. Sometimes you may desire to use duplicating stitch on part of the design and knit in other parts of the design. If the design is widely scattered and it would not be good to carry the yarn underneath, use duplicating stitch for that part of the design, and if part of the design uses colors clear across the row, knit in the design for that portion. You may work in single or double duplicating stitch. If you are working single duplicating stitch you will cover just *one* stitch. If you are working double duplicating stitch you will cover one stitch wide, but two stitches high. See diagram. It is easier to work the duplicating stitch before the pieces are blocked, because the holes are wide open and it is easier to get the tapestry needle into the holes. When you are working the duplicating stitch, you must start in the hole of an "up" stitch. Use full strength yarn. Do not fasten the beginning end—leave a three-inch end. Bring the tapestry needle up through the hole of the "up" stitch, drawing yarn from the wrong side to the right side of your work. Now, follow up with the stitch to the point where the stitch goes *behind* the point of the stitch on top of the stitch you are working. Take your tapestry needle through to the back under that stitch on top, coming out again where your stitch comes back to the right side, then insert the needle again into the base of the same stitch (back into the same hole where you started). You are indeed duplicating a stitch. You are laying a stitch on top of a stitch, following it in and out

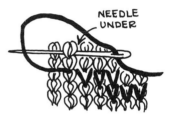

NEEDLE UNDER

SINGLE DUPLICATING STITCH

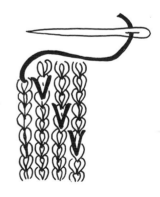

DOUBLE DUPLICATE STITCH

of the same holes. Each stitch will be a little "V". End each thread by skimming through threads of the same color on the wrong side of your work, then clip off. When you are working the duplicating stitch, you may either go from left to right or from right to left, from top to bottom or from bottom to top. Do not pull the stitches too tight. They should be lying flat on top of the stitch they are covering. Duplicating stitches are much more perfect than knit-in stitches, and they give a lovely three-dimensional look. Practice doing some duplicating stitch in single duplicating. You will be following your design on a graph as you did for knitting in designs. Try a little double duplicating stitch. This is worked the same as the single duplicating stitch, except that you are covering two stitches in length, but only one stitch in width. When working the stitches on your garment pieces, it is best to find the center stitch of the pieces, then work toward each side from the center to the edges.

If you should have an occasion to use duplicating stitch with mohair yarn over a smooth yarn knit, you will create a lovely frosted look to your design. See Photo.

Swatch of Duplicating Stitch with Mohair

Washing and Blocking Garments Knit of Two or More Colors

Sometimes, even with the most expensive yarns, colors will run or fade. You should test for this on a swatch knit of the two or more colors. If the colors *do* run, you *must* re-set the dye by putting the finished pieces in an acid bath of vinegar and water. For this bath, use ⅓ cup *white* vinegar to a small washbasin of cold water. Allow the pieces to stand in the bath for approximately three minutes, then go through the regular washing process.

Before washing and blocking pieces with colors carried across the back, examine the work to see if there is any puckering which may be improved. Turn the pieces to the wrong side, and pull up gently but firmly, with a knitting needle or crochet hook, on each and every loop which was carried across. This will help to flatten the work and even the stitches on the right side.

CHAPTER VI

Miscellaneous Knitting Procedures

SHORT ROWS

If your pattern asks that you work short rows, this will indicate to you that you are going to do some difficult shaping. When your pattern talks about short rows, they mean just that. *You do not work the entire row.* You turn your work around before you reach the edge, and thus enlarge the center section without enlarging the edges, for the seat of pants. Or, you enlarge the outside edges, as for a cape, without enlarging the center section.

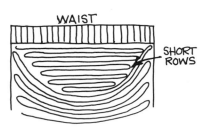

EXAMPLE.... FOR PANTS
ENLARGING CENTER
SECTION ONLY

EXAMPLE.... FOR CAPES
ENLARGING THE OUTSIDE EDGE
ONLY

Example for pants—Directions: "Starting at waistline with No. 1 needles, cast on 80 sts and work in ribbing of K1, P1 for $1\frac{1}{2}$." Change to No. 2 needles and P 1 row. Then work short rows as follows: K to last 6 sts, turn; Sl 1, P to last 6 sts, turn; Sl 1, K to last 12 sts, turn. Continue in stockinette stitch, working 6 sts less on every row until 10 short rows have been worked in all, and 20 sts are worked on last row. Turn, Sl 1, and work to edge. (Short rows completed.)

To do this, you work the ribbing for $1\frac{1}{2}$ inches and at the start of the short rows, you work until six stitches remain to be worked at the end of the needle. Then, turn your work around as if you had finished the row; (the six stitches are on the right-hand needle, not worked) slip 1 (as if to purl), then work until you reach six stitches from the other end of the needle, turn your work around and repeat the short rows leaving six stitches more at each end of the needle until you have worked ten "short" rows, or until there are only twenty stitches worked on the last row. Then, turn, Slip 1 stitch, and work all of the stitches clear across all rows. Your short rows have been completed and they will enlarge the center part of the pants for the seat.

NOTE: When you Sl 1 stitch after the turn of the short row, you must always slip the stitch as if to *Purl*, whether it is a knit stitch or a purl stitch. If you did not slip a stitch, there would be a hole left where you turned and worked back in the other direction.

KNIT-IN POCKETS

If you are going to knit-in the pockets, your pattern will give you the directions for the pocket liners and have you knit them and set them aside on holders to be used later.

EXAMPLE: "Pocket Liners—Make 2. With size 5 needles cast on 25 sts and work in stockinette st for 3" ending with a knit row. Slip stitches on a holder. Left front—Work until the front piece measures 7" ending with a purl row. Pocket opening—K32 sts, slip the last 25 sts onto a holder, K7. Next row—Purl to opening, purl across one pocket lining, purl to end of row . . . . Directions continue on for finishing the left front."

In diagramming this left front, all of these directions can be shown and you will know better what you are going to do. See diagram. On the row of the pocket opening, you will knit across 32 stitches, as the directions state, then you will thread 25 of those 32 stitches onto a yarn holder and slip them off your needle. That will leave 7 stitches on your right-hand needle. Then you will finish the row (18 stitches). On the next row (the purl row) you will work across 18 stitches until you come to where you put the 25 stitches onto the holder, then you will put one of your pocket liners onto the left needle, work these 25 stitches (since the liner is also twenty five stitches it will take the place of the 25 stitches put off onto the holder), then finish the row.

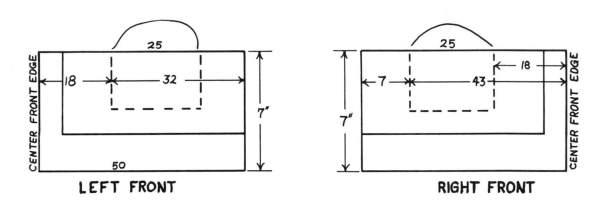

The directions for the right front say to reverse all the shaping and to work to correspond to the left front. When it is time to put in the right pocket, you will be putting it in from the opposite end of your work. Therefore, you will knit across 43 stitches and put 25 of them on a holder, then finish the row (7 stitches). On the following row: Purl 7 stitches, purl in the pocket liner, finish the row.

The 25 stitches on the holder will be picked up after the front is done and the pocket trim (flaps, or edge) can be knit on these 25 stitches.

NOTE: You can see from these diagrams that the pockets are inserted 7 stitches in from the side edge and 18 stitches in from the center front edge.

When blocking this front with the half-finished pocket, smooth out the pocket liner first, then lay the rest of the left front on top of the liner.

When it is time to add the trim to the pocket, you want to be sure that both pocket trims will match. Thus, you will have to put the stitches on the needle so that they will be worked in the same direction on each of the two pockets. If you do not, the edges of the trim will be bound off in opposite directions and your pockets will not look alike. To make sure this does not happen, attach a scrap of paper to each front showing, with an arrow, the direction in which you intend to insert your needle into the stitches. Then after you work the trim (8 rows in ribbing, for example) your two bound-off edges will be identical. CAUTION: When binding off, make the edge loose. If you do not, the trim will draw in and spoil the looks of your pocket. See page 244 on how to sew the pockets and the trim to your sweater.

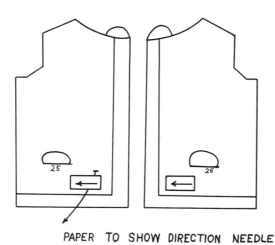

PAPER TO SHOW DIRECTION NEEDLE
IS TO BE INSERTED

SHAPING A FRONT "V" NECKLINE

In most pattern books when they ask you to shape the front for a long "V" neckline, they give you the directions to shape, for example, on every 6th or every 8th row. If you are off the stitch gauge row-wise, or have made your sweater longer or shorter, many times you will find that you are up to the shoulder and still have neck stitches to be taken off. Or you may have all of the neck stitches taken off long before time to shape the shoulders. This does not seem to be a good way for the directions to read. You should use inch measurements instead. Suppose you are going to work such a sweater and the pattern reads, for example: "work until 11" from start. To shape neck: Dec 1 st at front edge, then dec 1 st at same edge every 4th row 6 times more, then every 6th row 8 times, and at the same time, shape shoulders same as back when armhole is same length." This would be hard to do if you are working a cable, and the cables must be turned every 10th row. It is easy to do this work if you tie in a colored yarn marker at the beginning where the neck shaping is to start. Lay the partially finished front on top of the back (which you finished first). Measure the distance from the yarn marker you have just inserted (at the beginning of the neck shaping) up to the *finished back neck*. Make a notation on your diagram of the number of inches. Assume the distance is 12 inches. Now read through your pattern to find out how many times you are to decrease at the neck. ("Dec 1 st at front edge, then dec 1 st every 4th row *6* times, then every 6th row *8* times.") In the example all decreases at the neck add to 15. Now show on your diagram how you will space

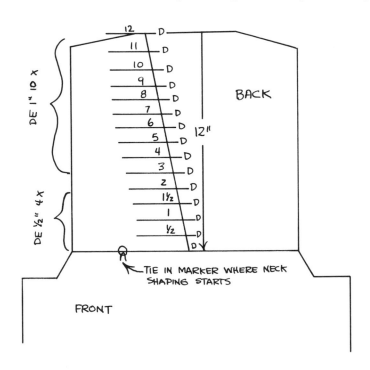

the 15 decreases so that you will get in all of the decreases by the time you finish off the shoulders. See diagram. Notice that the first decrease was placed immediately at the point of the yarn marker, then decrease 1 stitch every half inch 4 times, then every one inch 10 times, always measuring up from the yarn marker. You will get in all of your decreases by the time the work measures 12 inches from the yarn marker, but at the same time you must shape the shoulders when your armhole measures the same as the back armhole. All of the decreases will be spaced nicely and evenly, and all in and accounted for by the time the piece is to be finished off. Keep track of the decreases on your diagram *as you do them* by circling them. The following diagram shows an example of a long "V" neck on a man's sweater, showing how all decreases should be placed.

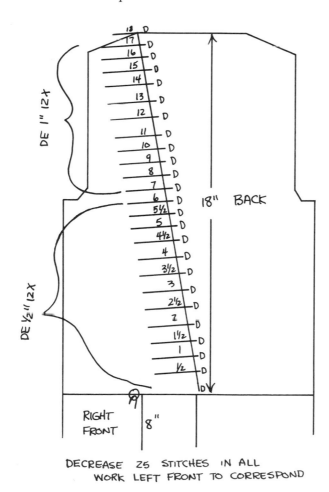

DECREASE 25 STITCHES IN ALL
WORK LEFT FRONT TO CORRESPOND

HOW TO WORK FRONT BORDERS SET ASIDE

If your pattern requires that you work your front border later, it will ask that you set aside 10 stitches, for example, on a holder to be worked later on small needles for the front border. This type of border looks very professional because it is firmer than borders worked on larger needles. When your front is finished and you are ready to work this front border on the smaller needles, you must be sure you will knit this border to the right length. Your buttonholes will have to be placed in one of these borders. You must realize that this border is going to stretch considerably, and if you do not take that fact into consideration, you will knit in your buttonholes as you think they should be placed, then when the piece is blocked the border will be too long, and your button-holes misplaced. Another thing you must take into consideration is that your front center edge has a lot of stretch and sag, and when you put your border onto that center front edge, you will want to hold in that extra fullness so that the sweater will not hang longer in the front than in the back. Lay the back of your sweater down and lay the front down on top of the back. Hold in the excess material and make sure that the bottom edges are together. Now measure the distance you will need for your front border. Make a notation of that number of inches and put this measurement with your other knit measurements to be used later when blocking. When knitting that border you must allow for the fact that your border will stretch approximately 1 to $1\frac{1}{2}$ inches. Take that antici-pation of stretch into consideration when knitting the other side where the buttonholes are placed. If your pattern states that you are to place buttonholes up to the start of a low neck shaping, mark the position of the buttonholes right on the side of your sweater near the edge. When you are making *vertical* buttonholes, stretch up on your border a little between each buttonhole. (If the buttonholes go to the top of the sweater, you can mark the position of your buttonholes on the first border worked.) Then you will compare your second border to the first border to tell you when it is time to work the buttonholes. After the borders have been worked, wash and block your knit pieces according to the general directions given previously on page 62 and lay the little border alongside of the front edge when you block. Stretch out the border to the measurement you jotted down with your other blocking measurements.

CAUTION: When front bands are set aside and worked later on a sweater with a long "V" neckline, each of the bands is intended to be made long enough to border the front and half of the back of the neck, and are to be joined there. You must understand that you cannot join these bands by weaving unless these bands start and end with the same kind of stitch. In other words, the ribbing must match on the two pieces with purl stitches at the outside edge of both, or knit stitches at the outside edge of both. Your pattern will not alert you to this fact, and in most cases, knitters do not find out that the borders do not match until it is time to join them together. Then since they do not match, a seam must be sewed and it does not look as perfect as the invisible joining you can make by weaving the ribbing stitches together. Directions on page 234. If you are making this kind of border on your sweater, you can make sure that your ribbing is going to match at the back of the neck when you first cast on for the front pieces.

To make sure they will match, you should cast on an *odd* number of stitches to begin each front. In that way, your row will have knit stitches at the beginning and end of the row, or purl stitches at the beginning and end of the row. Since you will be making sure that your bottom edges match, and you will be marking the outside of the pieces, you can begin and end both pieces with knits (or purls) and they are sure to match. If your pattern asks that you cast on 48 stitches, for example, change the number to 49 (an odd number) so that you will be assured that the front borders will match.

How to Sew on This Border

If you sew this border onto your finished sweater properly, it will look as if it were knit right on. It is not hard to do if you use the side-to-side top-stitching seam. You will be laying the border over the top of the edge of the sweater. Pin the border to the top of the sweater front, pinning it so that the fullness will be evenly distributed all of the way up. With split yarn and a tapestry needle, join the yarn at the bottom point where the border

Front Border Set Aside Sewed On

is already joined to the sweater front. With a small side-to-side stitch, take a small stitch on the *back* side of the border right near the edge, then a small stitch on the sweater front. See picture. Make sure that the border is on top of the front with a very small seam on the wrong side. Make sure all stitches are hidden and very close together. Steam lightly to the length needed. Try on the sweater to see if the border is hanging correctly. If not, re-steam to the correct length.

NOTE: If you are seaming on a front border for a long "V" neckline and the border is to continue around to half of the back of the neck, pin the border carefully to the finished sweater and sew as per directions above until you have reached a point about one inch from the center back of the neck where the borders are to join. Occasionally the borders are too long, and some rows will need to be ripped out before joining. Be sure to do this if it is necessary, as it is most important that the back of the neck border must be a little stretched and firm, not loose. Your weaving will make another row and make the border just a little longer. After weaving, sew that last few inches. See Weaving Ribbing Stitches Together on page 234.

KNITTING ON CIRCULAR NEEDLES

To knit a skirt on a circular needle, you must get the length needle that will fit your skirt. Most department stores carry both the 24″ and 29″ needles. As you will be decreasing to a smaller number of inches for the waist, you cannot stretch 28 inches of stitches around a 29 inch needle.

When casting on, do so in the regular manner, watching carefully to keep stitches even and not too tight. When it is time to join your work, you *must* make sure there is no twist at the bottom edge when joining, because if there is a twist, you will knit that twist into your work. Now join and work the next round. See picture. If you are working in stockinette stitch, you will not purl. You will knit all of the rounds. When working on circular needles, put the wrong side of your work on the outside and the right side on the inside. If you do this, your circular needle will make a nice circle and it will be easier to knit on the circular needle. (If you were to knit with the right side out, there would be a big bend

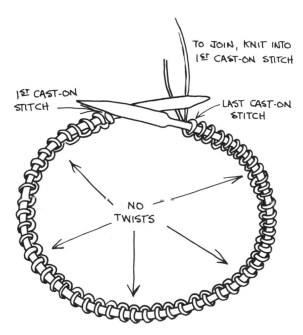

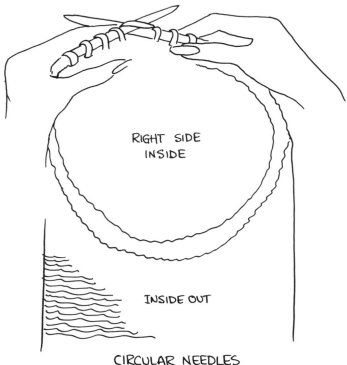

RIGHT SIDE
INSIDE

INSIDE OUT

CIRCULAR NEEDLES
KNIT ON FAR SIDE OF NEEDLES, WITH RIGHT
SIDE INSIDE AND INSIDE OUT.

in the circular needle which would make it difficult for you to knit with ease.) You will be knitting on the far side of the circle instead of the part near you.

If you need to change needle sizes for your skirt (because the edge is in ribbing, or seed stitch, or you are making a hem), when it is time to change to the larger needle, follow up from the tail of loose yarn left from the point of casting on and change to the large needle at that point. You do not actually change the needles, you simply knit off the smaller needle onto the larger needle.

If you are using circular needles on a cardigan at the yoke and you have a great many stitches on the needles, or whenever you start a sweater at the top and work a raglan knit in, and have a great many stitches on the needle (more than straight needles will hold), you use the circular needle as you would a pair of straight needles; that is, you knit over and purl back in rows instead of around and around. (You will not be making a closed tube.) Circular needles have two purposes: To knit in a tubular fashion for a skirt, or when there are too many stitches to fit on straight needles.

Attention! Some people tend to knit tighter or more loosely on circular needles. Be sure to knit a stitch gauge *on the circular needle* before using circular needles for your work.

KNITTING WITH FOUR NEEDLES

If you are using double-pointed (dp) needles for socks, mittens, etc., you will make a spiral tubing with no seams. The double-pointed needles will act as circular needles; that is, they allow you to go around and form a circle. Here, you will be working in rounds rather than in rows. When you come back around to the stitch where you started you have worked one round. If you are working in stockinette stitch you will not have to purl. You will knit all the stitches. If you are to work in a ribbing pattern, you will knit over knit stitches and purl over purl stitches. You will have stitches on three of the needles and the fourth needle is free to knit into the stitches on the other three.

To Cast on on Four Needles

If you are following a pattern, your pattern will read, for example, "cast on 60 stitches divided among three needles. Join and work in ribbing of K2, P2 for 3 inches." You will cast on 20 stitches onto each of three double-pointed needles. The stitches must be cast on loosely for a cuff. Since it is difficult to cast on onto the second and third needles without leaving a loose thread where the needles join, it is wise to cast on 3 extra stitches on the first needle, then transfer those 3 extra stitches onto the second needle, then continue casting on onto the second needle until you have 20 plus 3 on the second needle. Transfer 3 stitches onto the third needle, then cast on until you have 20 stitches on the third needle. Count stitches again before joining to make sure you have 20 stitches on each needle. See picture.

Joining and Knitting with Four Needles

Arrange the three needles into a triangle, making sure no stitches are twisted and that there is no twist between the needles.

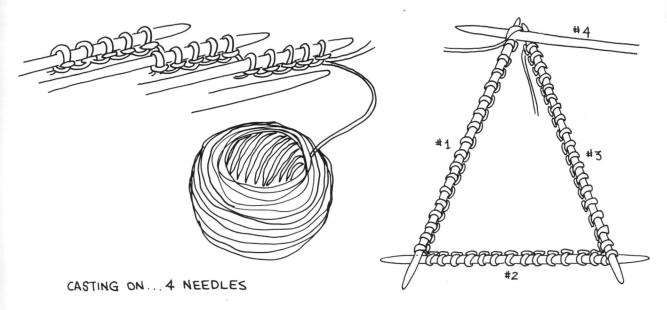

CASTING ON... 4 NEEDLES

NEEDLES 1 AND 4 ARE LYING ON <u>TOP</u> OF NEEDLES 2 AND 3.

Insert the fourth needle into the first cast-on stitch on the first needle and knit it. The two needles you are knitting with should lie on top of the other two needles. (In the picture needles 1 and 4 are lying on top of needles 2 and 3.) Hold your work so that you are knitting on the needles away from you instead of the ones near you. See photo. Needle 2 is near to you and needles 1, 3, and 4 are farther away from your body. Thus, you will be knitting "wrong side out". The back side or inside will be on the outside as you knit the tube. You want to knit it this way so that you will not have large separations between the stitches where the needles join.

NOTE: You are *not* knitting from the wrong side of your work; you are knitting from the right side, but by knitting on the far side of the tube, you are knitting the right side on the inside of the tube. See picture.

Continue working K2, P2, ribbing across the first needle. When the first needle is empty, take it in the right hand and use it as the empty needle. Always lay the two needles you are knitting with *over* the top of the other two needles. If you are to change to larger double-pointed needles after you have worked the cuff,

Knitting on 4 Needles

just knit off of the smaller needles onto the larger needles until you are using all four larger needles. If your pattern refers to the needles as No. 1, No. 2 and No. 3, they are referring to the needles as you started out. (Needle No. 1 is the first part of your round right after the tail of yarn left from casting on.) Later when you are working the heel or instep of socks, the pattern will again refer to the numbered needles. Follow up from the loose tail of yarn to find the position of the No. 1 needle.

Knitting Neck Ribbing with Four Needles

Often a pattern will call for you to pick up stitches around the neck of a sweater with double-pointed (dp) needles for making a turtleneck, or ribbing, etc. Do not pick up these stitches until your sweater has been washed and blocked and the shoulder seams (or raglan seams) sewed. The reason you are using the double-

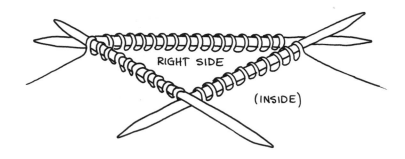

NECK STITCHES ON DOUBLE POINTED
NEEDLES

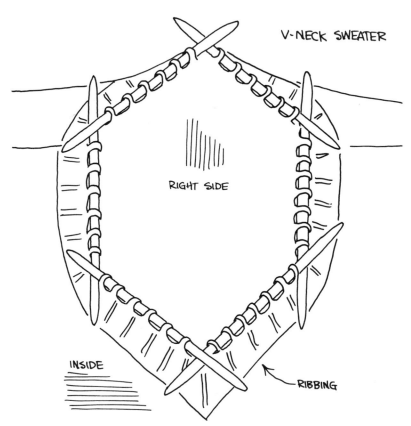

KNITTING ON SIX DOUBLE POINTED NEEDLES

pointed needles is so that there will be no seam in the turtleneck or ribbing. You will be working in rounds, and when you come back to the first stitch you continue going around over the stitches again in the same direction. You are working in rounds instead of rows. Turn your sweater inside out so that it will be easier for you to work on the double-pointed needles.

NOTE: Pick up the stitches from the *right* side. See picture. Pick up approximately the same number of stitches on each of the three needles, leaving the fourth needle free for knitting. Join the yarn at either the shoulder seam or the center back and follow the directions in your pattern. If you must pick up and knit stitches that are not on holders, the work must be sectioned off so that you will have an even look. See page 220.

If you have to pick up a great number of stitches on a long "V" neck pullover (more stitches than double-pointed needles will hold), use two sets of double pointed needles, knitting on 4, 5, 6, or 7 needles. See picture.

It is best to lay your work down on a table whenever you must work a neck on double-pointed needles. Then you can turn your work around on the table and there is much less chance of stitches coming off of the ends of the needles that you are not using. When it is time to bind off, start on the same needle you started with at the beginning of the "picked up" knitting. *Keep your bind-off stitches loose.*

CHOOSING THE CORRECT SIZE FOR:

How to Figure Size Needed if Cardigan Has Double Front Facing

If a cardigan has a double front facing with double button-holes to be worked, to figure out the size you need count all of the stitches you have just before you shape the underarm for the back and fronts. Then deduct the number of stitches in one over-lap. You deduct the stitches in *one front and facing,* plus the stitches in the *facing* for the other front.

EXAMPLE: If you have 9 stitches on the front and 10 stitches on the facing for each side of the front, you must deduct 19 stitches for one front plus 10 stitches for the facing of the other front, or 29 stitches.

How to Figure Size Needed if Cardigan Has No Band

If the cardigan has no front band and you will be making buttonholes in the front and using a ribbon facing, you must figure out how much of the front will overlap so that you can deduct one of the overlaps when counting up the stitches and adjusting them to your size. Read through the directions for the front with the buttonholes and see just where the buttonholes are being placed. Remember that the buttonholes will be in the center of the overlap.

EXAMPLE: Work buttonholes as follows: Knit 3 stitches, bind off the next 3 stitches, finish the row. On the next row, cast on 3 stitches over the 3 bound off on the previous row.

These directions tell you that the overlap is 9 stitches wide because the buttonhole is worked in the center of the overlap. The pattern asks you to work *3* stitches, then bind off *3* stitches. Then *3 more* stitches. (9 stitches total) must be counted as the overlap, with the buttonhole in the center of the overlap.

Importance of Row-Wise Gauge When Knitting Stripes

It is most important that you be on gauge stitch-wise first, otherwise your sweater will not be the desired size. Then, if your pattern is worked in stripes, either "knit in" colored stripes, or a pattern stitch in stripes, you must figure out how long your garment is going to be *before starting*. You may find that your sweater will be way too long, or perhaps too short. Are you on gauge row-wise? How long will the sweater be according to the pattern if you are on gauge row-wise? You may have to shorten the number of rows between stripes, if possible, or make some other adjustment to compensate for being off gauge row-wise, such as leaving out part of the striping pattern. Work all of this out on your diagram *before starting*.

LOWERING THE BACK OF THE NECK

Sometimes your pattern will ask that you lower the back of the neck of your sweater (usually when a large collar is to be added). This is done by binding off the center back of the neck stitches (or occasionally the pattern may ask that you put these stitches on a holder), then you must tie in another ball of yarn so that you can work each side separately and finish each shoulder. (This is done the same way you would knit the front neck shaping if you were making a pullover. See page 56.)

EXAMPLE: Work even on 96 sts until armholes measure 8″. *Neck and shoulders:* Work across 42 sts, tie in another ball of yarn, bind off center 12 stitches, work across last 42 sts. Continue working each side with a separate ball of yarn. *Shoulders and neck:* Bind off 4 sts from shoulder side 5 times, then 6 sts two times AND AT THE SAME TIME bind off 2 sts each neck edge 5 times.

Show these directions on a diagram and, as you do each part, circle it on your diagram.

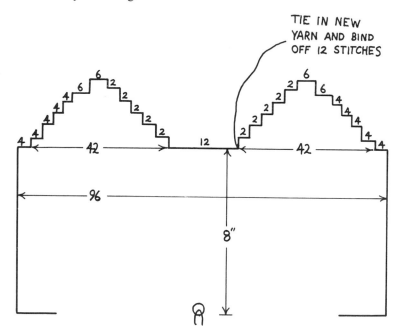

USING A DIAGRAM FOR ODD SOUNDING DIRECTIONS

If you are going to make a part of a garment with any shaping, it should be diagrammed so that you can see what the shape is and how the piece will be worked before you start working it. For an example, notice how this collar pattern reads, and how it looks on a diagram:

"Collar: 1st front piece: Cast on 3 sts. Mark end of row for outer edge. K1, P1, in ribbing, inc 1 st at outer edge every 4th row 3 times, ending at inner edge. Break off and slip sts on a holder. 2nd front piece: Work to correspond to first front piece reversing shaping. Do not break off. On next row, work in ribbing on 6 sts, cast on 13 sts for back of neck, work in ribbing as established on the 6 sts of other piece. 25 sts. Continue to inc 1 st each side of needle every 4th row, 3 times more. 31 sts. Work even until piece measures 5″ above cast on sts for back of neck. Bind off."

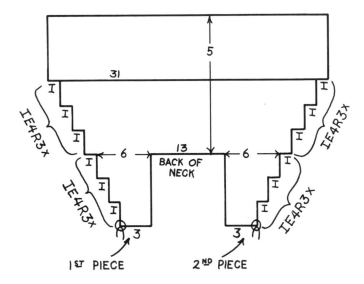

DIAGRAM OF COLLAR (ODD-SOUNDING DIRECTIONS)

MARKING PIECES RIGHT AND LEFT

If you are to make a sleeve or a sleeve piece that is different for the left side and the right side, you should pin a scrap of paper to the piece labeling it "right" or "left". If you are to join the piece to the right side of the back, for instance, you will be greatly helped by having these different pieces marked. An example of such pieces is the triangular sections of sleeves which are very much alike, but are different for the right and left sides. These sections are to be made first, put onto holders and used later when the back has been worked to a certain point.

"Description: Bias sleeve piece for right side of back: Cast on 6 sts. Work in stockinette st, inc 1 st at end of every K row and beg of every P row 32 times for underarm edge AND AT THE SAME TIME inc 1 st at opposite edge (sleeve edge) every 4th row 8 times. Slip on a holder. Work left bias sleeve piece by reversing shaping of first piece." See picture. The pattern will then go on to explain how you are to knit the back piece and when to set in the two triangular sleeve pieces. If you have them marked right and left, it will help you greatly.

Occasionally you will come upon a raglan sleeve in a pattern book that will have to be shaped just slightly lower in the front at the neck than in the back. These sleeves should be tagged "left" and "right" so that there would be no chance of putting in the sleeves in the wrong position, or knitting two sleeves for the same side.

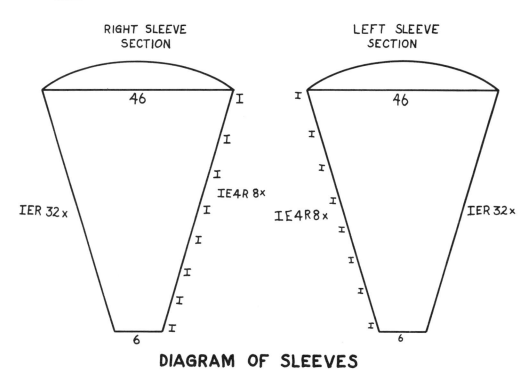

RIGHT SLEEVE SECTION   LEFT SLEEVE SECTION

DIAGRAM OF SLEEVES

HEMS AND FRONT FACINGS

Hems and Turning Rows

If the garment calls for part of the knitting to be turned under as a hem, this part should be knit on needles one or two sizes smaller than those used in the rest of the garment. Sometimes your pattern will ask that you knit the hem on the same size needles. Do not do this, for if you do, your finished garment will have a flared look at the bottom where the hem is. If you use smaller needles for the hem, the hem will hold in the bottom of your sweater or skirt to give that certain finished look you are striving for.

Cast on with the smaller needle, work for the desired number of inches, then also use the small size needle for the turning ridge, then use the regular sized needle thereafter.

Making the Turning Ridge

To make the turning ridge, you want to make a row of bumps on the right side. To do this, either purl a row on the right side, or knit a row on the wrong side.

Hem with Turning Ridge

Hem with Scalloped Edge

Occasionally, your pattern will ask that you form a turning row by knitting into the back loop of each stitch on a knit row. This method seems to be less desirable than that mentioned above. The above method may be substituted in your pattern with no difficulty.

A Hem with a Scalloped Edge

If you want a hem with a scalloped edge, on the turning row work one row of K2 tog, YO, across the row. Do this from the wrong side of your work. See page 244 for sewing hems and facings.

Hems or Facings with No Turning Ridge

About the only time you would use a facing or a hem with no turning ridge is when you are making a double neck ribbing or double cuffs, with facings turned under and tacked down. You should not go to smaller needles for this facing or hem. Ribbing will not flare out the way plain knitting does at the neck edge or hem.

Front Facings with a Turning Ridge

Sometimes your pattern will call for a double front facing with a turning ridge. The pattern may read, for example: "Cast on 77 sts and work Row 1: K1, P1, ribbing across 62 sts then on the last 15 sts work K7, sl 1, K7 for double front facing with turning ridge. Row 2: P 15 sts, K1, P1, to end of row." Whenever you are on a right side row, you will work the K7, sl 1, as if to *Purl,* K7. On the return row, you will purl all of the stitches for the facing. Slipping a stitch as if to *purl* gives you a firm turning ridge. On the other front facing, you will be placing buttonholes, one on either side of the turning ridge (the slipped stitch), and when the facing is turned under the buttonholes will come together to form one double buttonhole. See page 240 on hand finishing double buttonholes.

INCREASES EVENLY SPACED

If your pattern asks you to increase evenly spaced across a row, and you are to increase only a small number of stitches, just measure the intervals with your eye and insert straight pins into the work at each increase point. Then when you come to a pin, increase there. You can increase up to about six stitches with this method.

If your pattern asks that you increase a large number of stitches evenly spaced across a row, you must divide the number you are to increase (new stitches needed) into the number of stitches you already have on the needle, to find the right interval between increases.

EXAMPLE: "Cast on 63 stitches, work in K1, P1, ribbing for 3″. On the next row, purl, increasing 15 stitches evenly spaced across the row."

To work in these 15 stitches "evenly spaced", you must divide 63 by 15, which gives you 4, with a remainder of 3. This means that you will increase one stitch in every fourth stitch, with 3 stitches remaining. Use the 3 remaining stitches at the end of the row. To do this, start at the beginning of the row, and purling, count: one, two, three, increase in the *4th,* one, two, three, increase in the *4th* stitch, until you come to within 3 stitches of the end of the row, then just purl those last 3 stitches without increasing. They are the remainder. If you should have a large remainder to use up at the end, divide the remainder in half and work the halves at each end without increasing, then go into your intervals of increasing as explained above.

DECREASES EVENLY SPACED

If your pattern asks that you decrease evenly spaced across a row, and you are to decrease only a small number of stitches, just insert straight pins into the work and "eye" them in evenly. Then when you come to a pin, decrease there. You can decrease up to about six stitches with this method.

If your pattern asks that you decrease a large number of stitches evenly spaced across a row, you must divide the number of stitches you are to decrease into the number of stitches you already have to find the interval between decreases.

EXAMPLE: "Number of stitches on needle, 260. On next row decrease 40 sts evenly spaced."

To decrease these 40 stitches evenly spaced across the 260 stitches, you must divide 40 into 260 stitches, and you get 6 with a remainder of 20 stitches. This means that you will be getting rid of every 6th stitch, with 20 stitches you will not be counting. You must use up this remainder (20 stitches) at the beginning and end of the row. To start out, you would work 10 stitches (half of the remainder) then start counting from there and knit together the 5th and 6th stitches across the row, until you come to within 10 stitches of the other end, (the other half of the remainder), and just work them without decreasing. You should come out with 220 stitches left on the needle after decreasing.

RAVELING OUT AND RE-USING SMOOTH YARNS

If you must re-use yarn that has been knit, washed and blocked, the yarn must be hanked, washed and dried, and then rolled into a ball again before re-using. If you should try to knit with yarn that has been ravelled from pieces which were washed and blocked, the crimp is set into the yarn so firmly that you cannot knit evenly and this crimp must be taken out before re-using the yarn.

If you have not washed and blocked your pieces, you may ravel out the yarn and re-knit with it without washing.

IMPROVED PROCEDURES

How to Increase without Leaving "Purl Bumps"

There is a way to increase without leaving a purl bump. It should not, however, be used in most patterns, because there is no stretch to this stitch, and if you should use it up the sides of a sleeve, for instance, where many increases come on top of one another, the increase stitches would tend to draw a taut line at the edge.

But, if you are making a sleeve starting with ribbing, and then changing to a pattern of colors knit in, and the pattern asks that you increase (for example) 8 stitches evenly across the next row, the increase bumps would show and detract from the looks of the sleeve. In this instance, you can use the "increase without purl bumps". To do this, on the stitch requiring the increase, find the "bump" of the stitch in the row below. Knit into that bump to the right of the stitch, leaving the old stitch on. Then knit into

FIND THE BUMP OF THE STITCH
IN THE ROW BELOW — KNIT INTO
THAT BUMP, TO THE RIGHT OF
THE STITCH, THEN KNIT INTO THE
STITCH ITSELF.

INCREASE WITHOUT LEAVING PURL
BUMPS

the stitch itself. Or you can make an increase to the left of the stitch. On the stitch requiring the increase, knit that stitch, and *do* drop the old stitch off. Next, pick up the loop of the "bump" in the row below to the left of *that* stitch, put the loop on the left hand needle, then knit into that loop.

The Improved Horizontal Buttonhole

Starting at the front edge, work two stitches (or whatever your pattern calls for), bind off the next four stitches (or whatever your pattern calls for). Work to the end of the row. On the next row, work until you come to the hole, then turn your work around and "knit on" four stitches as in making the regular buttonhole, *then* pick up the front loop of the first bound off stitch and slip it onto the needle next to the knit-on stitches. Then turn your work around

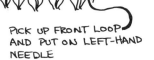

PICK UP FRONT LOOP
AND PUT ON LEFT-HAND
NEEDLE

IMPROVED HORIZONTAL BUTTONHOLE

again and work to the end of the row (2 stitches). On the following row, work two stitches then knit together the "picked-up bound-off stitch" and the last stitch of the knit on stitches.

This buttonhole may be used whenever you are working with knotty or nubby yarns and cannot plan on hand-finishing the buttonholes. If you are working with smooth yarn, you will be hand-finishing the buttonholes, and it is not necessary to use this improved buttonhole.

The No-Stair-Step Bind Off

If you would like to eliminate the "stair-steps" on the shoulder, it can be done by working "short rows" at each shoulder as follows:

Bind off the first row as usual. On the second row bind off as usual, except that as you approach the end of the row, work until one stitch remains on your left-hand needle, then turn your work around. The one remaining stitch is now on the needle in your right hand. Now slip the next stitch as if to purl from the left-hand needle to the right-hand needle. On the right-hand needle bind stitch No. 1 over stitch No. 2. Then bind off the rest of the stitches in the regular manner until the desired number of stitches are bound off. Do this on all the rest of the bind-off rows. You will not have a stair-step because you do not work the very last stitch, and when you turn your work around you slip the next stitch. There are two stitches that were not worked on the new row and the end stitch on the row before was not worked.

Improvement on Slip, Knit and Pass Slip Stitch Over

For full-fashioned raglan shaping on the right end of the needle where you were to K2, Sl 1, K1, PSSO—improve on this by doing the following: Knit the first two stitches. Now take the next stitch you were to have slipped and turn it around so that it is on the left-hand needle backwards (back half of the stitch is closest to the point of the needle). Now knit that stitch and the next stitch together through the *back* loops.

BACK HALF OF STITCH CLOSEST TO THE POINT

KNIT THAT STITCH AND NEXT ONE TOGETHER THROUGH BACK LOOPS

Shortening Sleeves

If you have knit your sleeves too long, they can be shortened from the bottom. Decide how much too long they are, then measure that amount from the top of the cuff ribbing. Starting at the bottom of the sleeve, open up the sleeve seam to a point about halfway to the underarm. Then, snip a knit stitch right on the edge at the point where you need to start ripping. *See picture.* Pull out the knit stitches, across the row a half stitch at a time, and put the stitches on a needle. When you have all of the stitches

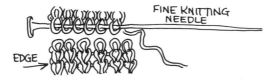

FINE KNITTING NEEDLE

EDGE →

PULL OUT STITCHES —
½ STITCH AT A TIME
AND PUT ON THE
NEEDLE

picked up, work the ribbing again on the small size needles you used before, then bind off loosely. If you must re-use the yarn you had after ripping the cuff, you must hank, wash and rinse the yarn before using it again. (The next time you knit a sleeve, see page 58 on measuring for sleeves, and you will not knit your sleeves too long again.)

CUFFS

To make sure that your cuff fits the wrist perfectly, remember that most patterns will give directions for a cuff too large for the average wrist. Take some ribbing already worked from another place on your sweater, for example, the ribbing at the bottom of the back of your sweater, and hold it around your wrist until it is just snug enough to please you. Then count that number of stitches, plus two or three for the seam, and that will be the number you will cast on for *your* cuff. Subtract the new number of cuff stitches from the number given to you in your pattern. This will tell you how many stitches you will have to add as you progress up the sleeve in order to arrive at the proper number when it is time to shape the cap of your sleeve. All increases must be in and accounted for approximately 2 inches before you reach the point where you shape the cap of your sleeve. You may add four stitches safely, evenly spaced at the end of the ribbing when you are changing to the large needles without showing any noticeable fullness there. Then, at intervals add the other stitches. The intervals will be shorter than in the original pattern. *Review "plot of sleeve" on page 58.*

FITTING THE BOTTOM EDGE OF A PULLOVER

Many pullover patterns need adjustment at the bottom edge for a good fit. This is especially true for men's pullovers. They want a snug fit through the hips.

Before you start your project, take the person's Actual and Knit Measurements and record them at the top of your pattern page (see page 42). Include one more measurement there—the hips where the sweater will fit at the bottom. On the *left* side of your page, the Actual Measurements, use the exact hip measurement. On the *right* side of your page, the Knit Measurements, add 2″ allowance to the hip measurement.

EXAMPLE:

Actual Measurements	Knit Measurements	
Chest 39	Chest	42
Hips 37	Hips	39
	Length	17
	Sleeve length	19
	Overall	—
	Overall sleeve	—

Work some ribbing on the size needle suggested in your pattern for working the ribbing. Cast on 28 to 30 stitches and work enough rows in ribbing to measure two inches. Put the little sample from the needles onto a yarn holder. Stretch out the ribbing and count the number of stitches needed to equal four inches. Divide the number by four and you now know your stitch gauge on the ribbing.

You may need to adjust your pattern for a good fit through the hips. Most pullover sweater patterns start out at the bottom with the same number of stitches required through the chest. If this is so in your pattern, then using the above example measurements you will need 1½ inches less at the bottom edge of the front and back. At 5 sts equals 1 inch, for example, you will need to cast on approximately 8 stitches less than the pattern calls for. On the last row of ribbing, you can increase 8 stitches evenly spaced across the row to get the required number of stitches called for in your pattern.

CHAPTER VII

Raglan Sweaters

RAGLAN SWEATERS STARTING AT THE BOTTOM

If you have chosen a sweater with raglan sleeves, it is most important that you meet the stitch gauge as to row count, or the raglan will be too long or too short. A diagram may be drawn up for the back of your sweater, and according to your pattern you will probably be decreasing every other row to form the raglans until you have a certain number of stitches left for the back of the neck. Your pattern may read for example: "Back—Cast on 87 sts, work in K1, P1 ribbing for 1″. Change to larger needles and work in pattern st until piece measures 15″. Shape raglan armhole: With right side facing you, bind off 2 sts at the beg of the next 2 rows. Then dec 1 st at beg and end of row every other row 28 times. Slip remaining sts on a holder for back of neck."

To do this, work as your pattern states until it is time to shape the armhole. Bind off the first two stitches, then tie in a colored yarn marker in the middle of your work. Bind off the other two stitches on the next row (the wrong side row). Now every time the yarn marker is facing you, decrease as the pattern states until you have 27 stitches left. You need not count the number of times

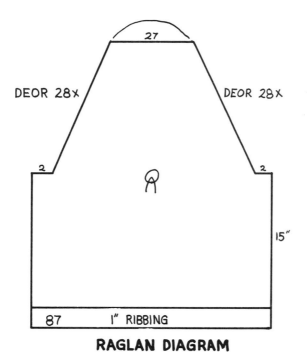

RAGLAN DIAGRAM

you decrease for the raglan as you are decreasing every time the marker is facing you and, by subtraction, you will find that you would have 27 stitches left.

     87 stitches on the needle
  − 4 bound off for the beginning of the raglan (two each side)
     83 stitches left
  −56 bound off for the raglan decreases (28 each side)
     27 stitches left for the back of the neck stitches.

    Everything will work out fine if you are obtaining the row-wise gauge the pattern is asking for. But if you are not, some adjustment must be made. In the above example the row-wise gauge given in the pattern was "6 rows equal 1 inch." If your knitting is on this gauge, your raglan will measure $9\frac{1}{2}$ inches straight up from the yarn marker. This was figured out by adding up all the rows from the point of the first bind off for the raglan shaping (where the yarn marker is). If you were to decrease every other row 28 times, it would take you 28 times two, or 56 rows to do the raglan shaping. Now divide the 56 rows by six (six rows per inch) and you get nearly 9½ inches. Suppose when you make your original stitch gauge of nine stitches equals two inches and six rows equals one inch, you were on gauge in one direction, getting nine stitches in two inches, but when you measured your gauge lengthwise, your little gauge measured only 3½ inches instead of four inches. If your finished raglan was supposed to measure approximately 9½ inches and you were losing one-half inch in every four inches, your raglan would measure approximately eight inches instead of the needed 9½ inches. You will need about eight more rows to make your raglan long enough. The best way to do this is to put in "skip rows" as you are working your raglan. Go back to the diagram and show the "skip rows". To put in skip rows means that you will *not* decrease every other row, but will skip the decrease on certain rows, i.e. the "skip" rows. Everytime you skip the decrease row you will actually be adding two more rows, because you were

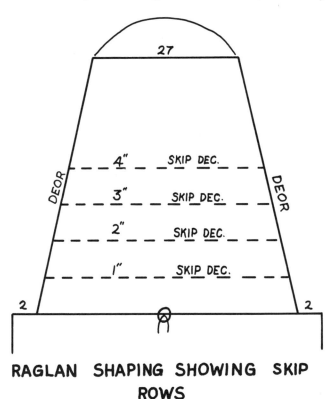

RAGLAN SHAPING SHOWING SKIP ROWS

supposed to decrease every other row. Normally you work a row without decreasing on the wrong side anyway, so if you skip a decrease row, you are in reality getting in two extra rows at every "skip". If you need eight extra rows you will need to skip the decreases four times, proceeding as follows from the beginning: Bind off the two stitches at the beginning of the next two rows for the start of the raglan shaping. Tie in the colored yarn marker on the row of the first bind-off. Then, make the decreases every time the yarn marker is facing you (every other row) until your piece measures one inch from the yarn marker. Then take your first skip row as shown on the diagram. Then work as before until your piece measures two inches from the yarn marker and then take your second skip row. Continue putting in the rest of your skip rows as shown on your diagram until all of the skip rows are in. Then decrease every other row until the 27 stitches remain. Your raglan will measure approximately $9\frac{1}{2}$ inches from the marker.

If, when you were working your stitch gauge you were off gauge row-wise only one-fourth inch in the piece which should have been four inches, you would need to put in only half as many skip rows as you did in the above example. You would draw up your diagram showing skip rows at one inch and two inches above the marker which would give you the extra four rows you need.

Since all raglans must be exactly the same, whatever you did for the back in the way of skip rows must also be done for the fronts and sleeves. If you put in skip rows every inch four times on the back, you must put in skip rows every inch four times on the fronts and sleeves.

When it is time to shape the front neck, draw up the front neck shaping on a diagram.

If a Cardigan

EXAMPLE: "Left Front. Cast on 52 sts, work ribbing for 1″. Change to large needles and work pattern across 45 sts, then ribbing of K1, P1 on the last 7 sts for the front border." (Always follow what was already established in ribbing on those last stitches for the border, knits over knits and purls over purls.) "Work until piece measures the same as back to underarm. Shape raglan armhole: Bind off 2 sts at arm edge once, then dec 1 st at arm

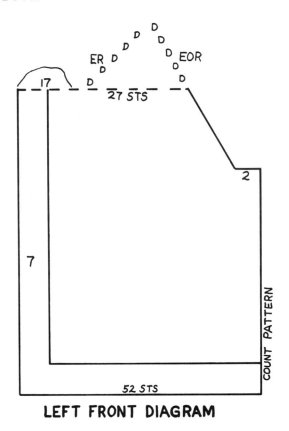

LEFT FRONT DIAGRAM

edge every other row *23 times* ending at center edge. Shape neck: At center edge work 17 sts and slip these sts on a holder. Continue to dec 1 st at arm edge every other row 5 times more and at the same time, at neck edge, dec 1 st every row 5 times."

To do this, you need not count the number of times you are to decrease at the arm edge. Simply subtract 23 (the number of times you were told to decrease) from the total number of stitches on the piece and you will know how many stitches are to be left on the needle just before you start shaping the neck.

$$
\begin{array}{rl}
52 & \text{stitches on the needle} \\
-\ 2 & \text{bound off for the start of the armhole} \\
\hline
50 & \text{stitches left} \\
-23 & \text{raglan decreases} \\
\hline
27 & \text{stitches left}
\end{array}
$$

You will work until you have 27 stitches left, then it will be time to shape the neck and finish the raglan. Draw up your diagram.

It will be easy for you to do each step because your diagram shows you what is going to happen. You will be decreasing *every other* row on the raglan as before and while you are doing that, you will be decreasing *every* row at the neck edge. You will use up all of the stitches by the time you have put in all of the decreases. Be sure to circle your decreases as you are doing them so that you will know where you are at all times.

If a Pullover

EXAMPLE: "Front: Work same as back, taking raglan decreases as for back and when there are 35 sts left on needle, work across 14 sts, tie in another ball of yarn, bind off the center 7 sts, work last 14 sts. Continue working on each side with a separate ball of yarn, or work 1 side at a time if you wish. Continue to dec for raglan armholes every other row as before 5 times more, and at the same time, bind off 2 sts from neck edge every other row 3 times, then dec 1 st at neck edge every other row 3 times." If you do not draw a diagram you will have a hard time doing this neck shaping, but if you do have the diagram, it will be easy to see what you are going to do. You can circle your work as you do each step, and you will know where you are at all times.

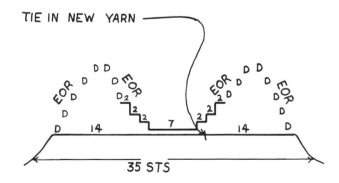

FRONT NECK SHAPING FOR PULLOVER

FULL FASHIONED RAGLAN SWEATERS

If you are making a full-fashioned raglan sweater, your shaping (or decreases) for the raglan will be set several stitches in from the edges. If the raglan is not full fashioned, the decreases are right on the very edge of the piece. Full-fashioned raglan sweaters if put together properly will look as though there are no seams at the raglans. If you are not on the stitch gauge row-wise, you must use the same method of lengthening your raglan by putting in skip rows as explained above.

Rules for Raglan Shaping

If a pattern calls for a "full-fashioned" raglan shaping, it means that the decreases will be several stitches in from the edge. If the decreases are right at the edge the sweater is not full fashioned. In order to produce this full-fashioned look, you cannot simply knit two together several stitches in from the edge. The two raglans would not look alike. That is why you find directions asking that you slip, knit, and pass on one end of the raglan and knit two together on the other end.

EXAMPLE: Pattern may read "K2, slip 1, K1, psso, work to within 4 sts of end, K2 tog, K2."

To do this knit the two stitches, slip the next stitch as if to *knit,* knit the next stitch, then pass the slipped stitch over the knit stitch. In other words, bind the slipped stitch over the knit stitch (a decrease made). In passing the slipped stitch over, bind the stitch without stretching it. Do it right on the tip of the needle. NOTE: You *must* slip the stitch as if to *knit,* because if you do not the raglan shaping will not look the same on both edges. You may not notice it until you have done several rows of the raglan decreases, then you will see that on the end where you slipped, knit and passed you have a twisted stitch. The reason it is twisted is that you slipped as if to purl instead of slipping as if to knit.

Be on the alert for errors in pattern books giving you raglan shaping. Many times the book will ask that you knit two together on the right end of the work and slip, knit and pass on the left end of the work. This is an error and if you should follow these directions the *two sides would not look alike.* To explain this better, you must understand that when you slip, knit and pass you are

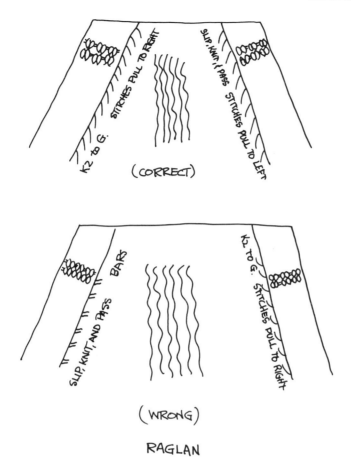

RAGLAN

pulling the stitches to the left side and when you knit two together you are pulling the stitch to the right side. Now, if you should have the directions for the two sides reversed, you would get an ugly bar on the left end of the needle where you slipped, knit and passed. Change the directions so that on the right end you always slip, knit and pass and on the left end you always knit together.

RAGLAN SWEATERS STARTING AT THE NECK

Many raglan sweater patterns start at the neck on circular needles and the raglans are knit right in, using increases at each raglan point. This eliminates any seams where the sleeves fit into the fronts and the back. After this raglan section is completed, the sleeves are finished, one by one, then the fronts and back are joined together at the sides and worked down in one piece to the bottom of the sweater. The only place where seams are needed, then, is on the sleeves.

As you progress on this type raglan, which is all knit in one piece, you will find that the work becomes very heavy and awkward to handle. You should knit so that heavy pieces are resting on a table to keep the stitches from stretching and throwing you off your stitch gauge.

Setting Up Raglans with "Yarn-Over" Increases

"With smaller size needles cast on 40 sts for neck edge. Work in ribbing of K1, P1 for 6 rows. Change to larger needles and begin raglan shaping. Row 1—wrong side row, and all wrong side rows, Purl. Row 2—K11 sts for left front, YO, K1 and mark this st for seam st, YO, K2 sts for left sleeve, YO, K1 and mark for seam st, YO, K10 for back, YO, K1 and mark for seam st, YO, K2 for right sleeve, YO, K1, mark for seam st, YO, K11 for right front (48 sts on needle)."

To do this, work the ribbing and change to the larger needles and purl the first row. When you begin on row two, knit eleven stitches, put in your yarn-over, then knit the next stitch. Stop right there and mark that stitch with a piece of colored yarn on the row below, then put in your next yarn-over, then continue to finish the row, marking all of your seam stitches the same way. After you have finished that row count your stitches to make sure you have the 48 sts required. Then examine your work and you will see that you have four marked stitches. On either side of the marked stitches, you have an eyelet hole made from your yarn-over. As you follow your pattern you will always purl on wrong side rows and on right side rows you will yarn-over before and after the marked stitch. You can see your yarn-overs lining up right on top of each other, row after row, with the central stitch in between them. And, you can see that on each right side row you are gaining eight stitches, two at each raglan point. See diagram.

On this particular pattern the directions read to continue increasing at all raglans as before until there are 200 stitches on the needle. Caution! If you were off the stitch gauge row-wise and

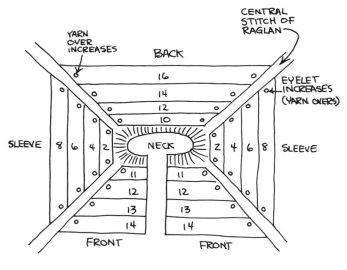

RAGLAN

need extra rows, you cannot put them in with the yarn-overs or you will get too many stitches on the needles and your sweater will be too large. If you need to add extra rows, you should work the extra rows after all of the eyelet rows have been worked, simply knitting over and purling back just before you come to the dividing row.

Dividing Row: Purl 31 stitches and place them on a yarn holder for the right front, purl 43 stitches and place them on a holder for the right sleeve, purl 52 stitches and put them on a holder for the back, purl 43 stitches for the left sleeve (leave these stitches on the needle), then place the remaining 31 stitches for the left front on another holder.

Left Sleeve: Work in stockinette stitch casting on three stitches at the beginning of each of the next two rows (you must use the "knitting on" method). Then the directions continue telling you how to finish this sleeve.

Next, you will work the right sleeve the same as you did the left. After both sleeves have been completed, put the body stitches back on the needle except the stitches from the left front (because those stitches were not worked when you were working across to the left sleeve on your dividing row). Join the yarn and purl these left front stitches, (31).

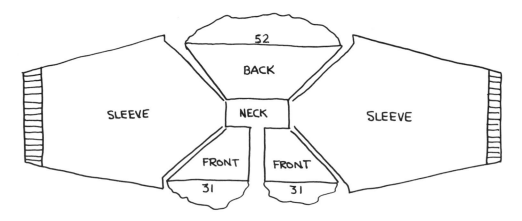

STITCHES ON HOLDERS FOR FRONTS
AND BACK.

SLEEVES FINISHED

Next Row: Work across the 31 stitches of the left front, "knit on" six stitches, work across the 52 stitches of the back, "knit on" six stitches, then work the 31 stitches of the other front. (You see, you are adding six stitches to each side at the underarm point and these will be seamed later when you are putting your sweater together.) Now you will work down on your sweater until it is the desired length, finishing off in ribbing. Crochet borders will be worked on this sweater later, after washing and blocking.

N O T E : The full directions for this sweater are not given here. The purpose in using these directions is to clear up certain things you will encounter in making a sweater of this type with eyelet raglan shaping.

Raglan Sweaters Starting at the Neck with Regular Increase Stitches

Some raglan sweaters which start at the neck use regular increases, (see page 153) instead of the yarn-over (eyelet hole) increase described in the previous paragraphs. In this type raglan, you will see the little "bump" looking stitches which you always see whenever an increase stitch is made. This makes the raglan quite attractive as these little increase marks make a pattern on each side of the raglan shaping.

Again, you *must* be on the row-wise gauge as you were when making the eyelet hole raglan shaping. If you are not on the row-wise gauge you will have to work extra rows after all raglan increases are made. You cannot put in any skip rows where increase marks (or eyelet holes) are used. If you did, there would be a greater distance between some increase marks (or eyelet holes) than others and it would spoil the symmetry of your work.

Example of directions for raglan with regular increases: "Cast on 23 sts on circular needle. P1 row. Set raglan as follows using ring markers. Inc 1 st in 2 sts, marker, inc 1 st in next st, K2 (sleeve section), inc 1 st in next st, marker, inc 1 st in next st, K9 sts (back section), inc 1 st in next st, marker, inc 1 st in next st, K2 (sleeve section), inc 1 st in next st, marker, inc 1 st in last 2 sts. Next row, purl. Repeat these 2 rows increasing in the first and last sts and in sts before and after markers on knit rows. Always purl back plain. When there are 8 sts on the needle up to the first marker, cast on 6 sts once at each end of needle. This completes the front neck shaping. Continue to increase before and after each marker on knit rows until there are 161 sts on needle. This completes raglan shaping."

Note #1: This raglan with regular increases tells you to increase in two stitches right together for each raglan increase. There is no central stitch worked between these two stitches; however, if you examine this raglan closely, it will look as though there *is* a central stitch worked. The reason for this is that whenever you increase you form a little bump *after* the stitch (to the left of the stitch) then when you increase in the next stitch you see a plain stitch first, then the little bump. Your marker is placed between the two stitches and to the right side of the marker you immediately see a bump but on the left side of the marker, you see a stitch first, then a bump.

There is another way to form a raglan with regular increase using a central stitch in between the increase stitches. Your pattern will read (for the raglan increase): "Work until 2 st before the

marker, inc 1 st in next st, K1, move marker, inc 1 st in next st". This type raglan looks as though there are two stitches between the increase stitches instead of one. When it is time to divide the work for working the sleeves, usually the pattern will have you divide between these two stitches.

Note #2: This raglan differs from the raglan with yarn-overs in several other ways. In the first place, there is no ribbing worked at the neck, as was done on the raglan with the yarn-overs. This raglan has a front neck shaping; that is, the front is being gradually shaped at the same time that the raglan increases are being knit in. On the other raglan with yarn-overs, all the neck stitches were cast on at the same time and there was no front neck shaping.

With this raglan you will be increasing before and after each marker. You will have four markers on your needle and, at the same time on every right side row, you will also be increasing on the first and last stitch to form the neck shaping until there are eight stitches on the needle before you reach the first marker. On the next row, you will cast on six stitches at each end of the needle (you must "knit on" these stitches). This completes the front neck shaping. From here on the sweater progresses in the same manner as did the sweater with the eyelet holes. You will follow the same procedure as was followed in that example. That is, finish knitting both the sleeves first, then join the back and fronts together at the sides and finish the body of the sweater.

Raglan Sweaters Starting at the Neck with Ribbing and Front Neck Shaping

It *is* possible to make a raglan starting at the neck that has both ribbing and front neck shaping. You must do the "short row" method. If you have never worked "short rows" read the directions on page 116. After the ribbing has been worked, you will be enlarging the back and sleeve part of your sweater with the short row method and gradually adding the front neck stitches from straight needles until all of the front neck stitches have been added. (In the following example, the directions for forming the button-holes are being omitted.)

EXAMPLE: "With size 4 needles cast on 81 sts and work in K1, P1 ribbing for 10 rows. *Raglan Yoke and Short Rows—Row*

1: Work 8 sts in ribbing for front border, P next 9 sts and leave these 17 sts on straight needle. With size 7 circular needle, P 49 sts, leave remaining 15 sts on straight needle. Row 2: Turn, Sl 1, K2, *inc 1 st in next st, place a marker on needle, inc 1 st in next st; K8 sts for left sleeve; inc 1 st in next st, place marker on needle, inc 1 st in next st*"; K 20 sts for back; repeat between *'s once, K2 then K2 from straight needle. Carry up markers slipping them from left to right point of needle on every row. Row 3: Turn, Sl 1, P all remaining sts on circular needle, P2 from straight needle. Row 4: Turn, Sl 1, *K to within 1 st of marker, inc 1 st in each of next 2 sts*, repeat between *'s three times more, K up to straight needle, K2 from straight needle. Repeat Rows 3 and 4 twice more. Row 9: Turn, Sl 1, P all remaining sts on circular needle; then from straight needle P1 st and work remaining 8 sts in ribbing. Row 10: Work 8 sts in ribbing, repeat between *'s of Row 4 four times, K up to straight needle, from straight needle K1 st, work remaining 8 sts in ribbing. This completes short rows (all sts are worked off of the straight needles). Continue to inc 1 st each side of each marker every second row as before 26 times more working border in ribbing as before and repeating buttonhole every $3\frac{3}{4}$". End at right front edge with 329 sts."

After reading through that example and looking at the dia-

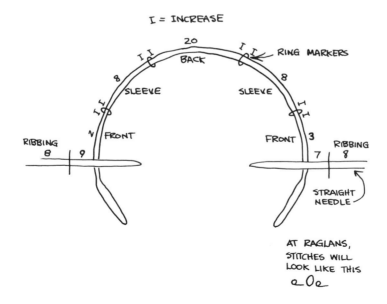

gram showing how the stitches are placed on straight needles at both ends of the work, and the rest of the stitches on a circular needle with the markers placed, the increase stitches shown and the number of stitches for the fronts, back and sleeves, you should be able to see how this type raglan is worked. To further understand this raglan you must realize that the stitches on the circular needle are the stitches *in between the short rows,* and you will be making the back of the neck and the sleeves deeper, and gradually adding the front neck stitches until all of the front neck stitches are added. When you come to the part of the instructions saying to turn, you turn your work around as if you had finished the row and you work back in the other direction. When you are told to slip one (after turning) you do this as if to *purl.*

Blocking Raglans Which Start at the Neck

When it is time to wash and block the raglan that was started at the neck and worked down, you have almost a finished sweater to block. Of course all the ends have been worked in but all trim such as crochet, pocket flaps, etc., will be worked *after* blocking. Baste the sleeves together with sewing thread with the right sides out so that they will not roll and curl while you are washing and blocking. Follow all directions for regular washing given on page 62 and block as follows: If your sweater is a cardigan, lay the back of the sweater down on your padded surface, *right side down* on the towel and smooth out the back of your sweater from the wrong side. From your blocking dimensions, measure the distance across the back just below the sleeves to get one-half of your knit measurement at the bust line. Measure your "overall" (see page 64) and make it conform to the "overall" you jotted down after you finished knitting. Now lay the fronts over on top of the back. Lay the side with the buttonholes down first, then the side with the buttons on top of the border with the buttonholes. Smooth out your garment getting it to size as you did when you worked with sweaters that were in pieces. Shape to the right lengths and widths. Work with the bottom and neck edges to make them straight and smooth. Lay out the sleeves as you would if you were blocking a finished sweater. That is, stretch them out away from the body of the sweater. Smooth out all of the wrinkles with the palms of your hands, bring out to width and length called for in your blocking dimensions. Let the garment remain there until dry. Or, you can change the towels under the garment several times to hasten the drying process. If you are blocking a pullover, follow the same process as described above, except that you will have to work with the back and front as they lie together.

Assembling Raglan Sweaters Which Started at the Neck

There is not much assembling to do with this type of sweater as there is no seam at the raglans, nor any seam on the sides of the sweater. You will have to seam only the sleeves. Use the back stitch starting just above the cuff and working up to the underarm of the sleeve. Then sew the cuffs, blending the ribbing on the cuff according to directions on page 75. There will be a little slit opening that resembles a half moon on each side under the arm. This must be sewed after you have steamed out the sleeve seam according to directions previously given on page 69. Turn the sweater inside out and pin that little slit together with the right sides together. Sew this seam with a back stitch from the wrong side of the sweater. Using split yarn, start at the very edge and sew this seam as any back-stitched seam is sewed, tapering off to nothing at the other end. Steam out this little seam. Any crochet or other trim is then put on, according to directions given on page 224.

HALF MOON SEAM

CHAPTER VIII

Skirts

CUSTOM MADE SKIRTS

You can knit a custom made skirt to match almost any sweater, and make yourself a good looking outfit.

Do not try to adjust a skirt pattern from a pattern book. Rather, you should draft up your own skirt pattern, just for you and to *your* own measurements. This is not difficult to do. First of all, decide upon the yarn and the needle size. If you are making a skirt to go with a sweater of knitting worsted, purchase approximately six four-ounce skeins of knitting worsted, in the same color number as was used for your sweater. If you are using a different yarn, purchase a little more yarn than you would need for a sweater.

In order to tie your skirt in with your sweater and to make a truly matching outfit, make a border on the skirt to match the border on your sweater. If your sweater has a garter stitch border, use a garter stitch border on your skirt; if your sweater has a hem with a turning ridge, use the same on your skirt. If your sweater has ribbing, use a small amount of ribbing for the border on your skirt (about $\frac{5}{8}$ inch). If your sweater is in a fancy pattern stitch,

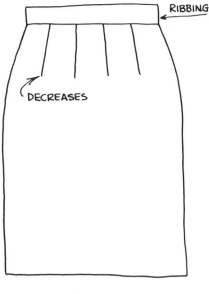

RIBBING

DECREASES

SKIRT

you may want to make a plain skirt, with no border at the bottom. This can be done nicely, and after your skirt is finished, you can add one or two rows of single crochet on the bottom edge to finish it off and to keep the edge from rolling and curling. If you use garter stitch, only one needle size is needed, but if you desire to use ribbing, seed stitch, or a hem, you will need to start with needles two sizes smaller for the trim or hem, then change to larger needles for the body of the skirt. Using smaller needles at the edge will keep your skirt from flaring out at the bottom.

STRAIGHT SKIRTS IN STOCKINETTE STITCH

Straight Skirts in Stockinette Stitch with Regular Decreases

The simple skirt suggested here is made on a circular needle. This is a straight skirt with no side seams. The decrease marks are spaced evenly around the skirt. If the decreases are lined up one right on top of the other, you will have a beautiful skirt with a custom made look. If, however, you are careless and do not have the decreases lined up properly and they are scattered and off center, it will look like a home-made job. Learn to do the decreases correctly.

This skirt has no side opening and is two inches larger around your waist measurement with elastic running through the waistband. This skirt has no definite back or front because it is the same all around.

Knit your stitch gauge first. Since you will be using a circular needle for your skirt, you should knit your gauge on a circular needle. You will be knitting only a four inch swatch so you will have to knit across and purl back to form stockinette stitch, *but* when you are actually working on your skirt, you will not be purling at all. (See page 6 and page 125.) Most people tend to purl looser stitches than their knit stitches, and many people find that they are way off stitch gauge later when they take a check on gauge on their skirt as they progress. This difficulty can be eliminated if you will purl *very tightly* when knitting your sample gauge, anticipating that your work on circular needles will be much tighter because you will not be purling when you actually work your skirt. For example, on #8 needles, and using knitting worsted, try for five stitches equal one inch. After the gauge has been determined, take your actual measurements. You may use fractions here, but when drawing up your pattern for knitting, round off the waist and hip fractions to the nearest inch. For the length measurement you may use the one-half inch fraction (nothing less). This skirt will fit you perfectly if you have taken accurate measurements. Always stand with feet together when having hips measured. This can make a difference in your actual measurement of up to two inches. Have a second person measure you if possible. Be sure to measure the number of inches between your waist and your hips. If the abdomen is larger than your hips, take your abdomen measurement and the distance down from the waist to the abdomen. (This will insure that the skirt will not cup in under the "tummy".) If the hips are larger than the abdomen, take the hip measurement at the largest point and measure the distance down from the waist to this point. If your hips are under 36 inches, your straight skirt should be *38* inches at the bottom; (a skirt measuring less than 38 inches at the bottom is rather constricting). If your hips are larger than 36 inches, you will start out at the bottom with hip (or abdomen) measurement, plus a two inch allowance.

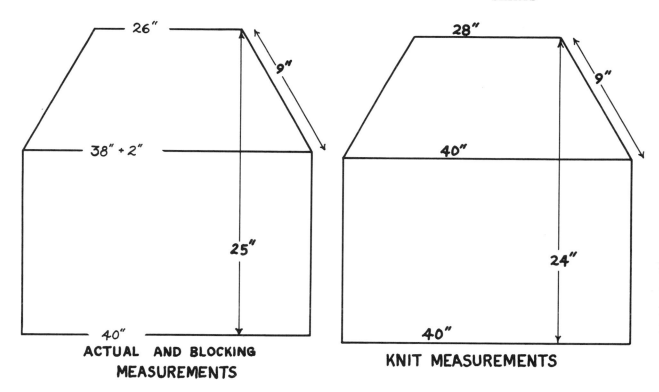

ACTUAL AND BLOCKING MEASUREMENTS

KNIT MEASUREMENTS

EXAMPLE: Hips 38″, measurement around bottom of skirt, 40″.

NOTE: This allowance must be added in order to insure a perfect fit.

Now, take three sheets of paper. On the first sheet show your actual and blocking measurements. On your second sheet of paper you will draw up your *knit measurements*. These measurements differ from your actual and blocking measurements at the waist by two inches, as the waist measurement is two inches larger. The knit measurement at the hips is the hip measurement plus two inches. The length from the waist to the hip (or abdomen) is the same, but the over-all length measurement is one inch *less,* to allow for a one-inch drop in blocking. See diagram above.

Now you are ready to translate inches into stitches and to draw up your basic skirt pattern on the third sheet. NOTE: Your Basic Skirt is drawn up on a gauge of five stitches equals one inch. Later you will be told how you can use the same pattern for all other stitch gauges. EXAMPLE: For 38″ hips you will start out with 200 stitches on your needle. (This number was arrived at by multiplying 40 inches by five stitches per inch—200 stitches.) After the border or hem has been worked, you will work in stockinette stitch for 15 inches from the cast-on row or from the turning ridge if your skirt has a hem. At 15 inches you reach the hipline. Mark this point with colored yarn markers in three or four places. *The first decrease does not start at the hipline.* You are only marking the hipline. The first decrease comes above the hipline. On your sheet of paper, make a large drawing of the skirt leaving plenty of room to show all markings. The drawing may look distorted (longer at the top above the hipline than from the hipline to the bottom), but you need the room to show all of the decreases and markings, so let it look distorted if necessary. You must decrease from the 200 stitches you started out with down to 140 stitches (28 inches times

START OF DRAWING OF PATTERN
AT 5 STITCHES = 1″ ; SHOWING
6 DEC. ROW TO 140 STITCHES

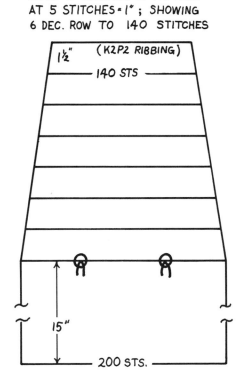

five stitches) at the waist. Show these figures on your pattern. You will want to reach 140 stitches at 1½ inches below the waist because the last 1½ inches will be worked in K2, P2 ribbing. You will be taking off two inches of stitches at each decrease; that is, ten stitches. You will need six decrease rows to accomplish this. See diagram. Now, determine how these decreases shall be spaced so that if any variation in tapering is needed, the larger spaces between decreases should be near the hips and the smaller spaces near the waist. The last 1½ inches will be K2, P2 ribbing, therefore you are left with 7½ inches to get six spaces between decreases. In this particular example it works out as follows: Work another 1½ inches after the marking at the hipline, then at 16½ inches the first row of decreases is made, dropping the number of stitches to 190. NOTE: All measuring must be done from the bottom of your work, or at the turning ridge if the skirt has a hem. *Never* measure the distance between decreases. Always measure from the bottom of your work. Work even for 1½ inches (18 inches from the bottom) then work second decrease row—180 stitches. Work even for 1½ inches (19½ inches) then work third decrease row—170 stitches. Work one inch even until you have 20½ inches, then work the fourth decrease row—160 stitches. Work even for one inch (21½ inches) then work fifth decrease row—150 stitches. Work even for one inch (22½ inches) then work sixth decrease row—140 stitches. Now work K2, P2 ribbing for 1½ inches. At 24 inches bind off loosely. NOTE: If your hips measure under 36 inches, adjust your pattern so that at the hipline your measurement will be your own, plus two inches. (You may have to work an extra decrease row *before* the hipline.)

It is not difficult to work the decrease rows. You must decide upon where your rounds start and then all of the decreases will line up perfectly, one on top of another. To do this, find the starting point at the bottom of your work where the tail end of loose yarn hangs. Follow that stitch up until you come to the needle. At this point put a ring marker on your needle and carry the marker up as you proceed. All decreases start from this stitch. Do not put your marker on the needle until it is time for the first decrease round. Many times a marker on the needle will cause a separation line which will not come out during the blocking process. If you see that you are leaving a separation line don't use a regular

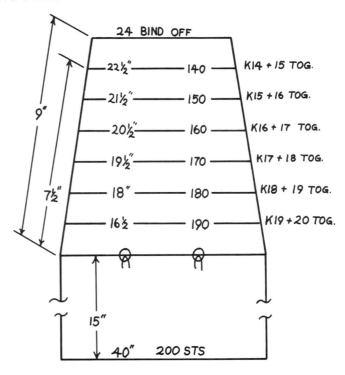

24 BIND OFF

22½" — 140 — K14 + 15 TOG.

21½" — 150 — K15 + 16 TOG.

20½" — 160 — K16 + 17 TOG.

19½" — 170 — K17 + 18 TOG.

18" — 180 — K18 + 19 TOG.

16½ — 190 — K19 + 20 TOG.

9"

7½"

15"

40"   200 STS

PATTERN #1 (COMPLETED) AT 5 STS = 1"

commercial marker. Make one out of sewing thread and move it from needle to needle as you would a regular marker.

To decrease ten stitches in a round of 200 stitches, at the same time keeping the decreases evenly spaced, divide ten into 200 and you get 20. This means you want to get rid of the 20th stitch ten times. You would knit stitches 19 and 20 together ten times around in one round. Start counting right after the marker; start with one and count to 18, then knit stitches 19 and 20 together; then start counting again with one and count to 18 again, then knit stitches 19 and 20 together. Continue doing this until you come back around to the marker again. The last two stitches you come to before the marker will be stitches 19 and 20 and you will knit them together. You should have knit 19 and 20 together ten times and have decreased ten stitches. Count your stitches. You should have 190 stitches. Then work even until the time for the next decrease. It works out as follows:

2nd decrease will be stitches 18 and 19 knit together (10 times)

3rd decrease will be stitches 17 and 18 knit together (10 times)

4th decrease will be stitches 16 and 17 knit together (10 times)

5th decrease will be stitches 15 and 16 knit together (10 times)

6th decrease will be stitches 14 and 15 knit together (10 times)

See pattern #1

This skirt pattern was simple to do because all figures used were divisible by 10. If your personal measurements do not come out to figures divisible by 10, see the next skirt pattern where five was used.

EXPLANATION: Whenever you use *even* numbers at the waist, hips, and bottom of skirt, your pattern will work out in numbers divisible by 10. But, if you must use *odd* numbers, your pattern will not be divisible by 10.

EXAMPLE: A waist measurement of 27 inches instead of 28 inches, which was used in the first example, and hip measurement of 39 inches instead of 40 inches, which was used in the first example. The first decrease you will take will be to decrease five times evenly around so that you can get your pattern down to a number divisible by ten—then stay in tens until you must go again to the fives at the very last decrease at the waist. See pattern #2. When you must decrease five times evenly spaced, divide the number of stitches you have (195) by five and you get 39. To decrease from 195 to 190 then, you will knit together the 38th and 39th stitches, five times. Examine the next two pictures—A and B—showing how the stitches will look on the circular needle, as if you were looking straight down from the top when it is time to decrease for the first time. View A shows the decreases from 195 to 190 stitches at the five decrease points. View B shows the ten decreases from 200 down to 190 stitches. You have 200 stitches on the needle, and you are going to decrease ten times evenly spaced around. You will knit together the 19th and 20th stitches ten times.

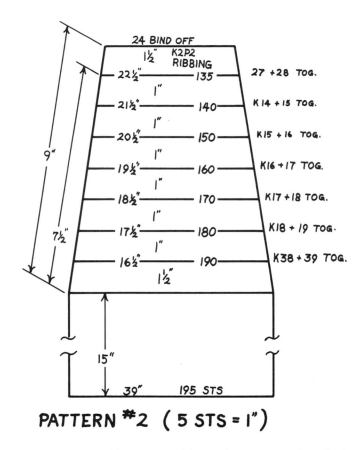

24 BIND OFF

1½" K2P2 RIBBING

22½"	135	27 + 28 TOG.
1"		
21½"	140	K 14 + 15 TOG.
1"		
20½"	150	K 15 + 16 TOG.
1"		
19½"	160	K 16 + 17 TOG.
1"		
18½"	170	K 17 + 18 TOG.
1"		
17½"	180	K 18 + 19 TOG.
1"		
16½"	190	K 38 + 39 TOG.

1½"

9"

7½"

15"

39" 195 STS

PATTERN #2 (5 STS = 1")

As you are working your skirt, take an occasional check on stitch gauge to insure a good fit. Make sure the decrease points are lining up one right on top of each other. If you must use five decrease points and then go to ten decrease points, you will notice that the five's come where every other one of the ten's comes. If they are not lining up properly, you have miscounted stitches and, of course, must rip out that row and do it again properly. *THE DECREASES MUST LINE UP!* After all of the decreases have been made and it is time to go into K2, P2 ribbing, you must be left with a number of stitches divisible by four, otherwise the K2, P2 ribbing will not work out correctly. Adjust this by decreasing one or two stitches on the last row (or leaving out one of the decreases, if necessary) to arrive at a number divisible by four. NOTE: The reason K2, P2 ribbing is used instead of K1, P1 ribbing is that it tends to pull in a great deal more than K1, P1 ribbing.

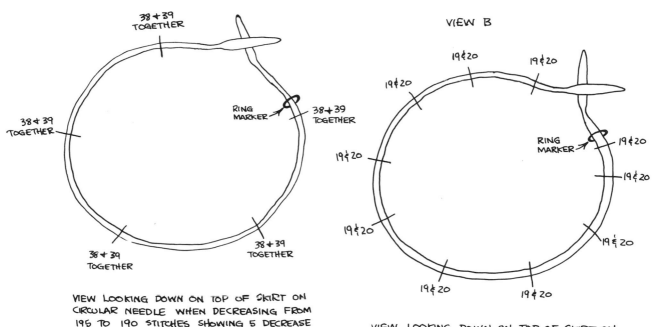

VIEW A

38 + 39 TOGETHER

38 + 39 TOGETHER

38 + 39 TOGETHER

38 + 39 TOGETHER

RING MARKER

VIEW LOOKING DOWN ON TOP OF SKIRT ON CIRCULAR NEEDLE WHEN DECREASING FROM 195 TO 190 STITCHES SHOWING 5 DECREASE POINTS

VIEW B

19 & 20

19 & 20

19 & 20

19 & 20

19 & 20

19 & 20

19 & 20

19 & 20

19 & 20

19 & 20

RING MARKER

VIEW LOOKING DOWN ON TOP OF SKIRT ON CIRCULAR NEEDLES AT 1ST DECREASE POINT

If your edging at the bottom is K1, P1 ribbing on smaller needles, it does not follow that you must also have K1, P1 ribbing on smaller needles at the waist. Always use K2, P2 ribbing on *regular* size needles for the waist. Now wash and block your skirt see page (182).

CASING FOR ELASTIC FOR SKIRT (CROCHETED)

With wrong side of skirt facing you, join the yarn at the top edge of the skirt and crochet a row of zigzag chain stitching as follows: Ch 4, 5, or 6 (or the amount needed to equal about $\frac{1}{2}$ inch of chain), slip stitch into a knit rib approximately $\frac{1}{2}$ inch below the edge, chain the same amount, slip stitch into the top of the next knit rib, continue around the top of the skirt with this zigzag chain; join and fasten off. Pre-shrink $\frac{5}{8}$ inch elastic cut to the waist length needed and weave it through the casing, either fastening with a hook and eye, or sewing securely. NOTE: You may desire to run in a row of basting thread $\frac{1}{2}$ inch below the top of the skirt to guide you while putting on your zigzag chain, to insure accuracy.

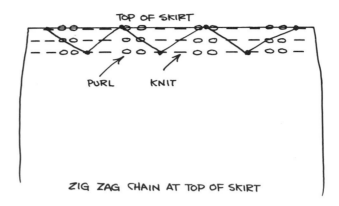

ZIG ZAG CHAIN AT TOP OF SKIRT

HOW TO USE THE SAME PATTERN FOR DIFFERENT YARNS AND GAUGES

Now that you have drawn up your basic skirt pattern to your personal measurements for five stitches equal one inch, you can use the same pattern for any stitch gauge on any kind of yarn with just a little change here and there. If you change your gauge to six stitches per inch, for example, all you will need to do is to figure how many stitches you must start out with. In the original example, you started out with 40 inches at the bottom of the skirt, or 200 stitches at five stitches per inch. With six stitches per inch, you will multiply 40 inches by six stitches per inch and you should start out at the bottom with 240 stitches. You will work for 15 inches on the 240 stitches, then mark the hipline with colored yarn markers as you did before. In the first example at five stitches per inch you took off two inches of stitches at each decrease (ten stitches at each decrease). At six stitches per inch on the second example, you will also take off two inches of stitches, or *twelve* stitches at each decrease point. It so happens that with all of these decreases, you will knit together the same numbered stitches that you did on the first example. On the first example you knit together stitches 19 and 20 (getting rid of the 20th stitch *ten times* leaving 190 stitches.) On the second example (at six stitches per inch) you knit together stitches 19 and 20, getting rid of the 20th stitch twelve times (leaving 228 stitches). On the next decrease, you will knit together stitches 18 and 19 as you did in the first example, then you will have 216 stitches left. You will make all of the decreases just as you did for the first example based on five stitches per inch.

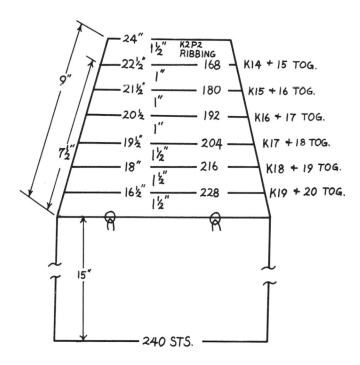

USE SAME PATTERN FOR ALL STITCH GAUGES (GAUGE 6 STS = 1")

No matter what stitch gauge you choose, it works out the same way mathematically.

However, when you are on a stitch gauge of 5½ stitches per inch, or any gauge containing a half stitch, you will be taking off an odd number of stitches at each decrease point, and your pattern will work out properly only if your basic skirt at 5 stitches equals one inch started out with a number divisible by 10. However, if your starting inch measurement was an odd number (such as 39) you would be starting out with 195 stitches on your basic skirt. It would not work out correctly to substitute 5½ stitches per inch into this pattern because, on the first decrease of one inch, you would be taking off only 5½ stitches and you cannot take off half a stitch. It would be better for you to adjust your pattern to start, with an even number of inches (40 instead of 39) whenever you must use a stitch gauge with half a stitch, such as 5½ or 6½ stitches per inch, etc. If you must go to an odd number of inches to decrease for the waist, just take off five or six stitches, leaving off the half stitch for your last decrease, and as your ribbing is coming right after that last decrease, it does not matter if those decrease marks do not line up properly since they will not show anyway right at the point of working the K2, P2 ribbing.

Straight Skirts in Stockinette Stitch with Full-Fashioned Decreases

If you are knitting a skirt in yarn of a lighter weight than knitting worsted, you may want to knit your skirt with full-fashioned decreases. This skirt does not look well in heavyweight yarns, because the decrease marks stand out too far and are too obvious. On the lighter weight yarns they show subtly and are very attractive. Again, as in the first skirt pattern given, the decreases *must* line up one on top of another or the skirt is spoiled. Again, you must take your measurements accurately and record them on a piece of paper titling the page "Actual and Blocking Measurements". See picture. On another piece of paper draw up your "Knit Measurements" as you did on the first skirt, allowing two inches more at the waist and hips, and showing the total length one inch shorter than the actual length. Determine the needle size needed for your yarn to have a nice firm texture, and knit an accurate stitch gauge. Multiply your skirt-bottom measurement by your stitch gauge to find out how many stitches you should cast on for the start of your skirt.

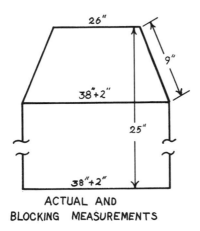

ACTUAL AND
BLOCKING MEASUREMENTS

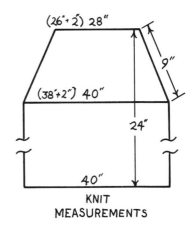

KNIT
MEASUREMENTS

EXAMPLE: Six and one half stitches equals one inch. If the bottom edge is 40 inches times 6½ stitches, you should start out with 260 stitches. You can have either six or seven decrease points for your full-fashioned skirt. Assume that you have chosen seven decrease points. You must then start out with a number of stitches divisible by seven and close to the needed number of stitches (260); that number is 259. That is the number of stitches you will cast on for the start of your skirt. You can work in stockinette stitch for 15 inches, then you will reach the hipline. Mark the hipline with scraps of colored yarn as you did on the first skirt. You must also find out how many stitches will be required at the waist. Multiply 28 inches (knit waist measurement) by 6½ stitches and

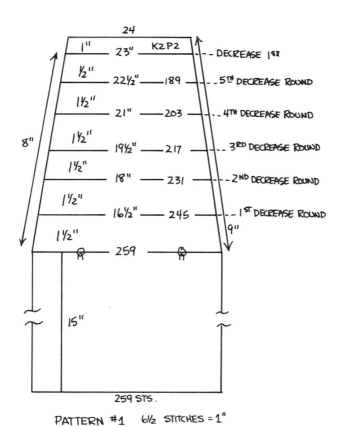

PATTERN #1   6½ STITCHES = 1"

you get 182 stitches. Since you have chosen 7 decrease points, you will lose 14 stitches at each decrease round, (two at each decrease). In order to find out how many decrease rounds you will need, subtract 14 stitches at each decrease round until you come to a number of stitches near to the number needed at the waist. Using the above example, show all of your figures as follows:

$$\begin{array}{ll}
259 \text{ sts} & \text{bottom of skirt} \\
-14 \\
\hline
245 \text{ sts} & \text{left after the 1st dec. rnd.} \\
-14 \\
\hline
231 \text{ sts} & \text{left after the 2nd dec. rnd.} \\
-14 \\
\hline
217 \text{ sts} & \text{left after the 3rd dec. rnd.} \\
-14 \\
\hline
203 \text{ sts} & \text{left after the 4th dec. rnd.} \\
-14 \\
\hline
189 \text{ sts} & \text{left after the 5th dec. rnd.}
\end{array}$$

NOTE: If you were to take another decrease round you would have less stitches than needed at the waist. Taking 14 stitches off on each decrease round, you will need 5 decrease rounds. Draw up your pattern showing the decrease rounds and find a good distance between decrease rounds. On this skirt the distance between decrease rounds should be equal, if possible. On the first skirt pattern, the distance could be tapered if necessary, because those decrease marks were not as prominent as these you will make on this skirt. The last one inch will be K2, P2 ribbing. You are left with 8 inches from the hipline to the start of the K2, P2 ribbing. Work $1\frac{1}{2}$ inches after reaching the hipline before the first decrease. Then your decrease rounds (rows) will be $1\frac{1}{2}$ inches apart. NOTE: After the last decrease is worked, $\frac{1}{2}$ inch is then worked before the start of the K2, P2 ribbing. This differs from the first skirt where the last decrease was taken just before working the K2, P2 ribbing. The reason for the change here is that these full-fashioned decreases are so prominent and they must show. If the last decrease was taken right at the K2, P2 ribbing it would not show. When it is time to go into the K2, P2 ribbing, decrease one

VIEW A

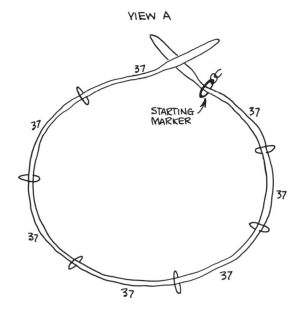

STARTING
MARKER

37
37
37
37
37
37
37

LOOKING DOWN ON TOP OF SKIRT ON CIRCULAR
NEEDLES WHEN TAKING THE 1ST DECREASE
ON A 7 FULL-FASHIONED DECREASE SKIRT

stitch so that the K2, P2 ribbing (requiring a number divisible by four) will come out right.

HOW TO WORK FULL-FASHIONED DECREASES

When it is nearly time to work the first round of full-fashioned decreases (about a row before), you must find the beginning of the round by following up the tail of loose yarn left from the casting on, and at that point put a marker on the needle. Count from the marker to 37 stitches, insert another marker, count 37 stitches and insert another marker. Continue counting 37 stitches and inserting markers after every 37th stitch until you come back around to the first marker. Mark the first marker in a special way so that you will know that it is the beginning of the round. Or tie in a colored yarn marker there to show that is the beginning of the round. Study View A showing how the skirt would look if you were looking down on the circular needle after you have put in your markers with 37 stitches between. The figure 37 was

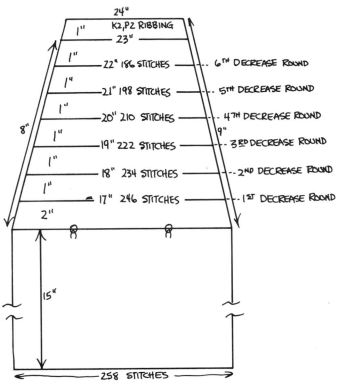

24"

K2,P2 RIBBING

1"

23"

1" 22" 186 STITCHES ———— 6TH DECREASE ROUND

1" 21" 198 STITCHES ———— 5TH DECREASE ROUND

1" 20" 210 STITCHES ———— 4TH DECREASE ROUND

8" 1" 19" 222 STITCHES ———— 3RD DECREASE ROUND   9"

1" 18" 234 STITCHES ———— 2ND DECREASE ROUND

1" 17" 246 STITCHES ———— 1ST DECREASE ROUND

2"

15"

258 STITCHES

PATTERN #2   GAUGE - 6½ STITCHES = 1"
6 FULL-FASHIONED DECREASE POINTS

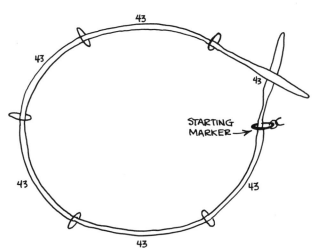

VIEW B

43

43

43

43

43

43

STARTING MARKER →

LOOKING DOWN ON TOP OF SKIRT ON CIRCULAR
NEEDLES WHEN TAKING THE 1ST DECREASE
ON A 6 FULL-FASHIONED DECREASE SKIRT

arrived at by dividing seven into 259, because you are going to use seven full-fashioned decrease points.

On the next round, move the starting marker to the right-hand needle, K2 tog, work until you come to two stitches before the next marker, Sl 1, K1, PSSO, move the marker, K2 tog. Continue in this manner until you come back around to two stitches before the starting marker, then Sl 1, K1, PSSO and move the starting marker. The first decrease round is now completed. You will work in stockinette stitch, carrying your markers along until it is time to work the second decrease round, and it must be done in exactly the same manner as the first decrease round. After each decrease round has been completed, count the stitches to make sure you have the number called for on your pattern.

If you should decide to work a skirt with only six full-fash-ioned decrease points, it would be worked in exactly the same manner, except that you would substitute six for seven in your figuring. As another example, carefully examine the next pattern, #2, to see how a skirt with six full-fashioned decreases would be worked out with another stitch gauge. Also, examine how that skirt would look in View B looking down on top of the circular needle showing the six full-fashioned decrease positions.

If these skirts seem too complicated and difficult for you to figure out, read and re-read through these examples until you can digest *why* you are doing what you are doing. There is no easy way to figure out a skirt that will fit the way these skirts fit. No skirt in any book will fit you as well as this skirt will. Once you master these skirts, they will not seem too difficult, but you must study through all of these patterns and directions.

OPTIONAL TREATMENT OF WAISTLINES

After you have made one skirt, you may feel that you would prefer a skirt with a narrower band. You may change your Knit 2, Purl 2 ribbing to a one-inch band, as was done on the skirt with full-fashioned decreases. Be sure to make the necessary adjustment on your skirt diagram.

Perhaps you would like a crocheted band over tube elastic. This may easily be done. Work out your pattern so that you will end the knitting one half inch short of the desired measurements. Do not go into the Knit 2 Purl 2 ribbing. Bind off. Block the skirt one half inch shorter than the blocking measurements. (The crocheted band will measure approximately one half inch.)

To work the crocheted band over tube elastic you must shrink the tube elastic, then cut it into four equal lengths, approximately six inches more than your waist measurement. Lay one length of the elastic along the top of your skirt and work a round of single crochet stitches through the bound off stitches and over the elastic. Join and finish off the round. Now work over the next strand of elastic as before, and so on, for three more rounds (to measure approximately one half inch) joining and fastening off after each round. Next, try on the skirt, and one by one, tie the ends of the elastic for each row, using a double hard knot for each row of

Crochet Band Over Tube Elastic on Top of Skirt

elastic, drawing it up to your correct waist measurement. (Caution! Avoid making the elastic too tight, or you will find the skirt uncomfortable at the band.) The ends should be worked back through the rows of single crochet on the wrong side, then clipped off.

STRAIGHT SKIRTS IN A PATTERN STITCH

A skirt worked *in a pattern stitch* will have to be made in *two pieces.* The decreases evenly spaced around the skirt on a circular needle would throw your pattern off after the first decrease row. When working in a pattern stitch all of your decreases must come at the sides and the side seams must be sewed. This skirt will have a zipper closing and a crocheted waist band.

Using your actual measurements, figure out your skirt pattern, allowing for a one inch drop. You must allow three inches more at the hips and approximately two inches more at the waist. (You are allowing more at the hipline for this skirt because you will be taking up some of the width in the side seams.)

E X A M P L E : Stitch gauge—6 stitches equal one inch. You must

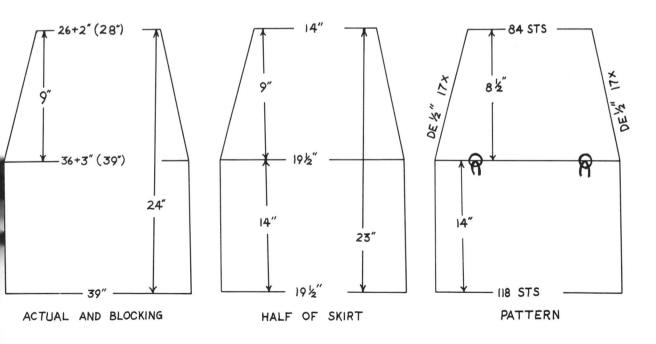

ACTUAL AND BLOCKING   HALF OF SKIRT   PATTERN

take your measurements (actual and blocking measurements) then use half those amounts for the front and half for the back of the skirt. (The front and back of a knit skirt should always have the same dimensions.)

EXAMPLE: Study the sketches and you can see that on the third drawing, (the pattern), stitches were substituted for the inches in drawing #2. Nineteen and one half inches multiplied by six stitches per inch equal 117 stitches, but the figure was rounded off to an even 118 stitches. You must have a number of stitches divisible by the multiple of your pattern stitch for your starting number, therefore, you would take the number nearest to 117 that was divisible by your multiple, which is 118. In this example, you would work even in your pattern stitch until your work measures 14 inches then mark the work for your hipline. The decreases are to come on each side of the work every one half inch, 17 times. (You had 118 stitches on the needles and needed to decrease to 84 stitches for the waist.) Subtract as follows:

118 stitches on needle at bottom of skirt
— 84 stitches needed for waist—therefore,
34 stitches must be decreased, or 17 decreases on each side of the skirt

NOTE: When working the decreases you must always measure from the bottom of your work, taking your decreases every one half inch, 17 times; the first decrease coming in at $14\frac{1}{2}$ inches, the second at 15 inches, the third to $15\frac{1}{2}$ inches and so on until you have taken all 17 decreases. Then, when your work measures $22\frac{1}{2}$ inches from the beginning, bind off for the waist. The last half inch will be your crocheted waistband.

If you must take more decreases than shown here (where they can come in every $\frac{1}{2}$ inch), you may have to decrease every $\frac{1}{2}$ inch for part of the way then every $\frac{1}{4}$ inch (which would be approximately every other row) near the waist. All of this can be worked out on your pattern before you start the skirt.

BLOCKING SKIRTS

Wash your skirt according to washing directions given previously and block the skirt made on circular needles, with no seams, with the right side out, as you would a finished skirt. That is, the skirt will have to be blocked double. Take the measurement of your hipline out to the measurement needed in your blocking dimensions, then measure the distance from your hips to the bottom of the skirt. The one inch drop you are anticipating must come from the hips to the bottom of the skirt. Make sure that the bottom of the skirt is drawn out to the same dimensions as your hips. Make sure that the side edges are straight and that the bottom edge is straight and even. Draw in the bottom edge just slightly so that there is no danger of a flare at the bottom. Now work with the top of the skirt, smoothing it and drawing it out and up to the right measurements. Draw the waist in to the actual waist measurement. The K2, P2 ribbing will draw in nicely. Let the skirt remain without moving it until it is dry. You will want to steam out the crease you will have on each side of the skirt. Do so with the "wet wash-cloth method" on your padded ironing table.

If your skirt was knit in two pieces, block the first piece with the right side up on your padded surface. Draw out the skirt at the hipline or push it back in to make it come out to the measurements you need for the blocking measurements. Make the bottom of the skirt straight and to the right measurement. Allow the one inch of stretch to come from the hipline to the bottom of the skirt. Then draw the upper part of the skirt out to the measurements needed. (NOTE: When measuring the over-all length, you must block this skirt ½ inch shorter than needed. After blocking you will be putting in the crocheted waistband, and that will account for the other ½ inch.) After you are satisfied with the looks of the first piece of the skirt, lay out the second piece on top of the first piece with right sides facing each other. Smooth out the skirt as best you can with the wrong side facing you. Make sure that the bottom edges are even and straight. Leave the two skirt pieces together during the drying process.

FINISHING SKIRTS

The two-piece skirt will have to be seamed on each side, (see directions for Sewing Seams on Knit Garments), the left side being left open from a point seven inches from the top of the skirt for the zipper. Caution! When seaming near the top of the left side, taper off the seam very near the edge so that the row of crochet

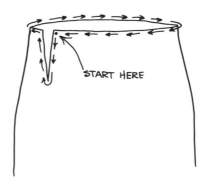

START HERE

CROCHET ONE ROW AROUND
ZIPPER OPENING, THEN CONTINUE
AROUND WAIST TO FORM FIRST
ROW OF BAND

around the zipper opening, which will be on the very edge, can be flat. Steam out the side seams and tack back the seams with sewing thread in a matching color. If one or two rows of crochet are needed at the bottom of the skirt, do it according to crochet directions given on page 224, making sure that the edge is not drawn in or too full. This edge *must* be flat.

Put one row of single crochet around the zipper opening on the left side. Make sure you follow the directions given on page 240 for working this edge. Measure the opening and make sure that it is the right length for the zipper. Do not fasten off the thread, because you will start the waistband using the same thread. Do not sew in the zipper until the waistband has been crocheted.

Now, section off one half of the waist of the skirt into about eight equal sections. You will want one half of the skirt waist to measure one half of your waist measurement. Take up the thread that is waiting at the top of your skirt (left front side), and put two stitches in the corner to allow you to turn, then work along in the first section keeping the work flat and counting your stitches. Jot down the number of stitches you took. Work across the second section using the same number of stitches, then measure that distance. If it is about right, continue on; if it is not right, you must re-do the first two sections making the necessary adjustment. When you have finished one row of single crochet, measure the skirt waist. If it is correct, put in three more rows of single crochet, and on the last row, make a chain loop (of about four chain stitches) and join the loop to the bottom of the crocheted band, and fasten off the thread and work in the end. Steam out the crocheted edge around the zipper closing, then carefully sew in the zipper according to the directions appearing on page 240.

You will need a length of ¾ inch grosgrain ribbon several inches longer than your waist measurement. Pre-shrink this ribbon, then cut a piece the length of your waist measurement, plus approximately ½ inch allowance for turned-under edges. Pin this length of ribbon to the wrong side of the crocheted waistband, about ¼ inch below the top of the band. Cover up the end of the zipper tape with the grosgrain ribbon. Divide the ribbon in half and make sure the half mark comes to the point of the side seam. If there is any fullness to be eased in, distribute this fullness so that the band looks smooth from the outside. With very small stitches, fasten the ribbon to the top edge of the band. When working the bottom edge of the grosgrain ribbon band, you will probably find that the ribbon extends beyond the crocheted waistband by about ¼ inch, and if you were to sew this edge down, you would be sewing into the skirt itself, and not the band. With sewing thread make an even row of outline stitch about ¼ inch from the bottom edge of the ribbon. See picture on doing the outline stitch. This will hold the ribbon firmly at the bottom of the band, and the outline stitch will add a pretty hand-finished look. Steam out the band with the "wet wash-cloth method", and sew a flat button in place opposite the loop.

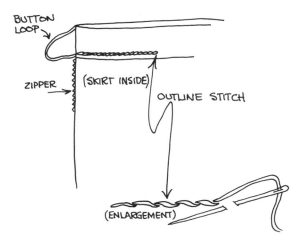

BUTTON LOOP

ZIPPER

(SKIRT INSIDE)

OUTLINE STITCH

(ENLARGEMENT)

CHAPTER IX

Dresses

GENERAL

If you could take a dress pattern directly from a pattern book, follow the instructions and the dress would fit your figure, you would be lucky indeed! Everyone has different measurements at the hips, the waist, the bust, the shoulders, the distance from the hips to the waist, the length of the skirt and the length of the bodice. If you see a dress pattern in a knit book which appeals to you, remember, it must be customized to fit your figure. Do not take the directions from the pattern book and commence to make your dress without first making sure that the dress will fit you when you have finished your knitting. Careful planning here can eliminate much ripping and re-doing later. When you make a dress, you are actually making a skirt with a bodice attached. Your basic skirt measurements will help you no end in making that part of the dress fit you. NOTE: If you have not made a basic skirt as yet, it is very advisable that you do so before attempting to make a dress, of which a skirt is an integral part. Your skirt can be an important stepping stone to making a good fitting dress.

Many dress patterns plan your work so that you knit the front in one piece and the back in another piece. If your dress is to be in stockinette stitch, you may wish to knit the dress on a circular needle, thus eliminating the side seams. All of the details can be worked out on your diagram. If the dress you choose is to be made in an all-over pattern stitch, you must knit the dress in two pieces and put the pieces together with side seams. Occasionally a pattern will be composed of panels of a pattern stitch set off by panels of plain stockinette stitch. In many cases you will be able to work such a dress on a circular needle and make regulated decreases on the panel of stockinette stitch. Keep in mind that whenever you work on a circular needle you will be working in rounds instead of rows. To form stockinette stitch you will be knitting all rounds and not working a round of knit and a round of purl as you would do when working a straight piece back and forth in rows (review instructions on knitting on circular needles on pages 125 and 126). Now, if your pattern panel directions ask you to purl every wrong side row (as so many pattern stitches do) you will simply *knit* those rounds. If, however, your pattern asks you to do some pattern work on the wrong side rows, then you will not be able to work on a circular needle and you must knit your dress in two pieces and sew the pieces together.

If you are working from a pattern using an all-over pattern stitch, you may find that the directions ask you to change the needle size from time to time. Such an example might be directions requiring that you cast on at the bottom edge of the dress working with size 6 needles, then when you reach the place where the decreases would normally start, the pattern will ask you to change to a number 5 needle and work so far, then change to number 4 needles, etc. By changing the size of the needles no decreases are required; therefore you will not disturb your pattern stitch and yet your dress will get the necessary shaping in this manner. Read and understand this type of pattern thoroughly. You may need to knit separate stitch gauges on each of the needle sizes required so that you will know exactly how much smaller you are making your garment at each of the key places on your basic dress measurement chart. See the paragraph for drawing your chart on page 189.

MEASUREMENTS TO TAKE FOR DRESSES

Take your actual measurements as you did when you were planning your basic skirt pattern (review material on pages 163 and 165). You may use fractions here, but when you draw the pattern for knitting, you should round off the fractions to the nearest inch. Wear a good foundation garment when you are being measured. Have a second person take all of your measurements. Stand with your feet together whenever you are having your hips measured. Make a drawing showing all of your measurements; your hips, your waist, the distance from your hips to your waist, your bust, the distance from your waist to where the armhole shaping will start and your shoulders. Have the second person measure the distance from the back of your neck to your waist and the distance from your waist to the bottom edge of your dress. Then measure the distance from the back of your neck to the bottom edge of your dress. Compare that figure with the length of the bodice from the back of the neck and the skirt length added together. If there is any discrepancy, take the measurements over again and make the correction. See Drawing 1 for an example of actual measurements required for making a dress. Keep in mind that Drawing 1 is *actual* body measurements, and on Drawing 2, Knit Measurements, notice that 2 inches allowance was made at the hips, the waist and the bust. If you do not allow at least two inches at the waist, you will not be able to get the dress on over your head unless you plan a side opening with a placket zipper. This is not necessary in most knit dresses, and many people feel that a zipper here detracts from the looks of the knit dress. Also notice that *no* allowance was made at the shoulders. Dresses require a closer fit than sweaters and they are usually made of lighter weight yarn. For these reasons, only two inches more at the bust is allowed as compared to the three to four inches allowed for sweaters.

HOW TO CUSTOMIZE A DRESS TO FIT YOUR FIGURE

Before you can adapt a pattern from a book to your own measurements, you must first diagram the pattern as it is given in the pattern book. When choosing the size you will work from,

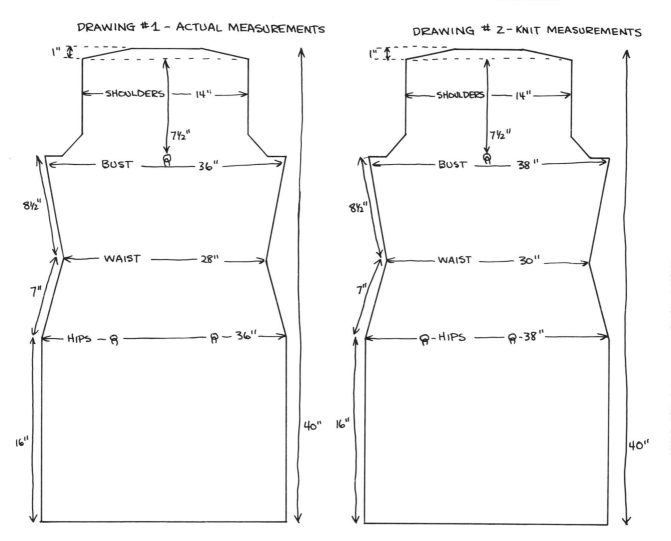

DRAWING #1 – ACTUAL MEASUREMENTS

DRAWING #2 – KNIT MEASUREMENTS

take the size nearest to your bust measurement. After you have drawn the diagram, change stitches into inches at the key points in the diagram (the bottom edge, the hips, the waist, the bust, the shoulders, the neck and any other important place where changes take place). Now you must compare that diagram to your knit measurements (Drawing 2), and make the necessary adjustments to conform to your measurements. Make sure you check on the length at this time, the length of the bodice, the skirt length, hips

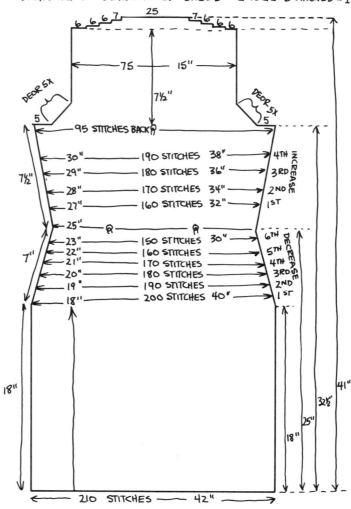

DRAWING 3   DIAGRAM OF DRESS — GAUGE 5 STITCHES = 1"

to waist, etc. You are now ready to draw the new adjusted diagram using your measurements.

A Dress on Circular Needles

In order to understand how and where changes were made from the original pattern to the pattern adjusted to your measurements, examine Drawing 3, diagram of example dress, and Drawing 4, diagram of the same dress adjusted to the example measure-

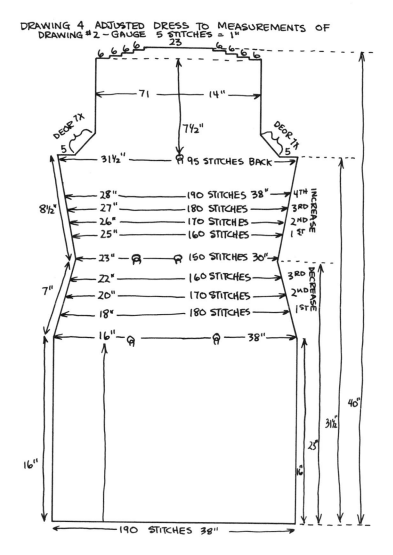

DRAWING 4 ADJUSTED DRESS TO MEASUREMENTS OF DRAWING #2 — GAUGE 5 STITCHES = 1"

ments of Drawing 2. The pattern for the dress in the example, Drawing 3, reads as follows:

"Gauge 5 sts equals 1 inch; 7 rows equals 1 inch. *Skirt:* With #7 needles cast on 210 sts. Work around in stockinette stitch for 18 inches. Mark beg of rnd. *1st Dec Rnd:* *K 19, K 2 tog, repeat from * around. Work even on 200 sts for 1 inch. *2nd Dec Rnd:* *K 18, K 2 tog, repeat from * around. Work even on 190 sts for 1 inch. *3rd Dec Rnd:* *K 17, K 2 tog, repeat from * around. Work even on 180 sts for 1 inch. *4th Dec Rnd:* *K 16, K 2 tog, repeat from * around. Work even on 170 sts for 1 inch. *5th Dec Rnd:* *K 15, K 2 tog, repeat from * around. Work even on 160 sts for 1 inch. *6th Dec Rnd:* *K 14, K 2 tog, repeat from * around. Work even on 150 sts until work measures 25 inches or desired length to waistline. Mark for waist.

Body: Work even for 2 inches. Next rnd: Inc 10 sts evenly around. There are now 160 sts on needle. Continue to increase 10 sts evenly around every 1 inch 3 times more. There are 190 sts on needle. Work even until piece measures 7½ inches above waistline marker. Divide sts as follows for back: With straight needles, work across 95 sts, slip the remaining 95 sts on a holder for front."

The directions for the rest of the back and front of the dress are not given here in words. The back directions appear in the drawing so that you may see just how they were to have been worked.

The next step in working over the original diagram (Drawing 3) is to change stitches into inches at all of the key points in the diagram.

Study Drawing 4 which shows how the dress pattern was adjusted to the measurements of Drawing 2. NOTE: In order to draw this diagram step-by-step, the shape of the dress was drawn first, then the new inch measurements were shown, then finally the inches were changed into stitches at the right places on the drawing.

A Dress Knit in Two Pieces

A dress knit in two pieces, a front and a back, will need adjustment to your measurements and careful planning as was done for the dress on a circular needle. Most dresses knit in an *all-over pattern stitch* will need to be made in two pieces. In order to adjust a pattern from a book to conform to your measurements, you will be working from your same basic measurements as shown in example Drawing 1 on page 189. Now draw your knit measurements allowing approximately 3 inches more at the hips, 3 inches more at the waist and 3 inches more at the bust (you are allowing more to take care of the side seams.) You must then draw half of the knit measurements using half of the amounts at the hips, waist and bust.

Study the example shown on Drawing 5, Knit Measurements, and sketch half of the knit measurements. Drawing 6 shows a diagram of the back of a dress taken directly from a pattern book of a dress in a pattern stitch. Drawing 7 shows the diagram of the back of the same dress adjusted to the half-measurements shown on Drawing 5.

NOTE: Whenever a dress is knit in two pieces (a front and a back) the decreases and increases *must* be made at the side edges of the pieces, otherwise the pattern stitch will be disturbed. The front and back of a skirt or skirt of a dress should always have the same dimensions. As you are studying the various examples given, note that stitches were changed into inches at all key points on the diagrams.

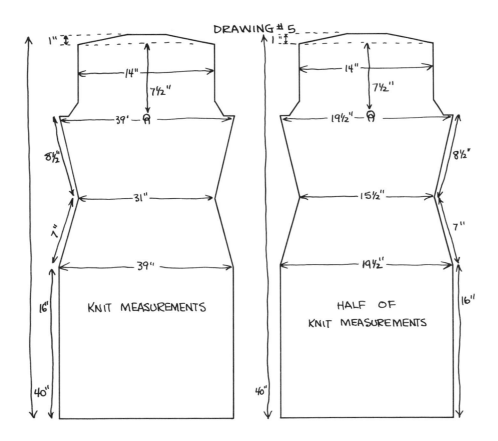

DRAWING # 5

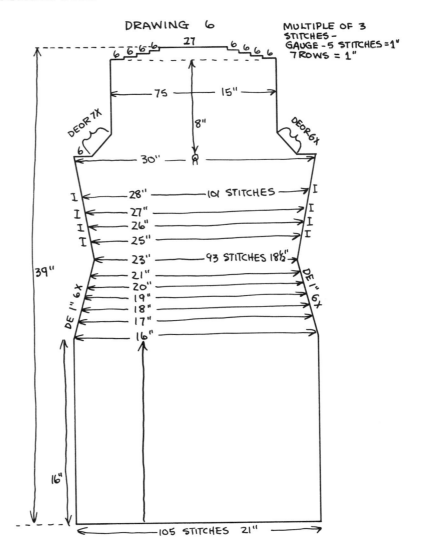

DRAWING 6

MULTIPLE OF 3
STITCHES -
GAUGE - 5 STITCHES = 1"
7 ROWS = 1"

Adapting a Dress Knit in Two Pieces to a Dress on Circular Needles

A pattern for a dress in stockinette stitch worked in two pieces can easily be converted to the same dress made without seams on a circular needle. Diagram the back of the dress as given directly from your pattern book. In most cases the front will be made the same as the back until you reach the point where you are to shape the neck. Change stitches into inches at all key points

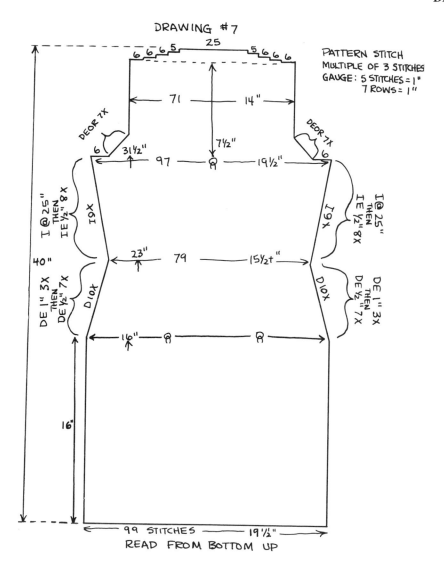

DRAWING #7

PATTERN STITCH
MULTIPLE OF 3 STITCHES
GAUGE: 5 STITCHES = 1"
7 ROWS = 1"

READ FROM BOTTOM UP

on the diagram, then compare the inches to *your* knit measurements for a dress on a circular needle, Drawing 2, substituting one half of these measurements since you are comparing just the back of the dress. You are now ready to draw your pattern. If your stitch gauge is 5 sts equals 1 inch, multiply the number of inches at the bottom edge of your dress by 5 to get the starting number of stitches. The skirt part will be identical to your original basic skirt

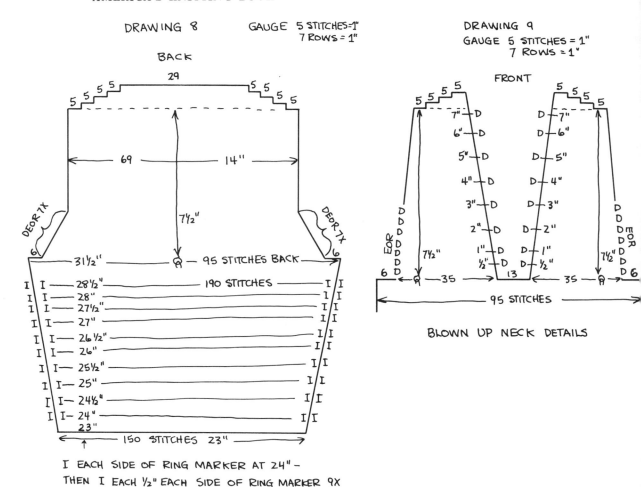

DRAWING 8   GAUGE 5 STITCHES=1"
7 ROWS = 1"

BACK

DRAWING 9

GAUGE 5 STITCHES = 1"
7 ROWS = 1"

FRONT

BLOWN UP NECK DETAILS

I EACH SIDE OF RING MARKER AT 24" –
THEN I EACH ½" EACH SIDE OF RING MARKER 9X

(see pages 163–171). You will not want to start any decreases until *after* you reach the hipline. (Many patterns will have you decrease right at the hipline, just where you *need* the full amount of allowance.) If your stitch gauge is 6 sts equals one inch, you will simply multiply your starting inch measurement by 6. When it is time to make the decreases above the hips, you will be taking off 2 inches of stitches at each decrease (or 12 stitches). This is exactly the same way you decreased on your basic skirt. (Review page 166 to refresh your memory.)

When you are planning the bodice part of the dress, you may

wish to take all of the increases at each side instead of using increases evenly spaced. This is a very satisfactory method to use and gives a very professional look to the dress. You will not separate the front from the back at this point, but you will need to place ring markers on the circular needles to show where each side is. Plan on increasing 1 stitch before and 1 stitch after each marker. This is a little hard to show on your diagram. You may find that it will be easier to "blow up" the diagram at this point, showing just the bodice. When it is time to shape the armholes and neck you may wish to "blow up" that part of the diagram also. Some dresses have openings in the front at the neck, or other neck details which may need to be shown in more detail. Do not hesitate to "blow up" any part if it will be easier for you to keep track of your progress. See diagrams on Drawings 8 and 9 of the bodice part of a dress altered from a two piece dress to a one piece dress on a circular needle. Notice the "blown up" neck details.

KNITTING THE DRESS

It would be a sad experience for you if you followed your newly adjusted diagram carefully, then when you had finished your dress and were blocking it, it stretched considerably, making the total length several inches longer than you want it to be. The work could also draw up in length and you would find yourself with a dress several inches shorter than desired. You must make sure to eliminate any danger of either of these misfortunes, and since you are concerned with such a long piece of work there is more danger of this happening. You will not want to guess about any phase of knitting a dress. If the dress did stretch or draw up in length after you blocked it, you would be forced to rip back all of your work until you reached the waistline point, and work the bodice over again.

Because the dress may stretch or draw up, the best procedure to follow is to put the stitches off on a long strand of yarn when you reach the place where you believe the waist will be. Block that much of your dress, leaving in the hip yarn markers, and block it as you would a skirt, to your own measurements, laying it flat, right side out.

When the piece of blocked dress is completely dry, try on the partly finished dress and see if it comes to your waist. Hold the dress to your waist and see how much too short or too long it may be. As you are examining the skirt part of your dress, notice if it fits nicely through the hips. Sometimes the skirt part may creep back in during the drying process, making the skirt too narrow through the hips. In re-blocking such a garment, you should be able to bring the skirt out to the needed hip measurement (if necessary, weight down the edges with fruit jars or drinking glasses), but in many cases, as you draw out the skirt in width, it may draw up in length. If you find that the skirt is too short, make a notation of how many inches short it is, and you will need to knit that much further to reach your waistline. Or if the skirt is too long, put in a new marker showing where the waistline is *now,* and the bodice measurements should be made from that *new waistline mark.* If you find that your skirt fits perfectly and is exactly the right length, mark that place for your waistline, put the stitches back on the needle and knit the bodice. You may wish to put all of the stitches off on a yarn holder when you reach the place where you believe the armholes should be shaped. Now try on the dress to make doubly sure you have measured correctly.

After you have made one dress, it is easy to knit another by comparing the second dress to the first one. Lay the partially finished dress on top of the first dress. However, do not eliminate the blocking process at the waistline. Because the skirt part did not draw up or stretch on the first dress do not assume that this will never happen to you. It might well happen on the second dress. Each new dress and new yarn presents a new problem. Be on the alert and leave out all possible guess-work. You should then be able to knit the dress right the first time.

TIPS FOR BETTER ASSEMBLING AND FINISHING

Read through the directions given in your pattern to see what the pattern suggests for finishing details. Many of these directions are very vague, and do not give the directions in the proper sequence for best construction. These can be improved upon.

After the dress is completely knit and the pieces blocked (if the dress was made in pieces) baste the pieces together at the shoulders, baste in the sleeves, baste the sides, baste waist and skirt together, then pin or baste the collar in place at the neckline. In the finishing directions of your pattern, there should be a sentence or two telling you where at the neckline you should place your collar. If these directions are not given, the collar edges should come to the center of the front band, or the center of the overlap, if there is an opening in the front of the dress. See page 236 on sewing collars.

Now try on the dress to make sure it is fitting properly before sewing it together. If you have blocked, measuring carefully, you should have a perfect fit. You would be foolish indeed, if you should completely and carefully sew the dress together without trying it on first to see if it is a good fit, if the neck is correct, or if the sleeves are right. Maybe you will need to knit a little part of the neckline over again to get it exactly as you want it. It is better to try on the dress and make some corrections than to suffer disappointment later. Now follow the proper sequence in assembling, using split yarn, if possible, and a fine tapestry needle.

Proper Sequence

A DRESS MADE IN TWO PIECES—FRONT AND BACK

All assembly should be done approximately as the sweater was done, (review pages 65–76), starting with the shoulder seams, if the dress has set-in sleeves. Sew the shoulder seams using the back stitch. Be sure to steam out all seams with the wet washcloth method before any cross seams are made. Then set in the sleeve with the back stitch. Put in your guide line as you were instructed to do for the sweater assembly. Review pages 69–71. Next, sew the sleeve and body seam all in one. When there are increases or decreases on the pieces to be joined, you must use the back stitch. When you come to the part of the skirt that is straight (no decreases), and if you are in stockinette stitch, use the pick-up-eye method.

If your dress has raglan sleeves, the only difference is that you will seam all of the raglans first, then sew sleeve and body seams as just described. You are now ready to add all trim—crochet, collar, pockets, etc. Consult your pattern finishing details for directions.

If your dress is to be worn with a belt, you may wish to put in a very lightweight elastic on the inside of your dress exactly at the waistline. This elastic will be very inconspicuous from the outside. Try on your dress and mark the waist. Turn the dress inside out and run a little basting line on the marked waistline to help you crochet this little edge straight. Then crochet a row of * slip stitch into a stitch directly on the line marked for the waist, then chain 2 or 3 stitches, skip about ½ inch at the marked waistline, and repeat from * around the waist and fasten off and work in the end of yarn. Take a length of ⅛ inch elastic (be sure to preshrink) and cut it slightly more than your waist measurement. Weave the elastic in and out through the crochet edge you just formed. Next, try on the dress and adjust the elastic for a comfortable fit and sew the elastic securely. This elastic worked into the waistline will help keep your dress from stretching and sagging as it might do if the entire weight of the dress were hanging from the shoulders.

A DRESS MADE IN TWO PIECES—BODICE AND SKIRT

Assemble the bodice according to former directions, then assemble the skirt. Steam all seams as usual with the wet washcloth method. Put in two rows of crochet over tube elastic at the waist of the skirt. See directions on page 179. Next, carefully pin the bodice *over* the skirt, matching the side seams, if there are any, and easing any fullness. You will be using sewing thread and with *very fine* stitches, stitch the bodice to the top of the skirt at a point *just below* the rows of crochet over tube elastic. The two rows of crochet over tube elastic will now be completely concealed on the inside of the dress. When you are sewing this seam, do not turn under the edge of the bodice. Be sure to stretch out the seam very often as you are sewing so that the seam will "give" with the elastic band when it is expanded.

Finish the rest of the dress according to the finishing details as instructed in your pattern. This elastic band crocheted over the tube elastic helps to carry the weight of the whole dress.

Your knowledge and skills will develop with each new garment you make, and each garment will help toward making the next garment better. Experience is a great teacher! Since it is impossible for you to personally knit every type of sweater or dress, you will find that you are constantly coming up against new problems. By following the basic fundamentals as outlined in this book and with your knowledge growing with each new knitting venture, soon you should be able to achieve a very professional look to your knits.

CHAPTER X

Knitted Accessories

KNITTING SOCKS

General

If you are going to knit socks without seams you will be using the four-needle method and you must cast on your stitches on three of the double-pointed (dp) needles, and the fourth needle is used to knit into the stitches on the other three needles. Review information on "Knitting With Four Needles", "To Cast On For Socks Or Mittens", and "Joining and Knitting With Four Needles" given on pages 127–129.

In making the socks, assume that you have cast on sixty stitches, divided between three needles. You have joined and worked in ribbing of knit two, purl two for three inches. Next, you will change to larger needles and work in stockinette stitch until the piece measures six inches. It is now time to divide the work and work down on the heel stitches.

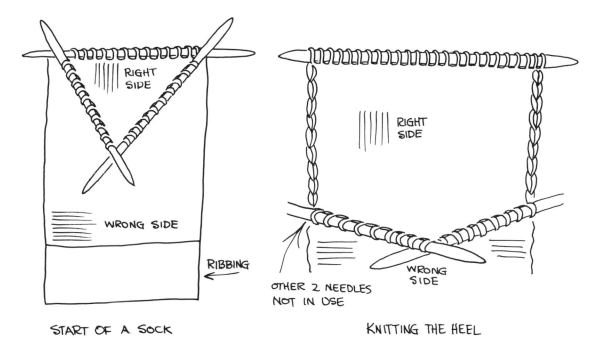

START OF A SOCK   KNITTING THE HEEL

Knitting The Heel

Most sock patterns read: "Divide for heel as follows: With 4th needle knit across 15 sts on 1st needle, turn and purl back across these 15 sts and also across 15 sts from the 3rd needle. Divide the remaining 30 sts equally on two needles for the instep." "Heel: Work as follows on 30 heel sts. Row 1—Purl. Row 2—*Sl 1, K 1, repeat from * across row. Repeat Rows 1 and 2 for 24 rows." See picture. NOTE: When you are working on the heel stitches, the other two needles are not being used.

TURNING THE HEEL

NOTE: To turn the heel you must work "short rows". If you do not know how "short rows" are worked, read through instructions on page 116 before starting to turn the heel.

"Row 1. From wrong side, P 20, P2 tog, turn.
Row 2. Sl 1, K 10, Sl 1, K1, PSSO, turn.
Row 3. Sl 1, P 11, P2 tog, turn.
Row 4. Sl 1, K 12, Sl 1, K 1, PSSO, turn.

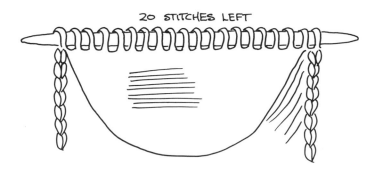

20 STITCHES LEFT

TURNING THE HEEL

Continue in this manner having 1 st more between the decreases on each row until 20 sts remain on heel needle and end with a knit row."

INSTEP AND FOOT OF SOCK

NOTE: After the heel has been turned, you will have to pick up the stitches on either side of the long heel flap and join to the instep stitches. You will be decreasing, according to directions, on either side of the instep stitches, forming little triangle gussets, then the foot is worked, then the toe and finally, the toe stitches are woven together.

Directions continue on: "With heel needle, pick up and knit 12 sts along side of heel (32 sts on heel needle). With the extra needle, knit across the next two needles (stitches of instep all on one needle now). With the extra needle, pick up and K 12 sts along the other side of heel and with the same needle, K 10 sts from heel needle (74 sts)."

"1st rnd: K each st around. Second rnd: K to within 3 sts of end of first needle, K 2 tog, K 1. Knit all sts on second needle, K1, S1 1, K 1, PSSO, K to end of round. Repeat the last two rounds until 60 sts remain. Work even on 60 sts until 2" less than foot measurement."

TOE

"1st round: K to last 3 sts on first needle, K 2 tog, K 1. On second needle, K 1, S1 1, K 1, PSSO, K to last 3 sts, K 2 tog,

K 1. On third needle, K 1, Sl 1, K 1, PSSO, K to end of round. Second round: Knit without decreasing. Repeat these two rounds until 16 sts remain. Weave toe stitches together."

NOTE: When you are picking up the twelve stitches along the side of the heel, stay in about one stitch from the edge, divide your work in half and get six stitches picked up in each half, making sure that they are evenly distributed and are not leaving any holes.

After all of the toe decreases have been made and you are left with sixteen stitches, they must be put on two double-pointed needles. With right sides out, weave the stitches together. See page 233. The instep gaps must be closed by using a little "side to side" stitch working with split yarn from the right side of the work. Block sock to measurements.

KNITTING MITTENS

General

Mittens are quite easy to knit. If you have had sufficient background, you should be able to follow the written pattern with no difficulties. There are directions available for mittens knit on two needles or four needles. The four-needle mittens will not have seams. There are two different types of thumbs; the gusset thumb and the thumb with no gusset, made from the original stitches. Do not fail to knit an accurate stitch gauge for any article. This includes mittens. You will want the mittens to fit well, therefore the proper stitch gauge must be obtained.

Two-Needle Mittens

Cast on and follow your pattern instructions until you come to the thumb directions. Many patterns will have you work across the thumb stitches with a contrasting colored yarn, then slip the stitches which you have just knit with the contrasting color back onto the left needle and knit again across these stitches with the original strand of yarn. The mitten directions are then followed for finishing the hand.

To Work the Thumb

The contrasting colored yarn is now removed and you will find that you have loops at the bottom edge of the thumb and loops at the top edge of the thumb. Pick up these loops on three double-pointed needles, dividing the stitches evenly. *Caution!* When you pick up the loops and work the thumb stitches, the *wrong* side of your mitten must face you. You will be picking up the loops from the right side of the work. See note on page 128. Join a strand of yarn and work across the stitches until you come to the corner between the upper and the lower stitches. You must pick up one stitch at this corner, then proceed to work to the other corner, picking up another stitch at that corner. Work in rounds

Thumb Stitches of Mitten in Contrasting Colored Yarn

until the thumb is ½″ less than the desired measurement, then shape the top of the thumb according to the written instructions.

Wash and block the mittens before sewing the seams. Use split yarn and pick-up-eye stitch to close the seam.

Four-Needle Mittens

Mittens may be knit without seams. You will be using double-pointed needles and you will use the same procedure in starting out as you did for knitting socks. Make sure you understand that you are working "wrong side out." The back side or inside will be on the outside as you knit the mittens. Review pages 127 and 128.

When it is time to work the thumb gusset, put ring markers on your needle and increase the needed stitches as your pattern directs. When all of the thumb stitches have been increased, your pattern will ask you to set them off on a strand of yarn to work later. On the next row your pattern will have you cast on some stitches to take the place of the stitches set off on a yarn holder for the thumb and continue working around until time to shape the top of the mitten. Proceed to finish the hand of the mitten.

Knitting the Thumb

Most patterns read: "Slip 14 sts from holder onto one double-pointed needle. Join yarn and pick up 1 st in next corner, 2 sts over the cast on sts and 1 st in next corner. Divide the 18 sts on 3 needles and K 1 round, dec 1 st at each corner. K around on 16 sts until thumb measures ½″ less than desired length. Shape top: *K1, K2 tog, repeat from * around. K 1 round. On next round K2 tog around. K 1 round. Break off yarn. Thread yarn into needle and pull through all sts. Fasten firmly."

NOTE: Your mitten directions may not ask you to pick up a stitch in each corner, but it is advisable to do so anyway. By picking up one stitch at each corner you will avoid puckering or leaving unsightly holes at these corners. You will have a much more perfect thumb than you would have if you passed by that space and picked up only stitches over the cast on stitches. On the very next round, knit 2 together at each corner to get rid of the extra stitches.

GLOVES

General

In order to insure a perfect fit in gloves, measurements should be taken carefully. Measure the girth of the hand just above the thumb. Measure each finger. Since you are going to so much trouble to knit gloves, and they are not easy to do, it would be a disappointment if the fingers were too long or too short. There is no reason why they cannot be exactly the right length if you take the time to measure each finger before you start knitting. Make a little drawing showing the measurements you need. See drawing. Next, you should knit the proper stitch gauge.

You should have no difficulty in following your written pattern, and inserting the thumb stitches as previously described on

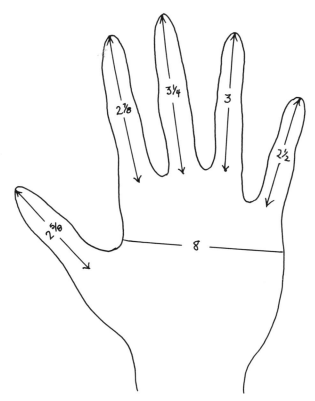

MEASUREMENTS TO TAKE FOR GLOVES

page 206 for knitting mittens. When the following things have been done:

(1) the thumb stitches have all been added,
(2) the thumb stitches slipped off on a strand of yarn to be worked later,
(3) the stitches cast on to take the place of the set-aside thumb stitches,

you will then work around on the glove until the glove, when tried on, reaches to the base of the fingers. Then it is time to work the fingers.

Working the Fingers

Read carefully through your pattern at this point to make sure you understand which finger is to be worked first. Some patterns will have you knit the index or forefinger first, then the middle finger, next the ring finger or 3rd finger, and last the little finger. Other patterns will instruct you to knit the little finger first, then the ring finger, then the middle finger and last the forefinger.

Your pattern may read, as an example: "*Index Finger:* On first needle K8 sts, sl next 50 sts on a strand of yarn for other three fingers. Cast on 2 sts between palm and back of hand, K last 8 sts. Divide these 18 sts onto 3 needles and K around in stockinette st until piece measures ½" from fingertip. Shape top: 1st rnd: Dec 3 sts evenly spaced. K one round even. Repeat the last 2 rounds once. Next rnd: K2 tog all around. Draw yarn through remaining sts and fasten off. *Middle Finger:* Join yarn and pick up 2 sts over the 2 sts cast on for the gusset of index finger, K next 9 sts from holder, cast on 2 sts between palm and back of hand, K9 sts from other end of holder. Divide these 22 sts onto 3 needles and K around in stockinette st until piece measures ½" from fingertip. Shape top to correspond to index finger."

Each finger is knit separately on double-pointed needles, casting on sts between the palm and back of hand to form a gusset. You should not run into any difficulties unless you are careless in picking up the gusset stitches. You may leave large holes where the stitches are picked up if precautions are not taken. Do not pick up these stitches too close to the edge; stay in far enough so that you do *not* leave any large holes.

The knitting of gloves becomes awkward when you knit the

fingers. The weight of the whole glove is hanging and dangling from the finger you are working on. You have so few stitches on each double-pointed needle that they twist and twine about while you are working. This makes for awkward knitting, but the results are gratifying.

Carefully wash and block your gloves to the correct measurements.

HATS, CAPS AND SCARVES

General

There are hats and caps knit on two needles and hats and caps knit on four needles. There are many different kinds of hats and caps and scarves made of a variety of yarns and different pattern stitches. You should have no difficulties in knitting these articles. You will be following your written pattern and you should not need any specific instructions. Do be sure to knit an accurate stitch gauge and measure carefully. Take the measurement of the circumference of the head whenever knitting hats or caps. Knit a sample of ribbing (if the cap has ribbing at the bottom edge) and measure the stretched out ribbing. Perhaps you will need to adjust the number of stitches you cast on for the start of the cap in order to get a good fit for the person's head.

Wash and block the finished articles as you would any other knit article.

CHAPTER XI

Knitting for Infants and Children

GENERAL

Children love sweaters. A child will be especially comfortable in a sweater because it can fit fairly close to the body and yet will stretch enough so that it does not restrict his every movement. Children do not like being confined in a bulky garment where they cannot move about easily at will. A child deserves a good fitting knit. You will want the sweater to fit the child *now,* not several years from now when the sweater is half worn out.

CHOOSING SIZE

In choosing the sweater size (to work from) for a child, you must not necessarily choose the age size corresponding to the child's age. If the child is average in size for his age, you can probably use the pattern size for his age. But, if the child is chubby, you may need the next size larger, or if the child is petite, you may need a smaller than average size. Do not guess at sweater sizes. Use the same process you used for choosing the correct size for yourself. Take the child's actual and knit measurements and record them on your pattern page, just as you did for yourself. Review page 33. Measure the child around the chest to get his actual chest measurement. An allowance of approximately 3″ more than the chest measurement should be added. (Do not allow too much or the sweater will not fit properly through the neck and shoulders.) This will be your Knit Measurements. At this time take the child's measurements for length and sleeve length, starting to measure from a point approximately 2″ below the armpit to the appropriate length. Measure the sleeve length from the same point (2″ below the armpit).

N O T E : A child will grow faster in height and arm length than he will in width through the body and shoulders. For this reason you may wish to knit the sweater and sleeves slightly longer than needed now so that the child can get longer wear from the sweater.

Now you must read through the pattern for a size you believe will be right and add up all of the stitches for the back and fronts as you did when you were determining what size you would choose for yourself. Don't forget to deduct one overlap if the sweater is a cardigan. Next, divide the total number of stitches at the underarm by your stitch gauge to get the finished measurement in inches.

Example for a child's cardigan sweater—age 4:

Actual size 25   Knit size—28
                        Length—9½
                        Sleeve length—11
                        Overall—
                        Overall sleeve—

Choosing the correct size—adding up the stitches before underarm shaping:

$$
\begin{array}{rl}
77 & \text{stitches back} \\
42 & \text{stitches front} \\
\underline{42} & \text{stitches front} \\
161 & \text{total stitches} \\
\underline{-\ 7} & \text{deduct one overlap} \\
154 & \text{total stitches at chest line}
\end{array}
$$

Now divide the complete number of stitches at the underarm (154) by the stitch gauge (given in your pattern) to get the finished measurement in inches. 154 divided by 5½ stitches per inch on the gauge equals *28 inches* (the size).

When determining what size to choose for teenage children, you must consider that they are growing more rapidly than younger children. For this reason, you should allow more inches over and above their chest measurement. A good allowance for this age group is 4 inches for a cardigan and 5 inches for a pullover. Infants, on the other hand, will need less allowance. Two inches more at the chest for allowance should be sufficient.

CHOOSING YARNS FOR CHILDREN'S GARMENTS

The types of yarn you may choose for knitting children's garments are unlimited. If you are knitting heavy outdoor type sweaters, choose a wool yarn for this garment. Wool yarns are warmer than synthetic yarns. Or, you may wish to try some of the machine washable yarns so popular with mothers everywhere. The busy mother will appreciate the fact that the garment may be machine washed and machine dried. It is true that these garments will not look as professional and flat as garments hand washed and hand blocked. You cannot make the corners square nor the edges straight, but for the busy mother these yarns are a boon. Try some of the new synthetic yarns available. Use up your odds and ends of yarns left from other projects. You can find a great variety of interesting patterns requiring several colors to be knit together, either in designs knit in, or stripes or squares of colors. You may be fortunate in finding reduced prices at your favorite yarn shop for odd dye lot yarns. You can combine them into interesting and useful garments for your children. Do keep in mind whenever combining yarns, to combine woolen yarns or synthetic yarns, but do not use some of each type. They block differently and your garment may be spoiled if it is stretching out here and drawing in there.

When you are knitting for infants, use the softest yarns available. There are yarns made especially for baby in both synthetic and wool. These are usually zephyr or fleece yarns made extra soft and extra refined.

KNITTING AND FINISHING THE CHILD'S SWEATER

Knitting for children can be pleasant and rewarding. To insure a perfect fit be sure to knit an accurate stitch gauge. Draw your diagram, and in general use all of the procedures learned previously. Try the partially finished garment on the child from time to time or compare the pieces to the child's body as you proceed. Block the knit pieces carefully and use the new improved assembling details. Be sure to knit the armholes long enough. A short armhole is very uncomfortable on a young child. A longer loose armhole gives the child freedom of movement.

If you have purposely knit the sleeves slightly long, you can turn under the cuffs and let them down later when the child needs longer sleeves, or you may wish to turn the cuffs up. See page 75 for sewing the cuffs.

Perhaps the sweater you are making will be handed down to the next child after the original owner has outgrown it. A sweater may be worn by both boys and girls. You simply knit buttonholes on each side of the fronts, then sew the buttons over the buttonholes on the left side for a girl's sweater or over the buttonholes on the right side for a boy's sweater.

If you like knitting for children, there are many patterns for pretty party dresses, sunsuits, pants and sweater outfits, caps, mittens, etc. Experiment and enjoy yourself creating pretty knits for children.

CHAPTER XII

Improved Finishing Details

PICKING UP STITCHES

If your pattern calls for you to pick up stitches up the fronts of your sweater and the pattern tells you how many stitches you need, you must divide the work into small sections so that you will have your stitches evenly spaced up the fronts of your sweater. Section off one front; dividing it in half and inserting a straight pin at the halfway point; then into fourths, into eighths, and into sixteenths if necessary, inserting a straight pin between the sections. Divide the number of stitches you are to pick up by the number of *sections* you have, and that will tell you how many stitches you are to pick up in each section. With the *right* side of your work facing you, start at the extreme right-hand end of your work, and pick up the number of stitches required in the first section. Stitches are not exactly picked up and knit. It is more like pulling a loop through the work and putting the loop on the needle. Using one needle only, insert the needle into a hole near the edge of the

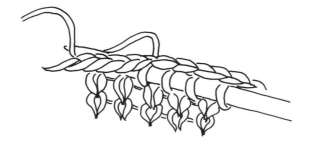

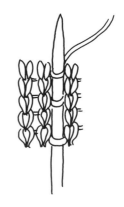

INSERT NEEDLES INTO HOLE NEAR EDGE
OF WORK. WRAP YARN AROUND NEEDLE
AND PULL LOOP THROUGH.

PICK UP STITCHES

STAY IN THE GROOVE

PICKING UP STITCHES

work (either one stitch in from the edge or one and one half
stitches in from the edge), wrap the yarn around the needle and
pull the loop through. If the edge is straight and there are no
decreases on this front edge, you must get in a groove and stay
in that groove all the way up the front. If the front edge has no
decreases part of the way up and then the neck edge tapers, and
you do have decreases, stay in the groove while you have no decreases,
then you should stay in far enough from the edge so that no large
holes are left where the stitches are picked up. Pick up the required
stitches in the first section, then examine your work to make sure
the stitches are evenly distributed, are not leaving holes, and are
in the groove if on a straight edge, and are firm on the needle.
If you are satisfied with the work so far, proceed to the next section,
working all sections meticulously. Keep track of the number of
stitches picked up in each section by jotting them down on a piece
of paper.

EXAMPLE: Stitches needed—66, divided by the number of
sections—8. Number of stitches to put in each section—8 in six
of the sections, and 9 in two of the sections.

When working the other front, pick up the same number of
stitches in each of the sections as you did on the first front, then
both sides will be exactly the same length.

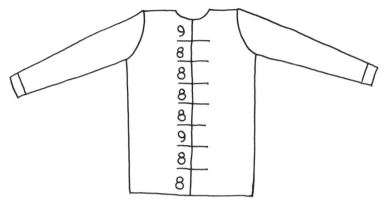

STITCHES NEEDED: 66

Failure in picking up stitches comes from trying to pick up stitches too close to the edge of the work, because at the edge the stitches are more uneven.

CAUTION! If you have changed the length of your sweater from the length given in the pattern, you cannot use the number of "pick-up" stitches prescribed in the pattern. If you have shortened your sweater, you will need less stitches, and if you have lengthened your sweater, you will need more stitches.

If the stitches are to be picked up, then worked in a ribbing pattern, you must realize that the ribbing is intended to be stretched clear out. It may look as though the new border is drawing up your front edge, but after you have worked the border, you will lightly steam out that border so that the ribbing is lying flat and stretched out. Do not bind off too tightly. If you have changed the length of your sweater, examine some ribbing you have worked elsewhere on your sweater, and count how many stitches per inch you are getting (remember ribbing must be stretched out when you are measuring). If you have added two inches to the length of your sweater, you will need to pick up enough more stitches to make two extra inches of ribbing.

If you have changed your pattern and desire to pick up stitches instead of using some other border asked for in the pattern, you will have to decide how many stitches to pick up. If, for example, you are knitting a cardigan with a long "V" neckline, and you want to pick up all of the stitches for a border up the front, around the back of the neck and down the other front, you can do this easily if you will follow these instructions: Of course the pieces have been washed and blocked, and the shoulder seams have been sewn and steamed. Lay the sweater out flat on a table, holding the bottom edges together, and with the fronts lying on top of the back. You will notice that on the center front edges there is a lot of excess material. This is caused by the stretch and sag you always get at the edges. When you pick up your stitches, this excess will be eased in and your sweater will not sag in the front. Take your tape measure and measure the distance from the bottom of the sweater up the front, along the long "V", and around to the center of the back of the neck. (As you are measuring with your tape, do *not* measure the fullness; measure the work as if the fullness were not there.). That will give you the number of inches you need for half the length of the border.

EXAMPLE: Distance from bottom of cardigan to center back of neck—28 inches. Your ribbing must measure 28 inches for half of your border. In order to find out how many stitches there are to the inch in your ribbing, *stretch out* the ribbing at the bottom of your sweater and measure off four inches. Count the number of stitches in the four inch space and then divide by four. In this example you counted off 20 stitches in four inches. Dividing by four, you find that you are getting five stitches per inch. Multiply 28 inches (the distance for half of the border) by five (stitches per inch) and you see that you will need to pick up 140 stitches with the size needle you used for the ribbing on the bottom of your sweater. NOTE: You will need to use a circular needle for picking up these stitches, because you will have a great number of stitches to pick up—many more than straight needles will hold. Section off the distance from the bottom and center back of the neck, dividing it into halves, fourths, eighths and sixteenths. You will find that in these sections you will pick up nine stitches in twelve of the sections and eight stitches in four of the sections. Alternate the sections which are to contain eight stitches so that they are not all side by side.

Now you have your plan and drawing set up showing the sections for half of your border, with the numbers of stitches to pick up in each section. With the right side of your work facing you, start at the bottom of the right front and pick up the number

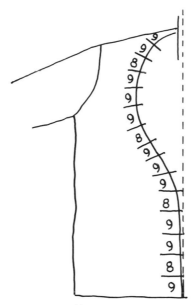

HALF OF SWEATER FRONT

ALTERNATE THE SECTIONS
WHICH ARE TO CONTAIN 8
STITCHES

of stitches you need in the first section, according to directions previously given on page 215. When you have picked up all of the stitches on half of the border, proceed down the other half in exactly the same way, picking up the correct number called for on your plan. After all of the stitches have been picked up for the entire sweater, work in the ribbing pattern for half of the number of rows you need. At this point you will place your buttonholes. Mark the position of each buttonhole right on the sweater front, (see directions for placing buttonholes on page 53). On the next row, when you come to the pin where the buttonhole is to be made, bind off the number of stitches needed. NOTE: You will have to decide how many stitches to bind off according to the size of the buttons. You may wish to make a buttonhole or two on a practice piece to make sure you are knitting the buttonhole to the correct size. On the next row, cast on the same number of stitches over the bound-off stitches. Complete the ribbing for as many rows as you decided upon, then bind off.

After the ribbing is completed, lightly steam out. Try on the garment to make sure that the two fronts are even and are not drawing up. If they are, re-steam for perfection.

Picking Up Stitches for Neck Ribbing

If your sweater is to be finished with a neck ribbing, and the stitches are to be picked up, your shoulder seam (or all raglan seams, if the sweater has raglan sleeves) should first be sewed. Then, slip all the stitches from the yarn holders onto the needle required, (usually the size will be the same as was used for ribbing elsewhere on the sweater), picking up the stitches from the wrong side of your work, and starting at the front edge of the *left* front. You will notice that there are large gaps where there were no stitches on yarn holders, at the places where you did your neck shaping. Just pass by the gaps and put only the stitches from the yarn holders onto the needle. Break off the yarn holders. Count the number of stitches you have picked up. Now subtract that number from the number of stitches the pattern asks that you pick up for the neck ribbing. Usually your pattern will be worded in this manner: "Pick up and knit 90 stitches, including stitches from holders." When you take the number of stitches you have put onto the needle from the yarn holders and subtract it from the number

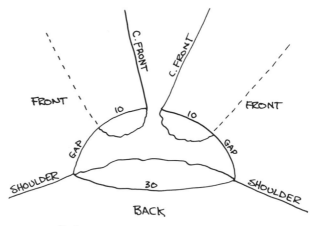

PICK UP 20 STITCHES IN EACH GAP

PICKING UP STITCHES FOR NECK RIBBING

asked for in the pattern, this will give you the number of stitches you lack, and these missing stitches will be picked up in the gaps. See diagram.

EXAMPLE: Thirty stitches were on a holder for the back of the neck; ten stitches were on holders for each front neck border, making a total of 50 stitches picked up from the holders.

> 90 stitches required
> 50 stitches picked up from holders
> ‾‾
> 40 stitches to be picked up in the gaps (20 in each gap)

Join the yarn at the *right* front edge, and if the border stitches were worked in K1, P1 ribbing, work across the ten stitches following your ribbing pattern. Now you are at the edge of the first gap. Whenever you pick up stitches, you can only pick them up by knitting. You cannot pick them up in the K1, P1 ribbing pattern. If you are going to get 20 stitches into the gap, divide the gap in half and insert a straight pin at the halfway point. Now you must pick up ten stitches in each half. The stitches in the gaps should be evenly spaced. Stitches are not exactly picked up and knit as the pattern asks that you do. They are more like pulling a loop through the work and putting the loop onto the needle. Insert the needle into a hole near the edge of the work, wrap the yarn around the needle, and pull the resulting loop through.

Pick up stitches in one section, then examine them to see if they are evenly spaced, are not leaving big holes, and are nice and firm on the needle. If you are satisfied so far, proceed to the other half of the gap, and pick up and knit ten stitches there. (It takes considerable practice to pick up stitches so that you do not leave any big holes in your work. It is better to skip over a space than to put a stitch in where a hole will be left.) After you have your 20 stitches picked up you must get back into the K1, P1 pattern for the stitches on the back of the neck, to be worked next. Count back over the stitches you have just picked up and find out where you would have been if those stitches had been in the K1, P1 pattern, then work across the 30 "back of neck" stitches in ribbing until you reach the next gap. Section off the second gap into halves and pick up the stitches as you did on the first gap, examining them to see if they are satisfactory. Count back over those stitches to see where you left off on the K1, P1 pattern,

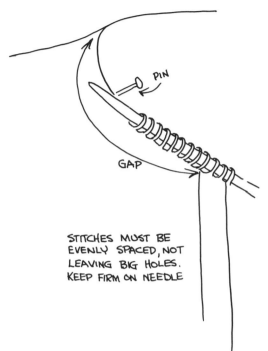

PIN

GAP

STITCHES MUST BE
EVENLY SPACED, NOT
LEAVING BIG HOLES.
KEEP FIRM ON NEEDLE

and if your pattern lines up properly with the last ten ribbing stitches, work them. If your pattern will not line up properly (if you would have two knits or two purls coming together where the border stitches and the gap stitches meet) take out one stitch in your gap (pick up 19 instead of 20) and then your ribbing will match. On the next row and all rows following work K 1, P 1 ribbing across all the stitches until the desired length is reached. Then bind off *loosely* in ribbing.

If the neck ribbing is to be doubled under, forming a double neckband, pin the bound-off edge in place, so as to cover the seam that shows where the stitches were picked up in the gaps. With split yarn, tack the neck ribbing in place using a small "side-to-side" stitch. Join the yarn at the fold point and sew the two edges together with a side-to-side stitch. When you sew through the bound-off edge, take the needle through the center of the bound-off stitch, then take a small stitch which just catches a few threads on the sweater side of the work. Working from side-to-side, take a stitch on the bound-off edge, and a small stitch on the sweater side. Do not pull these stitches tightly, or you will show an indentation on the right side of the sweater. Make sure there is enough "stretch" on this work. Finish this edge and work the two side edges together up to the fold, then fasten off the thread. This neck ribbing will not have a finished look until it is steamed out properly. Lay the neck out on your padded ironing table, wrong side up. Form the neck into a horseshoe shape. See Sketch. Steam the neck with the "wet wash-cloth method", then press the neck with the palms of your hands. Try on your garment to see if the neck is lying flat. You may have to go back to the ironing table and do a little more pressing. The neck may need to be drawn out a little bit more, or perhaps you have drawn it out too far and it will need to be pushed in some. You cannot tell until you try on the sweater, then you can adjust the neck to fit you.

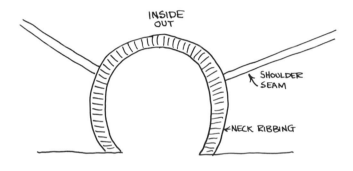

FOR A FINISHED LOOK, STEAM OUT NECK INTO HORSESHOE SHAPE

Picking Up Stitches for Neck Ribbing for a "V" Shaped Neckline

After your sweater has been washed and blocked and sewed together, and you are ready to pick up stitches for a "V" neckline, you should read through the directions to find out how many stitches the pattern wants you to pick up on the long "V" on one side. Many times the patterns will ask that you pick up more stitches than you need, and then your neck ribbing will not lie flat. This will certainly spoil the looks of the whole sweater. It only takes a few minutes to double check on the number of stitches you will need there, and you will find that you can do the ribbing right the first time. With your tape measure, measure the distance from the shoulder seam (or raglan) to the very point of the "V". Jot down that number. Next, read through the pattern to find out how many stitches are to be picked up there. From ribbing elsewhere on your sweater, preferably on the bottom of the sweater, count out that number of stitches, then measure that number with your tape. CAUTION! Whenever you are measuring ribbing, you must measure with the ribbing *stretched out.* If the number of stitches you are measuring at the bottom of your sweater is quite close to the number of inches you need, then use the figures in your pattern book. But, if you find that you are off by an inch or more, take just the number of stitches required to equal the measure you jotted down and pick up *that* number of stitches instead of the number called for in your pattern. See page 215 for further details.

CROCHET EDGES

If any crochet is required up the fronts of a sweater, around the neck or on the bottoms of sleeves, do not just start in crocheting without any order or plan to your work. You must have a plan and follow it to achieve an even look. The sweater should be washed, blocked and seamed together before the crocheting is done. Lay the sweater out on a flat surface, the back of the sweater down on the table and the fronts lying on top of the back. Notice that on the center front edges there is a lot of excess material, and it seems to hang down and curve back toward the side edges. This comes from the natural stretch and sag you always get on the edge of a garment. If you should crochet this edge as it is, with all of this excess sag, your sweater would hang much longer in the front than in the back. Hold the two bottom edges together and distribute this excess fullness. Now measure with your tape measure the distance from the bottom of the sweater up the front edge to the start of the neck shaping. As you are measuring this distance, do not measure the excess material. Measure this edge as if the fullness were not there. On scratch paper, jot down the number of inches you measured.

EXAMPLE: Distance up the front—18 inches. You must now divide this front into sections, inserting a straight pin at the end of each section. Divide into halves, then into fourths, and then into eighths. Start with the *right* side of your work facing you and "try out" for the number of stitches you will need in the first section. Whenever you are on a side edge, you will find that there is a long loose thread, then a hard knot, a long loose thread, then a hard knot all the way up the edge. It would be much easier to work into the long loose thread, but when you work into the hard knots the edge will be much prettier and you will not leave any holes. You must put your crochet stitches into the hard knots, working through two threads of the hard knot. CAUTION! Keep your stitches moderately loose and large and strive to make them even. You may have to add extra stitches in each section, because if you put one stitch in each hard knot it may draw the work up too much. Try putting in one or two or even three extra stitches in the first section. Whenever you must put in an extra stitch, put two stitches in the hard knot. Never put an extra stitch into the long loose loop between the knots. If you are trying for two or three extra stitches in the first section, distribute your increases so they will not all be together. Jot down how many stitches you used in the first section. Now go to the next section and put exactly as many stitches in the second section as you did in the first section. You must realize that your work must draw up a little to take up

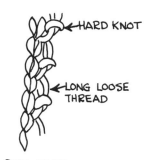

SIDE EDGE...
SHOWING LONG,
LOOSE, LOOP
AND HARD KNOT

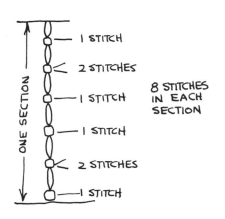

SPACING OF STITCHES IN ONE SECTION

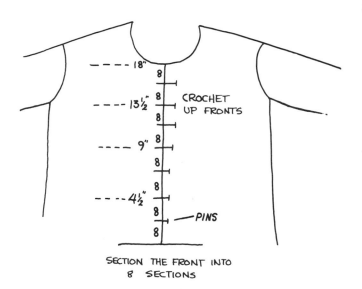

SECTION THE FRONT INTO
8 SECTIONS

CROCHET EDGES

the extra fullness you had on that edge. After you have worked the first two sections, measure the distance with your tape. The distance should measure $4\frac{1}{2}$ inches, or one fourth of the total of 18 inches. If your work measures more or less than the amount you need (one fourth of the total distance), try these first two sections over again, either adding extra stitches, or taking out some of the extra stitches, until you come out with the $4\frac{1}{2}$ inches you need. Now you know exactly how many stitches you need in each section, so continue up the front working all sections with the same number of stitches. It is a good idea to keep measuring, at the half way point—9 inches, and so on until, when finished, you have 18 inches.

At the end of the first row, if you are to crochet several rows, chain one and turn, then put a stitch in each stitch of the first row, putting the hook through both top loops. See photo.

CAUTION! When working the second row and all rows following, make sure you are working loosely. Measure your work after each row to make sure you are still coming out with the number of inches you need.

If you are to place buttonholes in the crochet edge, work the side without buttonholes first. When you start to work the side with the buttonholes, section off that front exactly as you did for the other front, and get as many stitches in each section as you got on the other side. When you come to the row in which you are to form the buttonholes, lay the sweater out on a table again and mark the spacing of the holes with your tape measure. Place a pin in the place where the hole is to be worked. (See page 53 on spacing of buttonholes.) As you are working the next row, when you come to a stitch or two before the pins, chain two then skip two single crochets of the previous row, then single crochet in the next stitch. Try placing the button through the hole. If the hole is too small chain more stitches, and skip more single crochets in the previous row. Continue to work all other buttonholes in the same manner. On the following row, work until you come to the hole, then if you skipped two single crochets for the buttonhole, put that same amount of single crochet stitches in the buttonhole, then proceed in each single crochet to the next hole. Work all the buttonholes the same. These buttonholes do not need to be hand finished. They will always lie flat. After you have finished the

Start of Crochet Buttonhole   **Finish of Crochet Buttonhole**

crochet border, lay the edges out on your padded ironing table, right sides down, and with the "wet wash-cloth method", lightly steam out each border, measuring them with a tape measure to make sure they are the same length, and the length you need.

Crocheting Around the Entire Sweater

In doing this, you will use the same principles you used when you were doing only the front edge; that is, you will be sectioning off your entire sweater and keeping track of the number of stitches you were able to get in each section. Start at the bottom edge, at the side seam of the right front, always working from the right side. Section off the right front bottom edge into four sections. Join the yarn at the seam and count the number of single crochet stitches you can put into the first section. Pass your crochet hook through two threads of each stitch on the edge (the cast on edge). You may find that by going into each stitch you will make your

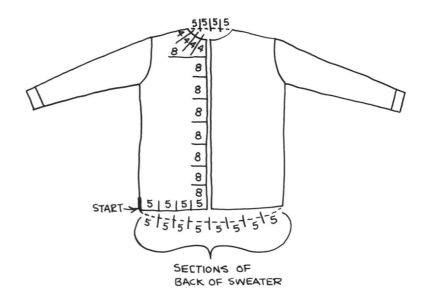

SECTIONS OF
BACK OF SWEATER

CROCHETING AROUND ENTIRE
SWEATER

work look too full, and you may have to skip over one or two stitches to make the work lie flat. If you do have to skip a stitch or two, space out the skips so that they are not right next to each other. Proceed to the next section with the same number of stitches you decided upon when doing the first section. Then go on to the third and fourth sections. When you come to a corner, put three stitches into one to make the turn. Now you are up to the center front edge; section off the front edge as mentioned previously, dividing into eight sections. Now you must go into the hard knots. Do as you were told in the previous paragraph. When you reach the top and are going to start on the curve of the front neckline, section off that part of the neck up to the shoulder seam. You must be careful here, because you are on a curve and it is difficult to find good places to put in your stitches because of the unevenness of the decreases. Do not go into any place that will leave a large hole. When you have finished the front, you will proceed to the back of the neck. Section off this part into about four sections, getting all sections alike. When you are coming around to the other side of the front of the neck shaping, section it off into four sections and put in the same number of stitches you put in on the other side at the neck shaping. Proceed down the other front, working exactly as you did the first front; turn the corner (with three stitches as before) and work the bottom edge of the left front exactly like the bottom edge of the first front. Now divide the back into halves, into fourths, into eighths. Find out how many stitches go nicely in the first section and proceed across all sections alike. If more than one row of crochet is required, as you return across the first row, you should put one stitch in each stitch of the first row, working through both top loops. When turning a corner, put three stitches in the center of the corner as explained before. On the neck it will be necessary to decrease on the second row (and third row, etc.) to give the neck a tapered look. (If you do not decrease, and continue to put a stitch in each stitch as before, you will find that the neck will stand up like a mandarin collar.) If more than two rows are worked, you should not decrease all in one row. Work off three or four decreases in each row. To decrease you simply pass by a stitch (skip a stitch in the previous row), then single crochet in the next stitch. The following is another way of decreasing in crochet: Draw up a loop in each of the next two stitches, yarn over and pull hook through both loops on hook. Of the two methods explained, the first method of passing by a stitch usually

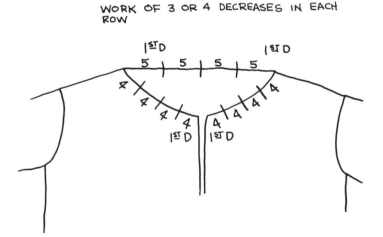

WORK OF 3 OR 4 DECREASES IN EACH ROW

NECK SHAPING SHOWING DECREASES TO TAPER IN ON 2ND ROW

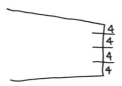

SLEEVE EDGE...
DIVIDE SLEEVE INTO SECTIONS

looks best, but you can try either and make the decision yourself. Keep track of your decreases on paper (see diagram page 228) telling you in what section they appeared, so that on the next row, you will not decrease in the same section in which you decreased before. Try on your sweater as you are working the rows to determine if more or less decreases are required. When crocheting around the sleeve edge, divide the sleeve into sections, and proceed as on the other parts of the sweater.

After you have finished the crochet, you must steam it out lightly with the "wet wash-cloth method". Work with the edge while it is damp to make it straight. Steam the neck edge out in a horseshoe curve. Make sure it is perfect, lest you ruin an otherwise beautiful sweater with uneven crochet work. Use Size 00 crochet hook for knitting worsted weight and Size 0 crochet hook for sport yarn weight.

EXTRA TIPS ON CROCHETING

If your pattern asks that you "put in one row of crochet around a double collar, double facing, double cuffs, or anything double, working through both thicknesses", do not do it. Put in your crochet using the sectioning method, but go through *only one* thickness—the outside piece. Then, carefully tack the facing to the outside with sewing thread. You will achieve a perfect, tailored look with this method.

If your pattern asks that you put on borders of crochet with a different color than was used to knit your sweater, work the first row of crochet with the main color used, then on the second row use the contrasting color. If you do not do this, your edge will have an uneven look on the first row, which will spoil the looks of your sweater.

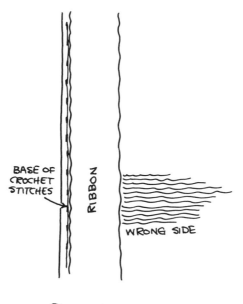

RIBBON FACING

RIBBON FACINGS

If your pattern calls for a ribbon facing to be used up the fronts of a sweater, it is usually because the sweater has stockinette stitch clear to the edge, and ribbon is needed to make that edge lie flat.

If buttonholes have been worked on one side, they should be hand finished in the regular manner, (page 239), then they should be basted shut, steamed and the bastings removed. One row of single crochet is required up the front edges. Do this according to directions given on page 224. Be sure to pre-shrink the ribbon. Pin the ribbon to the back side of one front edge of the *pre-blocked* sweater so that it does not pucker or stretch the garment. Make sure that the ribbon is not right up to the very edge of the crochet. The ribbon should be placed at the base of the crochet stitch, with the entire crochet stitch extending beyond the ribbon. See diagram above. Try on the sweater to make sure it is not sagging in front or drawing up. Readjust the ribbon if necessary, and try on the sweater again to make sure it is hanging exactly right. Then cut the other piece of ribbon exactly the same length as the first piece. Pin it to the other side of the front in the same manner as you did for the first front. Use sewing thread in a matching color. Start at the outside edge. Use very small stitches and place them very near the edge of the ribbon so that the stitches will not show. Pass the needle through just part of a stitch of yarn so that the sewed stitch will not show from the right side. When working the inside edge of the ribbon on the buttonhole side, make a slash in the ribbon to the far end of the buttonhole, then turn under the raw edges in a little "V" around each buttonhole (see diagram below). One reason this seems to be the best method is that one end of the buttonhole is not surrounded by ribbon, thus the hole can stretch and open up to receive the button. A much neater job can be done around the buttonhole by using the "V" method, because only one corner needs to be worked around.

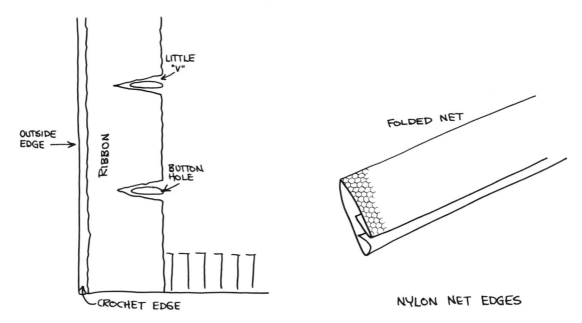

NYLON NET FACINGS

If your sweater is of lightweight mohair yarn, or some other extremely lightweight yarn, you may not want to use ribbon facings up the fronts of your sweater. You can use nylon net instead of the ribbon and it will not show through from the wrong side, and yet it will have enough body to hold your edges straight and even. Try to match the color as closely as possible. Cut a strip three times as wide as you will need finished, then turn under both raw edges and iron in the folds to the exact width you need. See picture. Now you are ready to apply the net facings and you will use the same principles explained above for applying ribbon facings.

CAUTION: Never use nylon net facings on heavy yarns. The net is not stiff enough to hold the edges even on heavy yarns. On all but very fine yarns, you should use grosgrain ribbon.

WEAVING STITCHES TOGETHER (KITCHENER STITCH)

This stitch is used for weaving Stockinette Stitch only.

You may have an occasion to weave stitches together on a straight shoulder or on the toe of a sock, etc. This is easily done and you will have an invisible joining. The stitches should not be bound off. Line the stitches up on two double-pointed needles, holding them parallel, with the wrong sides facing each other. You must have the same number of stitches on each piece. Use either the end of yarn left from your last row of knitting or attach a new strand of a length that is equal to one inch per each stitch on one needle. The end of the yarn must be coming from the extreme right end of the back needle, or the new strand must be attached to the base of *that* stitch at the extreme right end of the back needle. See diagram. Thread the yarn through a tapestry needle and work from right to left as follows:

YARN PASSES UNDER TIPS OF NEEDLES

KITCHENER STITCH

*Pass the tapestry needle through the first stitch on the front needle as if to *Knit,* draw the yarn through and take the stitch off. Pass the tapestry needle through the second stitch on the front needle as if to *Purl,* draw the yarn through and leave *that* stitch *on* the needle. Pass the yarn through the first stitch on the back needle as if to *Purl* and take that stitch off, then pass the yarn through the second stitch on the back needle as if to *Knit* and leave *that* stitch on the needle. Repeat from * until only one stitch remains on each needle. Now pass the yarn through the stitch on the front needle as if to *Knit* and take the stitch off, pass the yarn through the stitch on the back needle as if to *Purl* and take the stitch off. Even up the stitch and work in the end of the yarn. NOTE: It takes considerable practice on this to do a perfect job. You should practice on swatches. Remember that you always work two stitches on one needle before you go to the other needle, then work two stitches there, taking off the first of the two stitches and leaving on the second of the two stitches. When the yarn is being pulled through the stitches, it passes under the tips of the needles at the right end of the needles (see diagram page 233).

When it is time to even up the stitches, take the point of one of your double-pointed needles and start in where your stitches look loose. Pull up a loop on the line where you were weaving, and keep pulling up loop after loop across that row and make all of your stitches even in size. It is better to weave the stitches loosely and to even them up later than to weave tightly, as there will be no "give" and any unevenness cannot be remedied.

WEAVING RIBBING STITCHES TOGETHER

It is impossible to weave ribbing stitches together in the perfect ribbing pattern, but you can weave these ribbing stitches together in a simulated ribbing pattern which looks much better than a seam. For this work, four double-pointed needles are required. Each piece will be on two needles. Put the knit stitches on one needle and the purl stitches on the other needle for each piece. After the stitches are on the needles, proceed as follows:
1. Tuck the two needles with the purl stitches (the inside needles, #2 and #3—see diagram) down and out of the way. You are concerned with needles #1 and #4 only as

WEAVING RIBBING STITCHES TOGETHER

they carry the knit stitches. Weave these stitches together in the regular manner starting with yarn coming from the base of the first stitch at the right end of the rear needle (#4).

2. Next, work on needles #2 and #3 (purl stitch needles). Turn these needles around so that they become knit stitches. (The thread is there in the correct place waiting to be used.) Now, weave these stitches together in the regular manner. Even up the stitches and work in the end of the yarn.

    Needle #4, Knit stitches
    Needle #3, Purl stitches
    Needle #2, Purl stitches
    Needle #1, Knit stitches

NOTE: The two pieces of ribbing must be exactly alike or you cannot weave. That is, they should both start out with knit or both start out with purl stitches. If one piece starts with a knit stitch and the other with a purl stitch, the ribs will not match when joined.

BLOCKING SMALL PIECES

If you have a collar or a pocket or any small piece to be blocked, and you do not know what size to block it to, use your stitch gauge and divide the gauge into the number of stitches you used for the piece, and that will give you the number of inches the piece should measure after blocking.

EXAMPLE: Collar—"Cast on 68 stitches and work in pattern stitch for four inches." According to the gauge of four stitches per inch, your piece should measure 68 stitches divided by four, or 17 inches long and four inches wide.

When the collar is worked in a rib stitch, and you want the collar to fit exactly right, measure the neck edge where the collar is to be sewed on and then block the collar out to that measurement. That will be the neck edge. Then to give the collar a nice smooth look, flare out the outside of the collar about two inches more. The collar will fit nicely at the neck.

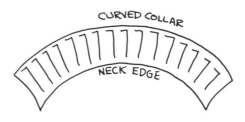

BLOCKING SMALL PIECES

SEWING ON A COLLAR THAT WAS KNIT SEPARATELY

Try on the sweater and make sure that the neck edge fits you correctly. If it does, take that measurement and jot it down on your scratch pad. If the neck is a bit too loose, hold the tape measure around your neck to the exact point you want your sweater neck to fit. Jot down that figure. If the neck of your sweater is quite a bit too large, several inches in fact, you should crochet an edge onto the sweater neck, holding the edge in to the desired number of inches, then apply the collar as explained. When doing your crochet work, you must section off parts of the neck edge so that the crochet work will be even. See page 224; Crochet Edges.

Now, pin the washed and blocked collar to the sweater. In the directions for finishing your sweater, you will usually find the place where the edge is to start. If your sweater is a cardigan, the collar should start at the center of the ribbing border, or front edge. If the collar fits at this point, then when the sweater is buttoned, the collar will just come together at the front edge and not lap over. Now, find the center back of your sweater and mark that point with a pin. In the same manner find the center of the collar.

Pin the two centers together. Holding sweater and collar together with the outside of the sweater and the wrong side of the collar facing each other, neatly pin the collar to the sweater all around that side. NOTE: You are not going to sew this seam the way it is pinned; you will be taking out each pin as you come to it and you will be sewing the seam from the right side. Now, measure the distance of the seam from the center front to the shoulder seam, and make sure that you have the same distance on the other side of your sweater to the shoulder seam. If you are particular that all sections are the same on each side of the fronts and back, your collar will not be lopsided, but will be accurate and even. Carelessness here, after all your careful work on the rest of your sweater, will result in your having produced just another amateur sweater.

PUSH RESULTING SEAM
TO WRONG SIDE

COLLAR

Join the yarn without a knot in the manner explained previously, (page 68), and sew from the right side (the right side of the collar to the wrong side of the sweater), using a small "side-to-side" stitch. Make your stitches very close together and very near to the edge. In doing this "side-to-side" stitch, you should make a small stitch on the collar piece very near the edge and running parallel with the edge of the collar, then take a small stitch on the sweater piece with that stitch also running parallel to the edge of the sweater piece, then with the thumbnail, turn both edges in to the wrong side to form a *very small flat* seam. You should be using split yarn, if possible, and short strands. Make sure you will come out to the right number of inches you jotted down for your seam. Check with the tape measure at the one-quarter mark, the halfway mark, the three-quarter mark, and at the finish. This seam must be lightly steamed out with the "wet wash-cloth method". Do not attempt to open out the seam with the fingers. Try on the sweater again to make sure that you are satisfied with the looks of the collar.

CROCHETED BUTTONS

Crocheted Buttons on Curtain Rings (Using ⅝″ Rings)

Make a slip knot in the yarn, then work single crochet stitches into the ring, counting the stitches until you have completely filled the ring. Jot down the number of stitches you worked. Cut off the yarn leaving about twelve inches. Thread it into a tapestry needle and take the needle through the back of every other stitch completely around the ring, drawing up on the yarn tightly so that the edge draws in and forms the inside of the button. Take several stitches to secure, and then with the yarn that is left, sew the button onto the sweater with an "X" stitch through the center of the button. When making the other buttons, use the same number of crochet stitches so that all of the buttons will look exactly alike.

Crocheted Button Balls

These buttons belong on dressy sweaters only. Try out the hook size to find the correct size to go with the yarn you are using.

Button Balls and Button Rings

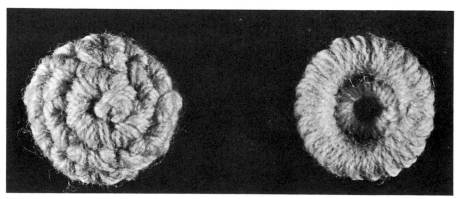

Directions: Chain 4, join with a slip stitch to form a ring. Rnd. 1: 6 sc in ring. Rnd 2: 2 sc in each sc (12 sc). Rnd 3: *2 sc in 1 sc, 1 sc in 1 sc, repeat from * around (18 sc). Rnd 4: (dec rnd) sc in every other sc around (9 sc). At this point stuff the button with cotton, as much as it will hold. Finishing rounds: 1 sc in every other sc until no stitches remain. Sew the button with the yarn left from the button.

N O T E : If you find that this button is too large, do not adjust the stitches or change the pattern. Change the yarn instead. If your yarn is four ply, take one ply away and make a button with just three ply. If it is still too large, try a button with two ply. This type of button should not be used on sweaters made of knitting worsted or heavy yarns.

HAND FINISHING BUTTONHOLES

All horizontal buttonholes in smooth or mohair yarns should be hand finished. Pieces should be washed and blocked first. Use split yarn if possible, or de-fuzzed mohair. Make a little running stitch all the way around the buttonhole near the edge. With your finger in the hole (to keep the hole open) work a blanket stitch around the hole, placing stitches evenly and keeping all stitches the same length. Count the stitches so as to have an equal number of stitches on each side of the hole. Place one stitch at each end of the hole. Do not put stitches too close together, as they tend to close off

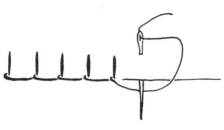

BLANKET STITCH

SAME NUMBER OF STITCHES ON EACH SIDE

ALL BUTTONHOLES ARE ALIKE

the hole. End the thread by running it through the back side of several stitches, then clip it off. The hole should then be basted shut and lightly steamed with the "wet wash-cloth method". Remove bastings when the holes are dry. Every time the sweater is washed and blocked, the buttonholes should be basted shut; they will then be flat and straight. Practice finishing some buttonholes before you attempt to do it on your sweater. Practice makes perfect, and perfect you must be.

Hand Finishing Double Buttonholes

Hand finish the outside buttonhole *only* according to the directions given above. Baste the buttonhole closed and lightly steam. Remove the basting and then, with sewing thread, carefully tack the facing buttonhole to the wrong side of the worked buttonhole. Caution! Do not ever attempt to work the double buttonhole through both thicknesses.

ZIPPERS

Sewing in Zippers

If your dress or sweater has a zipper to be sewed in at the back of the neck, or if you are putting in a zipper on a skirt, you will need to work one row of single crochet around that opening. Be sure to section off your work as you should do for any crochet (see page 224), so that your work will lie flat and both sides will be equal.

Pin the zipper in with the two edges of crochet coming together so that *NO* zipper teeth show. Since you are working on stretchy material, there is great danger of your zipper cupping in (becoming concave) or being put in with too much fullness. To get exactly the correct look, the zipper *must* go in flat. Use sewing thread of matching color and use the back stitch, sewing from the outside of the garment. Start sewing from the very bottom of the zipper and sew toward the neck edge on each of the sides of the zipper. Make very small stitches, holding the seam *over* your finger as you sew to make sure the zipper will not cup in. Try on your sweater or skirt to make sure you are satisfied with the looks, and

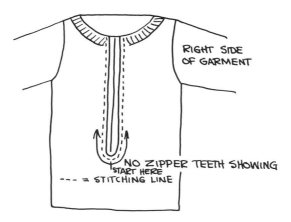

RIGHT SIDE
OF GARMENT

NO ZIPPER TEETH SHOWING
START HERE
--- = STITCHING LINE

REMEMBER: HOLD SEAM OVER FINGER AS
YOU SEW

if it pleases you, tack down the back side of the zipper carefully, hiding all stitches. See diagram above.

A Separating Zipper in the Front of a Cardigan

Since a zipper in the front of a cardigan will show whenever the sweater is worn with the zipper open, it is a good idea to knit a facing to cover the tape part of the zipper. It is not hard to do, and it will add much elegance to the appearance of your sweater. If you knit your sweater of knitting worsted or a heavy yarn, use a lightweight yarn for the zipper facing. If you cannot find a matching color in lightweight yarn, knit your facing of split yarn (splitting the yarn you used in the sweater) and you will have an exact match. See page 243 on splitting yarn. Use fine needles, about #2 or #3, and cast on enough stitches for approximately ⅝ inch, or about five or six stitches. Use stockinette stitch for this strip. Slip the first stitch on *every* row. Slip the stitch as if to purl. This will give a very firm edge on the strips. Steam out the strips with the "wet wash-cloth method". When your cardigan has been washed, blocked and put together, put in one row of crochet on each front edge. See page 224 for crocheting this edge. Next, pin the zipper in so that the bottom separating edge comes approximately one half inch above the bottom of the sweater, and the top of the zipper is at the point to make the neck or collar look correct. Pin the zipper to the wrong side of the fronts so that it is not puckered or fluted and make sure *NO* zipper teeth are showing. Use the back stitch, working from the right side, as explained in the previous paragraph on sewing in zippers.

NOTE: Examine your separating zipper. You will notice that at the very bottom end of the zipper each side has been coated with some plastic mixture to reinforce and give the zipper strength there. You cannot and must not try to start your sewing through this reinforced end. Make sure to secure the beginning of your sewing above the reinforced ends well, then start sewing from the bottom edge of each of the sides toward the top. Now pin in the strips you knit to the wrong side of the cardigan, with the edge coming near the teeth and covering over the threads from your hand back-stitching, placing your strips just above the loose reinforced end tips. Use sewing thread and put the stitches quite close together using a blind stitch. Sew both sides of the facing, and when sewing the edge on the knit material, take up only a part of a stitch to make sure no stitches show from the right side. Steam lightly on a padded board.

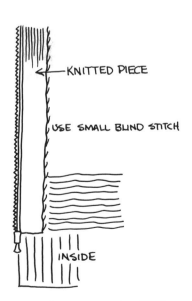

KNITTED PIECE

USE SMALL BLIND STITCH

INSIDE

COVERING ZIPPER TAPE
WITH KNITTED FACING

HOW TO SPLIT YARNS

If you need a lot of split yarn, you can split most four-ply yarns easily. To do this, you first roll the yarn into a ball, then pull out a length of yarn approximately 20 inches. At that point stop the ball from unwinding any further by inserting a tapestry needle through the ball holding your thread. Split the loose end of yarn and hold one half in each hand. Drop the ball of yarn down and let the yarn untwine as the ball turns. When you have split the 20 inches, let out another length of approximately 20 inches and repeat the untwining procedure. You may need two persons to roll your split yarn into balls as you split and attend to the untwining ball of yarn. See picture.

LET BALL
UNTWINE

SPLITTING YARN

SEWING SWEATERS KNIT WITH STRIPES

If you are putting together a sweater made of stripes of different colors, you should change the color of the yarn for sewing the garment as the garment changes color, whenever possible. If you are working on setting in a sleeve, and the colors coming together are not alike, choose the color used as the main color, or try out a small amount of each of the colors and decide which is the least conspicuous. Have needles threaded with all of the colors you need, ready to use when the colors change.

CUFFS WHICH TURN UP

If your cuffs are to be turned up you will not want a seam to show on the right side, where the cuff turns up. As you are blending the ribbing, blend to the point where the cuff turns up *from the wrong side,* then turn your seam at the turning point of the cuff and blend your ribbing *from the right side.*

TACKING HEMS, FACINGS AND POCKETS

Whenever you must tack back hems, facings or pockets, use split yarn if possible, or if you cannot split the yarn, you may use sewing thread in a matching color. Use the "side-to-side" stitch, keeping stitches quite close together for pockets, but a little farther apart for hems and facings. Do not pull the stitches up too tightly, because you may cause the hem, facing or pocket liner to show from the right side. You may use a catch stitch "X" on hems and facings if you so desire. See diagram. When you are steaming out these parts, be careful that you do not show an impression through onto the right side. Do not steam the part of the hem or facing that you have tacked down. Just steam the edge or fold. If you must steam the entire hem, you must first

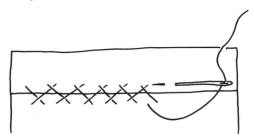

CATCH STITCH X ON HEMS AND FACINGS

place several thicknesses of cardboard along the edge of the hem under the wet wash-cloth. This will make a flat pressing surface for the iron and will prevent a line showing on the right side.

REMEDY FOR SAGGING SHOULDERS, NECKS, ETC.

After you have finished your sweater and as you are wearing it, you may feel that the shoulders or the neck are sagging. You can remedy that fault by attaching a single strand of heavy duty thread at the end of one seam and working along that seam with a small running stitch. Draw up the seam somewhat, and anchor the thread firmly at any other seam crossing the seam you are firming. In the case of neck ribbing, for instance, anchor the thread to the seam at the beginning of the neck ribbing, anchor again at the shoulder seams, or at each raglan seam, measuring the distance between the seams to make sure that all distances on like parts are exactly even. See diagram.

WRONG SIDE   ANCHOR AT ALL SEAMS

USE A LITTLE RUNNING STITCH

WORKING IN ENDS

Skimming

If you have worked a sweater with several different colors knit in or worked in, in colors, with duplicating stitch and there are many ends to work in, thread a tapestry needle with one of the ends and work in by skimming along through a yarn of the same color on the wrong side of the work. Just take up a tiny part of the yarn and weave through that thread. After you have skimmed

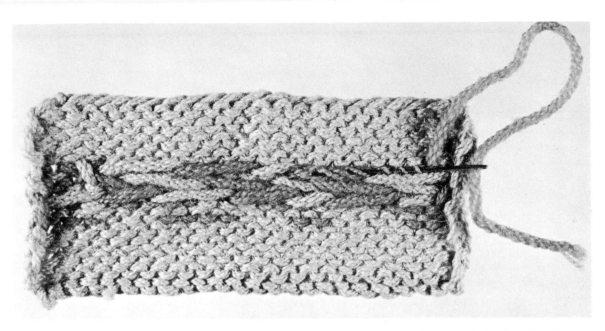

approximately an inch, turn back in the other direction and skim just a little way (about ½ inch) then clip off. See Photo. This is an excellent method to use, and the ends never come out, nor do they show at all from the right side. Ends which were left in the middle of your work may also be worked in by skimming. You must untie the knot and bring the threads to the wrong side, then proceed to work in the end by taking end #1 through hole #2 and end #2 through hole #1 (as you were instructed to do in working in ends on page 27) then instead of weaving the yarns through several back loops in the opposite direction, skim along through small parts of the threads on the back loops; turn around and skim back in the opposite direction for just a little way, then clip off. This is an excellent method to use for working in ends on knit skirts. The only ends you cannot work in this way are ends left in your work on nubby or knotty yarns.

Working in Ends Left from Yarn Holders

Any ends left from yarn holders may be worked in after the trim has been worked. The end may be worked in either skimming or along a seam and then clipped off.

Working in Ends on Vertical Buttonholes

Bring the ends through to the wrong side of the work, and thread one end through a tapestry needle. Reinforce the buttonhole edge by running the yarn through stitches on the edge of the buttonhole until you come around to the other loose end of yarn. Then take the yarn up one of the ribs for about four or five stitches, then clip off the end. Thread up the other end of the loose yarn and work along the opposite side of the buttonhole until you come to the place where the other end was, then work down one of the ribs for about four or five stitches, and clip off. See picture.

BIAS TRIMS

REINFORCE THE BUTTONHOLE
EDGE, THEN WORK UP AND
DOWN RIBS

Bias Trim with No Turning Ridge

Most patterns asking for a bias trim will give directions similar to the following:

"Cast on 9 sts. Row 1: (right side) Inc 1 st in the 1st stitch, K to the last 2 sts, K2 tog. Row 2: (wrong side) Purl all sts. Repeat the two rows for desired length."

Two Kinds of Bias Trim

Bias Trim with Turning Ridge

Since so many people have a great deal of trouble applying the bias trim evenly, you may find it easier and prettier to change your pattern from plain bias trim to the bias trim with a turning ridge.

Directions: Cast on 7 sts. Row 1: Increase one stitch in the first stitch, knit 1, skip the next stitch and leave on the needle, knit the next stitch, knit the skipped stitch, slip both stitches from left needle, knit 1, knit 2 together. Row 2: Purl all stitches. Repeat these two rows for the desired length. NOTE: You can make this strip any width you desire, simply by adding more stitches, always using an odd number of stitches, so that the two stitches twisting are in the center.

Upon examining this bias trim, you will find that the center turning ridge is not quite in the center of the strip. This is correct, and because this is so, the trim applies better to the garment.

Applying the Bias Trim

If the directions for your sweater call for a bias trim to be applied to the front, around the neck and down the other front, measure that distance and knit your bias trim with turning ridge that length. Do not bind off; put the stitches on a yarn holder, then block the bias trim, laying the strip out flat. With the widest half of the strip next to the sweater edge, carefully pin the strip up one side of the front. Try on the sweater and make sure that the bottom of the sweater is not sagging or drawing up. If you are satisfied with the looks of the bias pinned to the front, proceed to pin the bias around the neck of the one front and the back of the neck. Stop here and try on the sweater again. You may find that you will have to draw in the front and the back of the neck just a bit to make the bias lie flat. If this is so, adjust the trim and try on the sweater once more to make sure it is fitting just perfectly around the neck. Now, measure the distance from the shoulder seam to the point where the neck shaping and front meet on the side you have pinned. Make the other side exactly the same number of inches. Now measure the distance from the very top of the front of the pinned side to the bottom of the sweater. Make the other side conform to the same measurement. You will probably find that you have knit your bias strip too long and must rip out some, and then bind off. With the right side facing you, and using split yarn, (or de-fuzzed mohair, if you are working with mohair sewing thread if working with a fine yarn) of the same color as was used for knitting the trim, use a small "side-to-side" stitch, first taking a small stitch on the trim about $\frac{1}{4}$ inch in from the edge, and parallel to the edge of the strip; then take a small stitch on the sweater side, staying in a groove one stitch in from the edge. With your thumbnail, push the resulting seam to the wrong side as you go along. Be very careful that your stitches are very close together and very small (about $\frac{1}{4}$ inch long). Fold the bias on the turning ridge and using sewing thread, tack the narrow half of the trim to the small seam you have just made, on the wrong side, but do not make a regular seam there. With the "side-to-side" stitch, just cover over the seam. See picture and photographs of bias trim.

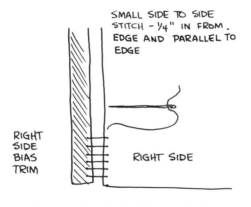

NOTE: As you probably know, whenever you work a piece of bias trim, the beginning and ending edges have a slant shape. To do away with the slant shape and make the bias strip straight at the bottom edge, you should first cast on three stitches. On the next row, and knitting, increase in the first and last stitch. On the wrong side row, purl all stitches. Repeat these two rows until you have the number of stitches required for the bias trim, then start your turning ridge. To finish off the piece, decrease one stitch at the beginning and end of right side rows, purl all stitches on wrong side rows until three stitches remain. Bind them off.

Sewing on Buttons

Buttons should be sewed on with split matching yarn. Sewing thread has a different texture and colors will not match exactly. If you have made horizontal buttonholes, you may sew on each button by sewing through the holes of the button as many times as you can pull the needle through without forcing.

If you have made vertical buttonholes, there is the danger of the little peak points forming on the border when the sweater is buttoned unless you use buttons with shanks. If you have selected buttons with *no* shanks, you will need to make a yarn shank on each button. To make the shank, anchor the split yarn on the wrong side, at the place where the button will be sewed. Sew through the holes of the button three or four times, leaving a space of approximately $\frac{1}{4}$ inch between the sweater and the button. This space will later form the shank. Now bring the needle and yarn through to the right side, and wrap the yarn around the threads of the $\frac{1}{4}$ inch space several times, then pass the needle and the yarn through to the wrong side and fasten off.

N O T E : If you are using crocheted button balls, sew these buttons flat against the sweater, with no shank.

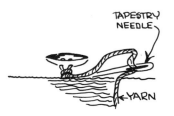

MAKING A YARN SHANK

SEWING ON BUTTONS

Binding off Front and Back Shoulders Together

Occasionally you may want to bind off the front and back shoulder stitches together instead of working the shoulders in

Kitchener stitch. This bound-off edge will give some firmness and strength which may be needed at the shoulders. If you are making a sleeveless shell or sleeveless dress and the pattern asks that you taper your shoulders, you may wish to change this so that front and back shoulders are bound off together. Do not taper the shoulders in stair step bind offs. These shoulders will have no shaping.

In order to do this, leave a sufficient amount of yarn on each of the shoulders to do the necessary binding off. (Approximately one inch for each stitch to be bound off.) The shoulder stitches should be put off on yarn holders. Then the pieces are washed and blocked. Using the size needle you used for knitting the garment, line up the left front shoulder stitches and the left back shoulder stitches on each of two separate needles. Hold the work so that the right sides are facing each other. Use a third needle to do the binding off. Pass the third needle through the first stitch on each of the two needles, and knit those stitches together; then knit the two second stitches from each needle together. You now have two stitches on the right-hand needle. Bind stitch #1 over stitch #2. Continue thus across all of the stitches on the shoulder. Steam the seam with the wet wash-cloth method.

THE JULIA BOWMAN BUTTONHOLES

All Julia Bowman buttonholes as described here are four stitch buttonholes. If your pattern asks that you use a different number of stitches, do so, but the number of loops involved will be different. All knitters are urged to practice these buttonholes many times before working them into garments. They are not easy to do, and beginners should use the other buttonhole described on page 29. The Bowman buttonhole differs radically from the original horizontal buttonhole in which you bind off a given number of stitches, then on the following row cast on the same

DRAWING OF LOOPS –
AFTER CONTRASTING COLORED
THREAD WAS REMOVED

number of stitches that you bound off on the previous row. When working the Julia Bowman buttonholes, instead of binding off the stitches as the pattern asks you to do, you will "knit in" a contrasting colored yarn at the point where these stitches were to have been bound off. Following the directions given in your pattern, when you reach the bind-off stitches for the buttonhole, instead of binding them off knit across these stitches with a contrasting strand of yarn, then slip the stitches which you have just knit with the contrasting color, back onto the left-hand needle and knit again across these stitches with your main colored strand. The contrasting color strand will remain in the work until after washing and blocking.

If your pattern calls for double buttonholes, you will be forming a buttonhole on the front of your garment, and also one on the facing, and sometimes the pattern will have you work a turning ridge between the front and the front facing. See page 138. Follow the directions given in your pattern for placing the buttonholes, then knit with a contrasting color the number of stitches you were to have bound off, as described above. The buttonholes will then not be hand finished until the garment pieces have been washed and blocked.

Hand Finishing the Bowman Buttonholes

DOUBLE BUTTONHOLES

Now pull out the contrasting colored thread, and immediately pick up the *bottom* edge loops of the buttonhole and put these loops on a cabling tool ——⌣—— or on a double-pointed needle, then put the *top* edge loops of the buttonhole on a strand of contrasting colored yarn. Repeat this on the buttonhole on the facing. See drawing, page 251 and how the loops are numbered, showing the outside view of the buttonhole. (The inside facing buttonhole will look the same.) Notice in the drawing that the loops are not placed one on top of each other; rather, the bottom loops come in between the top loops, and you have four full loops on the bottom of the hole, and on the top of the hole, you have three full loops in the center and a half loop at each end. This is the way it will appear in your work.

Thread a tapestry needle with full strength matching yarn,

Julia Bowman Double Buttonhole

(do not anchor the yarn at this time, as you may need to even up the stitches later), and draw the yarn through half loop #1 of the outside buttonhole. Fold the facing under so the two buttonholes are together with their wrong sides touching. NOTE: You will be working first from the outside buttonhole, then to the facing side buttonhole, working through each numbered loop. (The loops on the facing buttonhole are numbered the same as those on the outside buttonhole.) Also, you will find that you must turn your work from side to side to work through these loops twice, and each loop will be joined to the next loop with a stitch which looks like a "turning ridge" edge. With these things in mind proceed as follows:

1. The yarn is now in position to start work: Pass the needle and the yarn down through loop #2 on the outside buttonhole; then through half loop #1 on the facing and back through loop #2 on the facing.
2. Now bring the needle to the outside, up through loop #2

and down through loop #3. Turn the work over and on the facing side work up through loop #2 and down through loop #3. Next bring the needle to the outside through loop #3 and down through loop #4—and on the facing side work through loop #3 and loop #4. Continue in this manner working through each loop twice and working from outside to facing side and taking loops off the tools as they are worked until you have worked through all the loops on the bottom edge of the buttonhole and the yarn is coming up through loop #5 on the outside.

3. You are now ready to work the top half of the buttonhole, but these loops must first be put on the cabling tools or double-pointed needles.

4. Take the needle and yarn through half loop #6 of the outside, and on the facing side work once more through loop #5 and then half loop #6.

5. Continue in this manner until all loops have been worked on both sides. You are now back at the starting point of the half loop #1. Even up these stitches if necessary and then fasten off both ends. Caution! When "working in" the ends, do not pull tightly on the yarn at the corner, or you may find you have made a deep impression there which will spoil the smooth look of the buttonhole.

SINGLE BUTTONHOLE IN STOCKINETTE STITCH

The Julia Bowman single buttonhole in stockinette stitch will be knit in the same manner as was the Julia Bowman double buttonhole—that is, you will "knit in" the number of buttonhole stitches with contrasting colored strands of yarn as explained in the previous paragraphs. When the garment pieces have been washed and blocked, and you are ready to face the front with grosgrain ribbon, see page 231 on applying ribbon facings and proceed as explained there, including putting a row of single crochet on the front edge. NOTE: You must use grosgrain ribbon wide enough to extend past your buttonhole by more than 1/4 inch. Instead of slashing the ribbon at each buttonhole, you will cut into the ribbon to form an oval around the buttonhole just large enough to expose the contrasting colored stitches of the buttonhole on the wrong side. The buttonhole will then be worked *over* the raw edges

Cutting an Oval in Ribbon Around Single Buttonhole

of the trimmed grosgrain. See photo of the wrong side of a button-hole showing oval opening in the grosgrain. See the drawing showing numbered stitches as seen from the *wrong* side of the buttonhole.

DRAWING OF LOOPS —
FROM WRONG SIDE OF BUTTONHOLE

Leave the contrasting colored stitches in the work all this time. You will be working from the wrong side, and will start at the bottom of the buttonhole where the four loops are (#2, #3, #4, and #5). You will begin where the contrasting color yarn is coming out. You will be forming a turning ridge-type edge by making new loops with yarn of the garment color, using a crochet hook to form these loops, and leaving all loops on the hook to transfer later. The steps are as follows:

1. Holding a strand of the garment color to the back of the work, insert the crochet hook into loop #2 and pull a loop of this yarn through and leave this loop on the hook.
2. Now pull loops through #3, #4, #5 and half loop #6. You now have five loops on the crochet hook. Transfer these loops to a double-pointed needle.

Finished Single Julia Bowman Buttonhole from Right Side

Finished Single Julia Bowman Buttonhole from Wrong Side

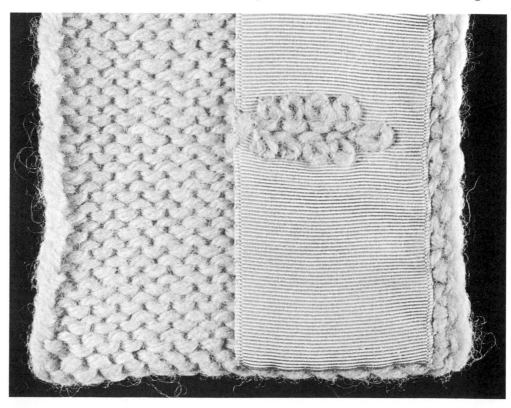

3. You will next pull up loops as before, with a crochet hook, through loops #7, #8, #9 and half loop #1. You now have four loops on the crochet hook. A fifth loop must be made through a loop (identified by arrow in drawing) to the side of loop #2. (This loop did *not* have contrasting color yarn passing through it.) Now you have five loops on the crochet hook and you must transfer them to another double-pointed needle.

4. Thread a sewing needle with matching sewing thread and anchor the thread through the ribbon near loop #2 which is on the bottom double-pointed needle. Using an "overcast stitch", fasten the #2 loop to the ribbon, stretching the loop over the cut edge of the ribbon. Then fasten the ends of the next loops (#3, #4, and #5) in the same manner. Four loops have been fastened down on the ribbon, covering the raw edge of the ribbon.

5. Loop #6 must be fastened down *at the corner* in the same manner as you fastened the other loops.

6. Now work all of the loops from the top double-pointed needle in the same manner working through loops #7, #8, #9 and half loop #1 stitching them to the ribbon on the top side. The extra loop coming through the side loop as shown by arrow in drawing will be the other corner loop and work it down as you did corner loop #6. Fasten off your thread.

7. The two ends of yarn which were left when you formed these loops must be worked in by skimming or working them under the grosgrain ribbon.

8. Now remove the contrasting colored yarn stitches one half stitch at a time to open up the buttonhole.

This makes a beautiful buttonhole!

BOWMAN BUTTONHOLES IN SEED STITCH OR GARTER STITCH

The single buttonhole just described may be used on seed stitch or garter stitch which has no ribbon facing. It is worked in the same manner, except *split* yarn is used to tack the loops down instead of using sewing thread. You may find that these buttonholes are quite loose and stretchy and must be made more firm. In this case, use split yarn (left from the overcasting of the loops)

**Finished Single Julia Bowman
Buttonhole on Fine Yarn**

and skim over to the first bump under the opened buttonhole. Working from the wrong side, take a little "back stitch" on each bump around the buttonhole to eliminate the excess stretch. Skim over to the edge and fasten off.

See photo of the neat buttonhole worked in very fine yarn.

CHAPTER XIII

Special Notes
on Yarns

NEEDLES AND YARNS GO TOGETHER

If the needles are too large for the yarn, your knitting will be loose and sleazy and with no body. For wearability, knitting should be firm and hold its shape. If the stitches are loose, the pieces will stretch during blocking and you will find it difficult to bring the pieces back into the measurements desired.

Knitting on needles too small for the size yarn will produce quite the opposite result. The knitting will become too firm, even very hard, and with too much body, and the pieces will not show the beauty of the twists of the yarns.

For best results, the knitter should obtain the ideal needle size for the yarn so as to show off the beauty and softness of the yarn, and yet keep the work firm enough to hold its shape and size.

Check the ideal needle size and the stitch gauge on smooth yarns.

Needle Size	Yarn	Stitches to the Inch
1	Dress yarns	9
2	Baby yarns, fingering yarns	8
3	Baby yarns, fingering yarns	7
4	Lightweight sport yarns (fingering yarn is borderline)	6½
5, 6	Sport yarns, 50/50 or 100% wool	6
7	Yarns slightly lighter in weight than knitting worsted but heavier than sport yarn	5½ or 6
8	Knitting worsted	5 or 5½
9	Combinations of yarns	4 or 4½
10	Combinations of yarns; bulky yarns that are heavier than knitting worsted	4
11	Combinations of yarns	3
13	Extra bulky yarns (heavier than two strands of knitting worsted)	2½
15	Extra bulky yarns	2

NOTE: You must realize this chart is dealing only with the yarns knit in stockinette stitch. If your pattern calls for another pattern stitch, it is very possible that a larger size needle may be used, and you can still maintain firmness. This is particularly true if the pattern stitch is such that it draws in the piece. On the other hand, any stitch which is similar to the seed stitch is usually quite stretchy and would require a smaller needle than that given in the ideal needle and stitch gauge.

MOHAIR YARNS

There are many, many kinds, brands and weights of mohair yarns. It is best to use the brand and weight your pattern calls for. There are lightweight and heavyweight mohairs, just as there are lightweight and heavyweight smooth yarns. They are not interchangeable. If you have already found your yarn and cannot find a pattern calling for that brand and kind of mohair yarn, it would be best for you to knit a stitch gauge with this yarn and try it out on several different size needles. Although the yarn may look lightweight to you, you will be surprised to find that mohair

MOHAIR

usually knits to fewer stitches to the inch than some smooth yarns. The reason is that the fuzz from the mohair fills in the holes and makes each stitch larger, and you will be surprised how heavy your little swatch seems. If you find that most of the fuzz is going to the wrong side, you are using needles much too fine for the mohair. Try out your swatch on needles several sizes larger.

There are mohair yarns of 100% kid mohair, 100% mohair, and combinations of mohair and synthetics. You must be sure to wet and dry your swatch before deciding on your gauge. Occasionally mohair yarns will draw up in length. You must know whether your yarn is going to do this so that you can knit each piece longer. If your stitches are very loose and with not sufficient body, you are knitting on needles much too large for your weight mohair. You will find that your swatch will stretch considerably and, should you knit a sweater with needles too large, your sweater will not hold its shape, and will stretch and sag, and be a great disappointment to you. Make sure you are satisfied with the look and "feel" of your stitch gauge before you begin your project.

Because it is more difficult to see what you are doing in mohair yarns, it is not advisable for a beginner to start out on a sweater of this material. It is quite hard to rip mohair. Also, you cannot re-knit with ripped yarn since you have disturbed the distribution of the fuzz, and if you were to re-knit with the ripped out yarn, your work would not look as fuzzy as before.

Do not be afraid to work with mohair yarns; but do not choose mohair for your first project.

Be sure to follow all of the methods suggested for choosing correct size, tying in colored yarn markers for measuring, drawing up your diagram, etc., and in general follow all of the procedures used before. When it is time to wash and block your sweater pieces, and assemble, note the few changes for mohairs.

Washing and Blocking Mohair Pieces

Many people are afraid to wash and block their own mohair sweaters. Do not be afraid to do this because your sweater will become prettier each time it is washed and blocked, if you use the correct process. Follow all directions for washing that you used before, given on page 62. Do not leave your pieces rolled up in a towel after washing. Block immediately and do not take out too much moisture. You will find that your mohair pieces "stay put" much better than pieces knit of smooth yarns. This is because there is very little twist in the yarn, therefore not as much elasticity. Instead of smoothing out the pieces with the palms of your hands, "tip-toe" through the yarn with the tips of your fingers, pushing out your pieces to make them larger, or pushing back to make them smaller. Use the *tips of your fingers* only, so that you do not flatten the hair of the mohair. Do not press your pieces with the palms of your hands as you did for smooth yarns. Lay like pieces together, right sides facing each other, and leave for several hours before separating them. When your pieces are *completely* dry, shake them very gently to restore fluffiness.

Assembling Mohairs

You should follow all of the general rules for assembling sweaters with very few exceptions for the mohair sweaters. If your mohair yarn has "globs" of fuzz, clip off these globs so as to have smooth matching yarn to sew with. Use quite short pieces. You cannot split this yarn. Use the back stitch and "pick-up-the-eye" seams according to former instructions. When it is time to steam out your seams with the "wet wash-cloth method", use the same procedure, but as you are pressing out the seams with your fingers, do not use much pressure. *CAUTION!!* "Easy does it" here. You do not want to flatten your precious fuzz. Then when your seam is dry, take a dry wash cloth and gently ruff up the closed seam from the right side to restore the fuzz. You want your seams to look opened, but definitely not flattened.

NUBBY AND KNOTTY YARNS

Knitting, Washing, Blocking and Assembling Garments of Nubby and Knotty Yarns

Follow all of the general rules for knitting, washing, blocking and assembling given previously with these exceptions:

KNITTING

1. Watch carefully for mistakes, they are hard to see, but may show up later.
2. Do not attempt to count rows as it is nearly impossible. You must measure with your tape.

KNOTTY AND NUBBY

3. It is not advisable to use a pattern stitch in knotty yarns. It is too difficult to see what you are doing, and it does not show up to advantage on these knotty yarns.

ASSEMBLING

1. When assembling, you will need to find a lightweight yarn of matching color to do your seams. If you cannot find such a matching color, you may use embroidery floss. Use all six strands. Your stitches will not show as they will disappear down amongst the knots. If it is difficult to pick up the eye, use the back stitch instead.
2. Do not attempt to hand finish buttonholes; you will make them worse. Use the improved horizontal buttonhole method, unless you can use the vertical type (in ribbing on the border). See page 141.
3. Be most careful in steaming out seams. You must steam the seams out, but, as with mohairs, do not flatten or smash your work. Do not lose that three-dimensional look which the pattern and texture of yarn has given your knitting.

CHAPTER XIV

Knitting with Sequins, Beads and Ribbon

KNITTING WITH SEQUINS

General

Knitting with sequins and beads is slow, tedious knitting, but the results are beautiful. The sequins for knitting are strung on long double strands of heavy thread. The strings of sequins must be transferred to the ball of yarn. The cup part of the sequin should be facing the ball of yarn so that when you are knitting with the sequins the cups will all face to the outside of your work. To transfer the sequins to the yarn, look for the loop at one end of the string of sequins. Pull the end of yarn coming from your ball of yarn through the loop several inches, then little by little transfer the sequins to the yarn. It is a good idea to look the yarn over carefully, re-rolling it to see if there are any knots in the yarn. The sequins will not transfer over knots, and you will need to cut off the knot, transfer the string of sequins to a thread, then back onto the yarn again. This can be eliminated if you carefully look the yarn over for knots before starting. If you find a knot, string part of your sequins onto the yarn, and when you come to the knot cut it off and string the rest of the sequins onto the rest of the yarn.

Look your pattern over carefully and figure which size you will work from. You must knit your stitch gauge using the sequins, yarn and needles suggested for the main body of the garment. You can practice your stitch and work your stitch gauge at the same time. The little gauge must be carefully blocked and dried before you decide if you are on gauge.

How to Knit with Sequins

In most patterns you will be instructed to knit a stitch with a sequin, bringing the sequin through the loop of the old stitch, then knit in the back of the next stitch. It is quite difficult to separate the sequins and to bring one sequin through the loop of

Sequin Swatch

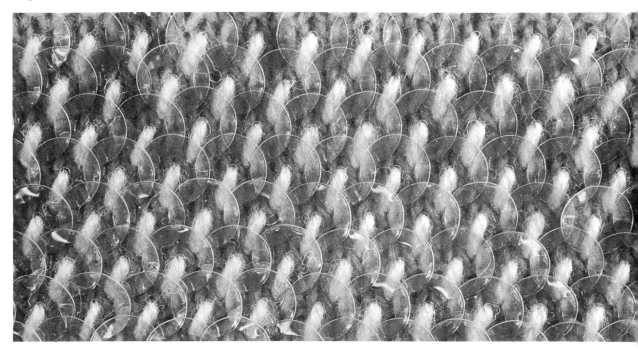

the old stitch and this process will slow you down considerably, but as with anything else you are learning you will improve with experience. On the second row, your pattern will require that you purl all stitches. On the following right side row, you will knit a sequin over the stitch you knit in back of the loop and *not* over the sequin of the previous knit row. In this way the sequins are staggered. Do not knit a sequin on the first or last stitch. You may have to knit two stitches at the beginning and end of some rows. It would be difficult to seam the garment if you had sequins knit right on the edges, and for this reason you should not knit sequins on these edge stitches regardless of what your pattern asks you to do. If you come to a place where you will need to add new yarn, tie in the new strand at the edge of your work. CAUTION! Try to detect errors immediately. Ripping with sequins is very difficult. Each sequin must be pushed back through the old loop to rip each stitch.

Here is a little tip to help speed your knitting after you have gotten used to knitting with the sequins. Spread the sequins out on your loose yarn about one inch apart. Spread about ten of them out, then they are in approximately the right place for knitting each sequin stitch. It is much faster than separating each sequin and bringing it into place for each stitch.

Washing, Blocking and Assembling

Your sequin knit pieces must always be hand washed and hand blocked. If the sequin knits are steamed with very hot steam the sequins will melt. If they are steamed with much cooler steam they will loose their luster. They *must* be hand washed and hand blocked.

Wash your knit pieces as you would any other pieces, with cold water and a good sweater soap. Do not roll the pieces in a towel to take out moisture. Block them quite wet on a good padded surface. You may replace the wet padding with dry towels after several hours. This will hasten the drying time. Review washing and blocking on pages 62–65. Lay each piece out separately, and with the fingers and palms of your hands make each sequin lie in the same direction with the cup of the sequin facing the outside of your work.

In assembling sequin garments you will use all methods

previously learned—that is, using split yarn if possible, and using back stitch seams and pick-up-eye seams where applicable. Do *not* steam any seams. Tack down the back-stitched seams with matching sewing thread as explained on page 76. If the seams still look as if they need flattening, you will need to wet them and press them with your fingers, then let them dry before moving them. Anything you would ordinarily steam in other garments will need to be done with water, such as added trim, picked up stitches, zippers and hems. In order to wet just part of your garment, lay the garment out on a padded surface and lay a wet washcloth under the part you need to flatten, then lay another wet washcloth over that part. After several hours remove the wet washcloths and that part will be wet enough for you to mold, flatten and press with your hands. Do not move the garment until it is dry.

KNITTING WITH BEADS

General

If the holes in the beads are large enough to thread the beads on the yarn, you should string the beads on the yarn and work as you were instructed to work with sequins. As you are knitting

Bead Swatch

with the beads you must bring the bead through the loop of each stitch just as you did when working with sequins. Your pattern will tell you where to place the beads.

If the holes in the beads are too small to string on your yarn, you must sew the beads on the completed pieces with heavy duty thread. When you are planning to knit an all-over scattered design with beads to be sewed on, work a purl stitch at each place where you will later sew a bead. This will facilitate tedious bead-sewing.

Block and assemble your pieces using the same instructions just given for sequins.

CAUTION! Do not use any wooden varnished beads which will not wash well, nor should you use beads which will tarnish. If the beaded design is quite elaborate and many beads are used, your garment may become quite heavy. Choose beads of a light weight if a large quantity of them is going to be knit in or sewed on.

KNITTING WITH RIBBON

General

There are spools of ribbon made especially for knitting. They come in a variety of different materials from silk to rayon and combinations of silk and rayon. If the ribbon is woven the edges are finished as a selvage. Some less expensive ribbons have fused rather than woven edges. Ribbons of this type are inferior because they are rough and scratchy.

Ribbon can be knit in a variety of garments, either knit alone or combined with a strand of yarn. Considerable practice may be necessary before starting a garment of ribbon. The technique is quite different from knitting with regular knitting yarns. The ribbon must be kept flat and uncrushed for best results. You will find that if you hold the ribbon with considerable slack you can form the stitches without twisting the ribbon and each stitch will be flat on the needle. You may wish to let out a length of ribbon from the spool, insert a pin into the ribbon and spool to keep more ribbon from unwinding, then knit that much ribbon, untwist, draw out another length of ribbon and repeat the process. Since there is no elasticity to ribbon, you cannot knit in stockinette stitch in

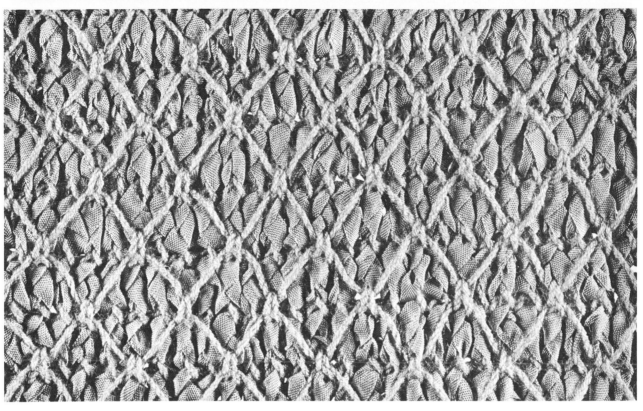

Ribbon Swatch

Ribbon Swatch with Mohair

the ordinary manner because your knitted piece will take a diagonal slant. For this reason your pattern will instruct you to knit in the back of all knit stitches and purl in the regular manner. If you are working in a pattern stitch, your pattern will tell you which side of the stitch to knit or purl into if there is any deviation from the regular directions for the knit and purl stitches. Some patterns requiring ribbon and yarn knit together will direct you to work two rows with ribbon, then two rows with yarn. This gives a pleasant effect and works up much faster than knitting with ribbon alone. Another pretty combination is ribbon knit with mohair—two rows of each.

BLOCKING AND ASSEMBLING RIBBON KNITS

As a general rule, ribbon knits should not be hand washed and blocked like other hand-knitting materials although it has occasionally been done successfully. After you have knit your stitch gauge you can experiment by getting the gauge wet and hand blocking it. The big danger in getting the ribbon wet is that it may wrinkle or water streak. If this happens it will be impossible to remove the wrinkles or spots which will spoil the elegant looks of the ribbon knit. Most ribbon knit pieces should be lightly steamed using a light weight, damp pressing cloth. When pressing these pieces do not stretch them in any place. In fact, the work looks prettier if the stitches are pushed close together and are flattened with slight pressure.

Use matching sewing thread and use the back stitch entirely, making small seams with stitches very close together. All of the seams should be pressed open. You may wish to insert a piece of cardboard between the garment and the open seam to keep an impression of the seam from showing on the right side. If any crochet is required as a finish, remember that the ribbon must be kept flat. The finished edge should be pressed with slight pressure to flatten it.

When the garment needs cleaning, it will need to be cleaned professionally.

CHAPTER XV

Adapting Patterns

CHANGING STITCH GAUGE FOR DIFFERENT YARNS

If you have found a pattern you like but want to use a yarn that does not meet the stitch gauge, you can change the stitch gauge from the original to a new stitch gauge. First of all, you must choose the correct size for you according to the directions previously given on page 33, *using the gauge given in the pattern.* After you have determined the correct size you need, proceed to draw your diagram using the *gauge given in the pattern.* Then, on the same drawing change *stitches* into inches by dividing the number of stitches by the *original gauge* (i.e., the number of stitches per inch), to get the number of inches required at all key places on the diagram.

EXAMPLE: "Gauge 5 sts equals 1''; 7 rows equals 1''. With #4 needles cast on 105 sts. Work in stockinette st for 7 rows, ending with a knit row, knit next row for hemline. Change to #6 needles and work in stockinette stitch until piece measures 13½'' above hemline. *Armholes:* Bind off 6 sts at beg of next 2 rows. Dec 1 st at each edge every other row 6 times (81 sts). Work even

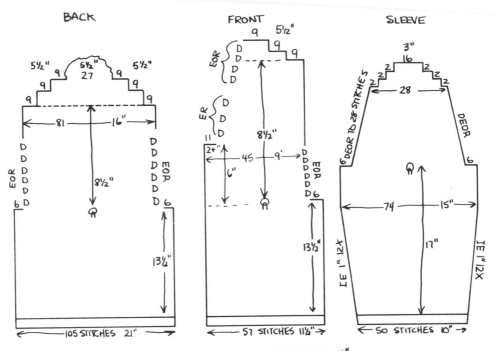

BACK

5½" 9   5½" 9   5½"
              27
        9   9
    9   9
    9   9
←——— 81 ———→ 16" ←——
D   D
D   D
D   D EOR
EOR D   D
D   D
6 D   D 6
                8½"
              105 STITCHES 21"
              13½"

FRONT

          9   5½"
EOR D   9
     D   9
     D ———
     D
              8½"
ER D
     D
     D
11 D
2+"
←— 45 — 9" →
6"
                D EOR
                D
                D
                D 6
                13½"
←— 57 STITCHES 11½" →

SLEEVE

        3"
        16
    2   2
  2   2
←—— 28 ——→
                    DEOR
6 DEOR TO 28 STITCHES
←——— 74 — 15" →
              17"
IE 1" 12X   IE 1" 12X
6   6
←— 50 STITCHES 10" →

DIAGRAM A   FOR CHANGING STITCH GAUGE   5 STITCHES = 1"
                                          7 ROWS = 1"

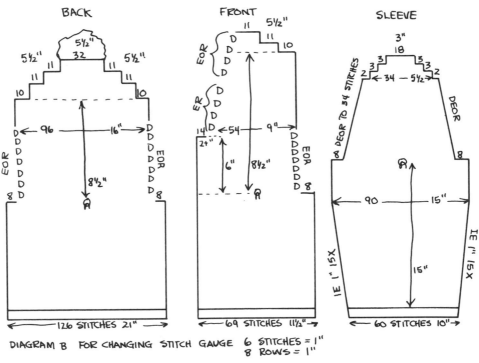

BACK

5½" 11   5½" 11 5½"
              32
        11   11
    11   11
    10   10
←——— 96 ——— 16" ——→
D   D
D   D
D   D EOR
EOR D   D
D   D
8 D   D 8
                8½"
←—— 126 STITCHES 21" —→

FRONT

          11 5½"
EOR D   11
     D   10
     D ———
     D
                    8½"
ER D
     D
     D
14 D ←— 54 — 9" →
2+"
6"
                D EOR
                D
                D
                D
                D
                D 8
←— 69 STITCHES 11½" →

SLEEVE

        3"
        18
    3   3
  2   2
←— 34 — 5½" →
                    DEOR
8 DEOR TO 34 STITCHES
←——— 90 — 15" →
              15"
IE 1" 15X   IE 1" 15X
8   8
←— 60 STITCHES 10" →

DIAGRAM B   FOR CHANGING STITCH GAUGE   6 STITCHES = 1"
                                         8 ROWS = 1"

272

until armhole measures 8½". *Shoulders:* Bind off 9 sts at beg of next 6 rows, slip remaining 27 sts on holder for back of neck."

The directions in words for the fronts and sleeves are not given here. They appear in the diagrams so that you see just how they are intended to be worked.

See *Diagram A* showing the pattern worked out on 5 stitches equals one inch, seven rows equals one inch. After the diagram was drawn, the number of stitches at each key point was changed into inches.

Then on *Diagram B,* the sweater pieces were drawn up again using the inches at each key point and they were multiplied by the new stitch gauge of six stitches equals one inch, and eight rows equals one inch. This pattern could have been worked out using *any* stitch gauge.

After the pattern has been drafted you must consider the finishing. The original pattern asks that you pick up and knit 85 stitches around the neck including stitches from holders. (Assuming that you would be getting five stitches per inch in ribbing on needles two sizes smaller, the neck would measure seventeen inches. This is a cardigan and has an overlap up the front, so that seems to be about the right number of inches.) You would need to pick up eighteen stitches in each gap if you were following the original pattern. Now to follow the new pattern with six stitches per inch, multiply seventeen inches by six stitches to get the 102 stitches required for the neck ribbing. You have sixty stitches waiting on holders so 21 stitches will need to be picked up in each gap.

If your pattern is such that it requires you to knit any part of the sweater according to the row-wise gauge, you must figure out how far that would be in inches and how the new pattern will come out row-wise. One such pattern is any raglan with decreases up each raglan shaping. These patterns are always figured out row-wise and it has been thoroughly discussed previously that you must adjust your pattern if you are off gauge row-wise in a raglan. Re-read that information given on page 149.

CREATING DIFFERENT SIZES

You can make a sweater larger than the largest size or smaller than the smallest size. It is not wise to make your pattern a great deal larger than the largest size, nor a great deal smaller than the smallest size. There is too much chance for error because of the neck shaping, armhole depths, sleeve widths, etc. If you must enlarge your sweater by more than an inch or two, you should look for another pattern in a larger size. There are pattern books available now which specialize in large and extra large sizes. If you must go to a pattern very much smaller than the smallest size, look for another pattern in a book specializing in teen sizes.

How to Enlarge Patterns

If you have chosen a pattern and the largest size is not quite large enough for you, you can enlarge the largest size an inch or two by adding more stitches to the large size pattern. Keep in mind that the sleeves will be only slightly larger than the largest size. (Sleeves do not change as rapidly nor in the same proportion as do the back and front.) The first step in changing a pattern to a larger pattern is to find out exactly what size you need by measuring yourself at the bust line, then find out exactly what size the largest size is at the bust line.

EXAMPLE: If the actual bust measurement is 41 inches, the knit size for this cardigan should be 44 inches. Now add up all of the stitches given in the original pattern for the fronts and back of the cardigan at the point just before the underarm shaping as follows:

```
105 stitches on the back
 57 stitches on one front
 57 stitches on the other front
219 stitches back and front
 −9 deduct one overlap
210 stitches
```

Now divide this total number of stitches by the stitch gauge of five stitches equals one inch and you will find that the sweater size of this pattern is 42 inches. You will thus need to enlarge this pattern by about two inches or ten stitches. See example Diagram A of the large size and notice that at the key points the stitches were changed into inches. (NOTE: The example being used here is the same pattern used when the stitch gauge was changed from one gauge to another gauge on page 271.)

Now notice the example Diagram B of the same pattern

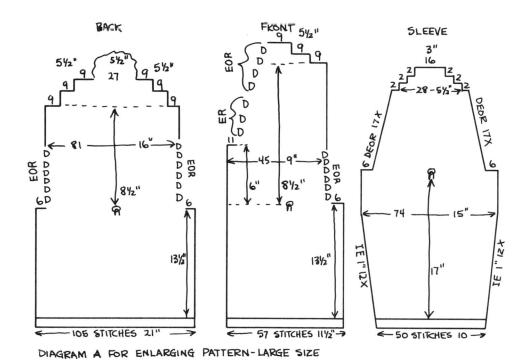

BACK

5½" | 5½" | 5½"
9 | 9 | 27 | 9 | 9
9 D | | | | 9
81 ← 16" → D | EOR
EOR | DDDDD | DDDD | EOR
6 D | | D 6
8½"
13½"
← 105 STITCHES 21" →

FRONT 5½"
9 | 9
EOR { D D D D }
9
ER { D D D }
11
45 — 9" → D DDDDD EOR
6" | 8½" | 6
13½"
← 57 STITCHES 11½" →

SLEEVE
3"
16
2 | 2 | 2 | 2
2 ← 28 - 5½" → 2
6 DEOR 17X | DEOR 17X 6
74 — 15" →
IE 1" 12X | IE 1" 12X
17"
← 50 STITCHES 10 →

DIAGRAM A FOR ENLARGING PATTERN - LARGE SIZE

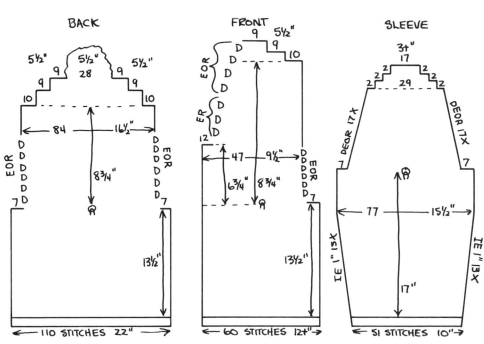

BACK

5½" | 5½" | 5½"
9 | 28 | 9
9 | | 9
10 | | 10
84 ← 16½" →
EOR | DDDDD | DDDD | EOR
7 D | | D 7
8¾"
13½"
← 110 STITCHES 22" →

FRONT 5½"
9 | 9
EOR { D D D D } 10
ER { D D D }
12
47 — 9½" → DDDDD EOR
6¾" | 8¾" | 7
13½"
← 60 STITCHES 12+" →

SLEEVE
3+"
17
2 | 2 | 2 | 2
2 | 29 | 2
7 DEOR 17X | DEOR 17X 7
77 — 15½" →
IE 1" 15X | IE 1" 13X
17"
← 51 STITCHES 10" →

DIAGRAM B - FOR ENLARGING PATTERN - LARGER THAN LARGE SIZE

275

enlarged to a size 44. Changes were made at key points, such as the cast on row (from 21 inches to 22 inches in the back) and at the shoulders of the back (from sixteen inches to 16½ inches) and on the fronts (from 11½ inches to twelve plus inches) at the cast on rows. Notice that the sleeve pattern was enlarged by only one-half inch in width.

How to Make Patterns Smaller

If you want to make a pattern smaller than the smallest size by just a few inches, the procedure is the same as was used to make the pattern larger. That is, first find out what size you need then find out what size the smallest size of the pattern comes to.

EXAMPLE: If the actual bust measurement is 31 inches, the knit size for this cardigan should be 34 inches. Now add up all of the stitches given in the original pattern for the fronts and back of the cardigan at the point just before the underarm shaping:

```
  90 stitches on the back
  48 stitches on one front
  48 stitches on the other front
 186 stitches back and front
 − 7 deduct one overlap
 179 stitches
```

Now divide this total number of stitches by the stitch gauge of five stitches equals one inch and you will find that the sweater size of this pattern is almost 36 inches. You will need to make this pattern nearly two inches smaller. Notice the pattern drawn up in Diagram C of the small size, and notice that at the key points the stitches were changed into inches. Then notice the example Diagram D of the same pattern reduced to the size 34. NOTE: The armhole distance was shortened by only one-fourth inch. The sleeve width and sleeve cap were not changed. A sleeve any narrower would be dangerously narrow, even on a small person.

OTHER CHANGES TO PLAN FOR BEFORE STARTING (WHAT TO LOOK FOR IN A PATTERN)

An advanced knitter should always read completely through the pattern before starting any garment than she may decide if

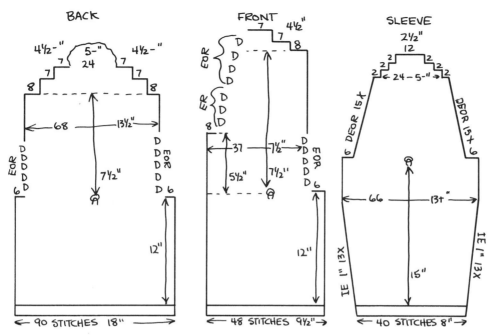

BACK

4½-" 5-" 4½-"
7   24   7
8   8
←— 68 —→ 13½"
7½"

EOR
D D D D D D
6   6

12"

←— 90 STITCHES 18" —→

FRONT

7   4½"
7   8
EOR { D D D D
ER { D D D D
8   D D

37   7½"
5½" 7½"

EOR
D D D D D D
6

12"

←— 48 STITCHES 9½" —→

SLEEVE

2½"
12
2   2
2 ←24—5-"→ 2 2

6 DEOR 15x   DEOR 15x 6

←— 66 —→ 13†"

IE 1" 13X   IE 1" 13X

15"

←— 40 STITCHES 8" —→

DIAGRAM C - FOR MAKING PATTERN SMALLER - DIAGRAM OF THE ORIGINAL SMALL SIZE

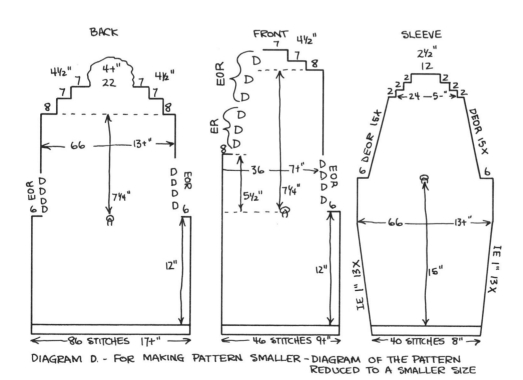

BACK

4†" 4+" 4½"
7   22   7
8   8
←— 66 —→ 13†"
7¼"

EOR
6 D D D D   D D D D 6
EOR

12"

←— 86 STITCHES 17†" —→

FRONT

7   4½"
7   8
EOR { D D D
ER { D D D
8   D

36   7†"
5½" 7¼"

EOR
D D D D D
6

12"

←— 46 STITCHES 9†" —→

SLEEVE

2½"
12
2   2
2 ←24—5-"→ 2 2

6 DEOR 15x   DEOR 15X 6

←— 66 —→ 13†"

IE 1" 13X   IE 1" 13X

15"

←— 40 STITCHES 8" —→

DIAGRAM D. - FOR MAKING PATTERN SMALLER - DIAGRAM OF THE PATTERN
REDUCED TO A SMALLER SIZE

277

she plans to make any changes. Anticipate the finishing details before starting your garment. Read the finishing directions suggested in your pattern to see if you need to knit anything differently for different finishing procedures. As you are reading through the directions, look for the following to see if you wish to make changes at any of these points:

1. See if the pattern tells you to make increases up the sides before you reach the armhole shaping. If the pattern does have increases, it will mean that you must use the back stitch method when you assemble the sweater. Perhaps you would prefer to start with the total number of stitches that you need at the armhole shaping, so that you can use the "pick up eye" method (much prettier) when assembling. Be sure to use your diagram and make your changes on the diagram.

2. How are the fronts finished if the sweater is a cardigan? Keep in mind that a double front facing with double buttonholes belongs only on a heavy, sporty-looking sweater. If your sweater does not fall in that category, you may want to change your pattern so that you will have a single front border finished with ribbon. Also, double buttonholes are very difficult to hand finish, especially on heavy yarns. (See page 240 on finishing double buttonholes.) If you are changing from double front border to single, make sure the proper deduction of stitches is made on your diagram.

3. Buttonholes—how are they made? If you are changing double buttonholes to single, because you are changing a double front facing to a single, make sure that your *horizontal* buttonhole is worked in the *middle* of that facing. The only time you should ever use the vertical buttonhole is when you have ribbing or garter stitch on the border. NOTE: Never make a vertical buttonhole if you intend to use ribbon facing up the fronts of your sweater. If you have occasion to have buttonholes worked in by machine (if you forgot to put in any buttonholes), you can cover up this machine work by using split yarn to carefully overcast the machine buttonholes.

C A U T I O N : As you are reading through your pattern,

if you come upon directions asking that you put in button-holes on every 23rd or 24th row, for example, you must question these directions. You must draw up your diagram and place the buttonholes according to the inch measurement. If you do not, you may find that the buttonholes are misplaced either because you had to lengthen or shorten your garment, or because your stitch gauge was off row-wise.

4. You should consider the neck or collar. Make sure you are satisfied with the looks in the picture. If the neck looks quite low or quite high, and you believe you will need to raise or lower it, diagram the neck as given in the pattern and then diagram the neck with your raised or lowered adjustment. If you have an unusually short, broad neck it would be to your advantage to lower the back of your sweater at the neck by approximately one inch. If you must do this type of alteration, you will have to work each side of the back with a separate ball of yarn (see page 132). If your neck is long and thin, you would never want to use directions that ask you to lower the back of the neck. Change your diagram so that the back of the neck is bound off last (or put on a yarn holder), after the shoulders have been worked.

5. Notice how the sleeves look in the picture. You may want to lengthen the sleeves. If you are changing a three-quarter sleeve to a full-length sleeve, you will probably have to cut down the number of stitches on the cuff.

    Some patterns will ask that you make increases above the cuff, then go straight up to the armhole without any more increases up the sides (or with very few increases up the sides). If you do as the directions ask, you will have a bell-like sleeve. If you do not want this type of sleeve, plot your sleeve and use increases up the side gradually. (See page 58.)

6. Notice how the side edges start. Oftentimes a pattern will have to be adjusted just slightly so that when the side edges are put together the pattern will come out right. For instance, if you are working a pattern with colors knit in, you will want your pattern to flow along through the seam and not

be interrupted. You may have to add a stitch or two on each side so that the sides will match, or maybe you will have to take a stitch or two away to make the sides match. Remember, when you are "picking up the eye" to join your seams, you are picking up one stitch in from the edge on each piece. So you must have an extra stitch on each side.

7. Notice the ribbing. In order to form a perfect blend when sewing K2, P2 ribbing together, you must plan for this before casting on any stitches. Adjust the number of stitches, if necessary, so that you start with K2 and end with K2 (or start with P2 and end with P2). When you blend the ribbing, blend between the 1st and 2nd stitches on each piece for a perfect blend.

CHAPTER XVI

Care and Storage
of Knit Garments

Knit garments, both ready-made and hand-made need special care. They should never be hung up on coat hangers. They should be folded and carefully put away after each wearing. When folding the garments, you should not make any vertical folds. To fold a sweater, lay the sweater out flat, right side up (do not button if the sweater is a cardigan); fold the sleeves over the front, then make one fold bringing the bottom of the sweater up to the top. There will be no deep creases in the sweaters, because the sleeves raise up the fold. They may be stacked ten or twelve high if necessary. They should be placed either in a chest, or a drawer, or on shelves. To store your skirts, place a sheet of tissue paper on top of the skirt, then make two horizontal folds in the skirt, then they will not show any fold marks, if cared for in this manner. To store a knit dress, place several sheets of tissue paper over the dress, then lay the sleeves over the top of the front. Make two folds in the dress, dividing the dress into thirds, folding over the

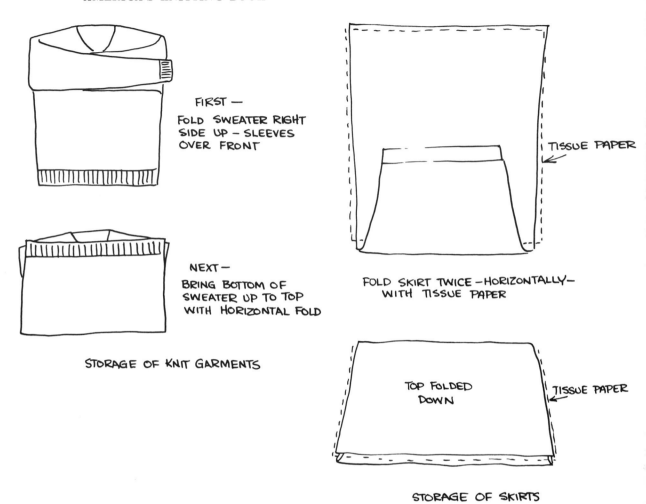

FIRST —
FOLD SWEATER RIGHT
SIDE UP – SLEEVES
OVER FRONT

NEXT —
BRING BOTTOM OF
SWEATER UP TO TOP
WITH HORIZONTAL FOLD

STORAGE OF KNIT GARMENTS

TISSUE PAPER

FOLD SKIRT TWICE —HORIZONTALLY—
WITH TISSUE PAPER

TOP FOLDED
DOWN

TISSUE PAPER

STORAGE OF SKIRTS

tissue paper. If you have a knit coat, use the same process as was used in preparing the knit dress, with one exception; make only one fold horizontally in the coat over several layers of tissue paper. See pictures. Do not place your knits in plastic bags. The garments may sweat in the bags and this dampness may be bad for the yarn. If you care to protect your knits with plastic, just place a sheet of plastic over the top of the folded knits to keep out extra dust.

It is not advisable to hand wash and block ready-made knits.

FOLD ARMS AS
FOR SWEATER

NEVER BUTTON

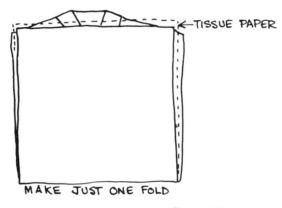

←—TISSUE PAPER

MAKE JUST ONE FOLD

STORAGE OF COATS

The yarns used in ready-made knits are usually not of the quality that hand knitting yarns are and they may stretch or fade. It is safer to send these knits to a good dry cleaning establishment. Hand knits, on the other hand should always be hand washed and hand blocked. (The exception to this rule is a knit garment which has a lining. A garment with a lining should be sent to a good dry cleaner.) If the garment has become quite soiled, you should carefully wash it, using the amount of soap called for on the package. Do not double up on the amount of soap. Instead, you should go completely through the washing process twice, using the correct amount of soap. Try not to let your knits become badly soiled. If your knits become out of shape, and "elbows" and "knees" appear, it is time to wash and block whether your garment is soiled or not.

Before washing the garment, take the following measurements: Width at bust (or chest), width at sleeve just below armhole, length, sleeve length, overall, and overall sleeve lengths. Baste the buttonholes closed if your sweater has buttonholes. You will find that the sweater seams will tend to hold the sweater together, and measuring will be easier than when working with the pieces before assembling. If the seams have been tacked down with sewing thread, they will always stay opened and flat.

If the sweater is a cardigan, lay the back of the sweater down on your padded surface, right side down on the padding and smooth out the back of your sweater from the wrong side. From your blocking measurements, measure the distance across the back at the point just below the sleeves. Bring out the back to one-half of the bust measurement. Measure the length, making it conform to the measurement taken before washing. Now lay the fronts over on top of the back. Lay the side with the buttonholes down first, then lay the side with the buttons on top. This is so that your buttons will not make a raised place on the buttonhole side. Smooth out your garment, getting it to size just as you did when you worked with sweaters that were in pieces. Shape to the right lengths and widths. Work with the bottom edges and neck edges to make them straight and smooth. Work with the shoulder seams (or raglans) making them lie straight. Lay out the sleeves, extending them straight out at each side of the sweater. Check the sleeve width at the underarm. Smooth out all of the wrinkles with the palms of the hands. Change the towels or padding under the sweater once or twice to hasten the drying time.

If you are blocking a pullover, take all of the measurements as were taken for the cardigan, then follow the instructions above. You must work with the back and front as they lie together, which is a bit more difficult than working with first the back and then the front.

INDEX